SHADES OF BELONGING

Religion in Contemporary Africa Series

The Religion in Contemporary Africa Series (RCAS) aims at publishing innovative research relevant to the diverse and changing religious scene in contemporary Africa. One of the principal objectives of the Series is to facilitate the dissemination of research by young African scholars. The Series includes books from a range of disciplines: the academic study of religions, anthropology, sociology and related disciplines in the human and social sciences.

Series editors are JAMES L. COX, Professor of Religious Studies in the University of Edinburgh, and GERRIE TER HAAR, Professor of Religion and Development in the Institute of Social Studies, The Hague, Netherlands. They can be contacted at: <j.cox@ed.ac.uk> or <terhaar@iss.nl>.

Previous Publications in the Religion in Contemporary Africa Series

1. James L. Cox and Gerrie ter Haar (eds.). *Uniquely African? African Christian Identity from Cultural and Historical Perspectives.*
2. Matthews A. Ojo. *The End-Time Army. Charismatic Movements in Modern Nigeria.*
3. Leslie S. Nthoi. *Contesting Sacred Space. A Pilgrimage Study of the Mwali Cult of Southern Africa.*
4. Gerrie ter Haar (ed.). *Imagining Evil. Witchcraft Beliefs and Accusations in Contemporary Africa.*
5. Asonzeh Ukah. *A New Paradigm of Pentecostal Power. A Study of the Redeemed Christian Church of God in Nigeria.*

SHADES OF BELONGING

African Pentecostals in Twenty-first Century Ireland

Abel Ugba

Africa World Press, Inc.

P.O. Box 1892
Trenton, NJ 08607

P.O. Box 48
Asmara, ERITREA

Africa World Press, Inc.

P.O. Box 1892
Trenton, NJ 08607

P.O. Box 48
Asmara, ERITREA

Book and cover design: Saverance Publishing Services
                           (www.saverancepublishing.com)

Library of Congress Cataloging-in-Publication Data

Ugba, Abel.
   Shades of belonging : African Pentecostals in twenty-first century Ireland / Abel Ugba.
      p. cm.
   Includes bibliographical references.
   ISBN 1-59221-658-7 (hardcover) -- ISBN 1-59221-659-5 (pbk.)
   1. Pentecostal churches--Ireland. 2. Blacks--Ireland. 3. Blacks--Religion. I. Title.

BX8762.A45I74 2008
289.9'4089960417--dc22

                                    2008028988

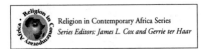

Religion in Contemporary Africa Series
Series Editors: James L. Cox and Gerrie ter Haar

To Eileen Lelmkhul

...at whose invitation we went to Ireland and began a new and exciting chapter of our lives. She provided a home and stability when they were the two things we needed most.

CONTENTS

LIST OF DIAGRAMS

ACKNOWLEDGEMENTS

This book is based on four years of ethnographic work in the Greater Dublin Area, beginning in 2001. I was based in the Department of Sociology, Trinity College Dublin (TCD), researching for a PhD dissertation. It has often been said that the road to PhD is long and lonely. In my case, they were busy, exciting and productive years, thanks to the tremendous support I received from within the department and outside of it. Dr. Ronit Lentin, my supervisor, showed enormous faith in me from day one. I couldn't ask for a better mentor. Prof. Bob Holton, head of department at the time, was very accessible and helpful. So was Dr. Andrew Finlay, the postgraduate coordinator who also served as my internal examiner. I owe a debt of gratitude to the many colleagues who provided helpful insight at different stages. I particularly want to thank Dr. Elaine Moriarty for her friendship.

The most profound gratitude goes to my respondents. They generously gave of their time and offered useful and frank views. Many welcomed me into their homes and provided refreshments. Others became acquaintances and our friendship has outlasted the project. I'm grateful for the opportunity to meet so many nice people.

I have changed the names of many respondents in the interest of anonymity and because of the sensitive nature of some of the issues highlighted in this book.

Silke, my wife, has remained a supportive and loving friend. She's a great gift to our children and me. Ebose and Benahi, our children, make our world go around. They perfected the act of tip-toeing around the house and talking in hushed voices because 'daddy is working in the office.' Many thanks for being so considerate. Thanks to Eileen, my mother-in-law, Auntie Marie and Sigi for their continued interest in and support for my family and me.

Finally, thanks to Gerrie ter Haar, co-editor of the Religion in Contemporary Africa Series, for encouraging me to write this book but also for the genuine interest she has shown in my professional advancement.

Thanks to JEHOVAH for the gift of life and for the sort of wisdom that comes from Him alone.

CHAPTER ONE

INTRODUCTION

This book is the result of ethnographic observations of and detailed interviews with Pentecostal African immigrants in Dublin, Ireland's capital city. At the beginning of the twenty-first century when I commenced the research, Dublin was undergoing a cultural, socio-demographic and economic transformation. Trendy restaurants, many of them offering non-Irish cuisine, and modern shopping malls filled with crowds of mostly young people, lined glitzy streets. On newly repaved but congested roads, motorists, cyclists and pedestrians jostled for space while builders and planners were locked in a fierce race to erect new offices and apartment blocks to accommodate the city's burgeoning population. These changes, facilitated by a sudden rise in economic activities and prosperity (also known as the 'Celtic Tiger', see Kirby et al., 2002), were paralleled by dramatic shifts in the socio-cultural and demographic characteristics of the city.

One of the central features of the shift in the city's demography was a visible increase in the numbers of non-Caucasian immigrants and minority ethnic groups. The 2006 census returned a population of 1,187,176 for the Greater Dublin Area, compared to 1,122,821 in 2002 and 1,058,264 in 1996. Cork, the second biggest city, only had 481,295 in 2006 and 447,829 in 2002 (CSO 2006). The majority of non-EU immigrants live in the Leinster region and in the Greater Dublin Area. During the 2006 census, 75,885 people in the Dublin region said they were of non-Irish and non-EU nationality. Census data and media reports aside, the increase in the presence of other nationalities and cultures was discernable even to casual visitors to Dublin city centre. Shops specialising in ethnic foods, cosmetics, newspapers and other consumer goods had been set up by immigrant entrepreneurs from China, India, Pakistan and Eastern Europe (Spiller 2002; Hannon 2003).

Walking in O'Connell Street and the other main streets, a visible increase in the number of sub-Saharan African immigrants was noticeable. Colourfully-attired African mothers dressed in that uniquely African style could be seen, while young men and women, some of them adorned in attractively braided hair and fashionable clothes, walk the streets or huddle in front of 'ethnic' shops, especially in the predominantly immigrant business enclaves of Parnell Street and Moore Street. Increasingly, many Africans could be seen at the wheels of Dublin Bus, the state-owned transport company. In the Royal College of Surgeons and in other tertiary institutions and secondary schools, there was a visible increase in the number of Africans. In June 2007 a Nigerian, Mr Rotimi Adebari, was elected the Mayor of Portlaoise, the first 'black' person to occupy that position in Ireland (The Irish Times 2007). The election of Ireland's first black mayor marked a change on Ireland's political landscape and it signalled a deeper, wider and sustained involvement of African immigrants in the Irish society.

People of African descent[1] have been present in Ireland since the eighteenth century (McKeon 1997; Mutwarasibo 2002; Rolston and Shannon 2002). However, only since the last decade of the twentieth century has there been a large-scale presence and the formation of communities based mostly on national, ethnic, religious and special interests (Smith and Mutwarasibo 2000; Ugba 2003a). In 2002, the Census returned 20,981 nationals of African states in Ireland (CSO 2002). This number increased to 35,326 during the 2006 census. Both figures are generally believed to underrepresent the statistical strength of the community since, for example, they do not include Africans who are also Irish citizens or citizens of other European countries and the United

States. Whereas 35, 326 said they were nationals of African countries during the 2006 census, 42,764 identified Africa as their place of birth while 40,525 described their ethnic background as African. The two censuses and other official statistical sources confirm that Nigerians are the largest African national group in Ireland. They accounted for about two-third (or 8,969) of the 2002 census figure and less than half (or 16,300) of the 2006 figure (CSO 2006).

Little is documented or known about the motivations, routes and activities of African immigrants who came to Ireland before the twentieth century. However, some of those that arrived in the eighteenth century were said to be members of the 29th (British) Army Regiment that had set up a base in Dublin in 1757, and others were domestic servants who, as McKeon reports, incurred the wrath of natives for taking away their jobs. Barbara McKeon (1997) also acknowledges that among those Africans in eighteenth century Ireland there were a few very wealthy individuals who arrived with a retinue of domestic servants and helpers. Recent immigrant groups consist mostly of students, workers and asylum seekers (Ugba 2004). Media reports and official statistics suggest that many of those that arrived since the mid-1990s came as asylum seekers. For example, Nigerians have consistently topped the lists of asylum applicants since 2001. In some years, they have constituted more than one-third of total applications. Other African countries that have featured prominently on the asylum application lists include the Democratic Republic of Congo, Somalia, Sudan and Zimbabwe.

The prominence of Nigeria and a few other Sub-Saharan African countries on the asylum application lists has been matched by their near absence on the work permit/visa lists. For example, 60 Nigerians were granted work permits in 2004, compared to the 1,776 that applied for asylum. In 2005, 77 work permits were granted but there were 1278 Nigerian asylum applicants. Generally, the numbers of sub-Saharan Africans, and indeed other non-EU and non-Western migrants, coming to Ireland to work have decreased steadily, mostly since 2004 when the first 10 former communist countries joined the EU. But even in the pre-accession years when Ireland desperately needed immigrant workers, it did not target sub-Saharan Africans—see my analysis of relevant immigration policies in the next chapter.

The increased migration of Africans to Ireland has baffled commentators, mostly anti-immigration politicians, who argue that Ireland is an unlikely destination for migrants from Africa because it has neither colonial ties nor direct air links to the continent. Although the Irish state did not participate in the scramble for and the colonial domination of the African continent, interactions between Africans and the Irish date back many centuries. They have taken place through commerce, missionary activities, anti-slave trade movements and the arrival of Irish people in Africa as participants in the British colonial enterprise (Rolston and Shannon 2002; Ugba 2003a). Therefore, a critical analysis of the increased presence of African immigrants in Ireland in the twenty-first century must take into account these historical, economic and political connections between Africa and Ireland. It must also consider the post Second World War increase in global migrations, especially from East to West and from South to North (Ugba 2003b, 2005; Faist 2000; Martin 2001; Zlotnik 2001). The analysis should also focus on recent developments in Ireland's immigration policies and on the massive socio-political and economic upheavals in most parts of Africa since the 1980s (Kabbaj 2003; Harrison 2002; United Nations 1993; UNHCR1997). These upheavals and the resulting uncertainties have provoked more voluntary and involuntary migrations within and out of the African continent in recent decades than at any other time, except during the slave trade.

Several studies (e.g., Rotte and Volger 1997; Marren 2001; 1995; Massey 1998; Zlotnik 2001) demonstrate that people generally tend to migrate from politically unstable, socially insecure and economically poor regions to more stable and prosperous societies. In the case of Africa, Findley (2001) reported that in the 1960s refugees originated from only eight African countries, mainly those governed by white minority governments. But by 1997, refugees were fleeing conflicts in 21 Sub-Saharan countries. Sudan, Burundi, the Democratic Republic of Congo and Somalia were among the top five originators of refugees in 2004, according to the United Nations High Commission for Refugees. In Sudan, refugee outflows increased by almost 125,000 (+21 %) during 2004 alone as victims of renewed fighting in the country's protracted civil war fled. In 2005, Asia and Africa continued to both produce and harbour the bulk of the world's refugees (www.unhcr.org 2005). Given these social and political developments and their consequences on the economy and livelihood of African people, it is no surprise that many recent African immigrants to Ireland and other European countries are asylum seekers (Ugba 2004; also see www.unhcr.org; www.orac.ie).

Also, Africans from countries where English is the official or dominant language have migrated to Ireland because they believe it is less difficult for them to realise their ambitions or fulfil their dreams in Ireland than in non-English speaking European countries. The other factor that has contributed to the increased presence of African immigrants is Ireland's geographical proximity to the United Kingdom, where there has, for many decades, been a larger and more settled population of Africans. Experiential knowledge and available evidence suggest that many African immigrants in Ireland had either lived in the UK, have friends/relatives there, travel there frequently or consume ethnic products, including newspapers and magazines, manufactured by or procured through Africans in the UK. These interconnections and transnational activities have contributed to the development of vibrant African communities in Ireland, mostly since the mid 1990s.

In addition to external circumstances and the various interconnections between Africa and Ireland, internal developments in Ireland, especially the economic boom of the 1990s, have resulted in new immigration policies that opened avenues for greater migrant inflows. The 'Celtic

Tiger' economy was, among other factors, the result of direct foreign investment in the Irish economy after the government lowered (and in some cases eliminated) export taxes (Mac Éinrí 2001; Sweeney 1998; Kirby et al 2002). Expanded economic production resulted in increased demand for overseas workers, especially towards the end of the 1990s. International movement of goods and capital and international migration are interrelated strands of globalisation. The inter-connections are such that it is impossible for nation-states to choose one and reject the other, as Saskia Sassen (1988, 1998) and other authors (e.g., Marren 2001; Martin 2001) have made clear. The rise of Ireland to the position of a big international player by reasons of its newly-found economic prosperity and her insertion into regional and international organisations brought her to the attention, not only of investors and multinational corporations, but also of potential migrants, including refugees and asylum seekers (Cullen 2000; Mac Éinrí 2001). Africans have arrived in Ireland as labour migrants—in fewer numbers—and as asylum seekers.

FORMATION OF AFRICAN COMMUNITIES

One of the direct consequences of the larger-scale presence of Africans in Ireland is the formation of communities and special interest groups. As Steven Vertovec (2000) and others (e.g., Bhardwaj and Rao 1990; Dahya 1974; Williams 1992) have noted, the processes surrounding the formation of associations and other institutions by immigrants often reflect the size and development of the immigrant population itself. Richard Kolm (1971) notes that institutions set up by immigrants constitute vital links between the individual and the group and between the group and other groups in society. He also describes 'ethnic' institutions as the signposts of ethnicisation, or the metamorphosis from an immigrant group to an ethnic group. These institutions and immigrant participation in various civic activities often make the immigrant groups physically 'visible', offer opportunities for interaction with the dominant society, create channels for transnational exchanges and constitute strategies for articulating self-understanding and group orientation.

On the other hand, immigrant and 'ethnic' institutions are sometimes constructed as obstacles to integration, a throw-back to the past and sites of oppressive patriarchy and harmful traditions. For example, John Bodnar (1985:166-7), accused immigrant religious organisations in nineteenth century United States of harbouring "premodern cadre of leaders" who endeavoured "to centralize authority, revitalize faith, and maintain the loyalty of their flocks in a rapidly changing world." Noteworthy in earlier investigations of immigrant institutions (Marcuse 1997; Portes 1995; Portes and Bach 1985; Thomas and Znaniecki 1974; Waldinger 1993) is the excessive reliance on functionalism (Blasi 1998) to explain the various reasons for them as well their uses. The majority of studies have concentrated on the function of these institutions in providing an ethnic quilt or 'safe' places in a new and strange environment. Many of the early inquiries into immigrant settlements in the US fall into this category (e.g., Logan et al. 2000; Wellman 1979; Wirth 1969). Although such functionalist interpretations enrich our understanding of migration and settlement, I argue in the case of the activities of African immigrants in Ireland that they are inadequate because they tend to focus on one aspect of a complex and multi-dimensional phenomenon.

African immigrants in Ireland have, through socio-cultural, economic and, of recent, political activities, contributed to the evolution of Ireland into a multi-ethnic, multicultural and vibrant nation. Through these activities they are asserting their presence and inviting the larger society to acknowledge, debate and cherish 'difference'. For a variety of reasons, some of which I have outlined below, the churches initiated or led by Africans occupy a unique and important place among the various social and cultural institutions newer African immigrants have established. Before I discuss the reasons, it must be noted that religious activism among African immigrants in Ireland extends beyond Pentecostalism. The 2002 Census attributed the rapid growth of Muslim communities and the resurgence in the membership of many 'mainline' churches to the presence of immigrants. According to the 2006 census, the number of Muslims increased from 19,147 to 32,539 (almost 70%) between 2002 and 2006, a period that coincided with the recent dramatic increases in in-migration. During this period, the Hindus increased from 3,099 to 6,516 (96%), the Orthodox experienced 99% growth while the Buddhists increased by 66% to 6,516. The gains of the mainstream churches have been moderate. Membership of the Church of Ireland increased by 8.6% to 125,585 while Catholics increased by 6.3% to 3.7m (CSO 2006).

Despite these increases in the membership of established and mainstream religious groups, the most innovative and dramatic changes in Ireland's religious landscape in recent years is not the participation of immigrants in mainline churches but the birth and spread of immigrant-led religious groups (Ugba 2003b; 2006a 2006b, 2007b). The majority of Christian groups established by African immigrants fall under the broad categories of Pentecostalism and Evangelical. The 2006 census shows that membership of Pentecostal/Apostolic groups increased by 156% to 8,116 between 2002 and 2006 while Evangelicals grew by 40% to 5,276 (CSO 2006). Participation in African-initiated or African-led Pentecostal churches has been intense and voluntary, less problematic and apparently unhindered by precarious residence status or length of stay in Ireland. The majority (73%) of recent African immigrants are Christians, according to a survey I conducted in the Greater Dublin Area (Ugba 2004). All the respondents but one had religious affiliations and 26.3% were Muslims. The majority believe that their religious group, rather than their ethnic group or the Gardai (Police), cared the most about them. The majority also said they would consult their church group, not their national/ethnic group or the Gardai/other state bodies, about problems in their family.

The opinion on religion and religious participation expressed by the respondents demonstrates the primacy of religious ideas and activities in the lives of African immigrants in Ireland. Religious involvement appears to be the first affiliation cultivated, activated or reactivated by the majority of African immigrants once they have arrived in Ireland. As Warner (1998:3) notes, religious identities tend to mean more to individuals in situations of migration or exile than in their homes because religious institutions often become the places "where new relations among the members of the community—among men and women, parents and children, recent arrivals and those settled—are forged." Barbara Metcalf suggests a different reason for immigrants' heightened religious consciousness: "The sense of contrast—contrast with a past or contrast with the rest of society—is at the heart of a self-consciousness that shapes religious style" (Metcalf 1996:7) Similarly, Penny Logan (1988:124, cited in Vertovec 2000) discovered, in the case of Gujaratis in Britain, that many adults developed heightened religious awareness "as a result of belonging to a minority group in a predominantly irreligious society."

In Ireland, while the churches established or led by Africans have flourished, many African community groups have waxed and waned. According to Smith and Mutwasaribo (2000: 8), the lack of "regular sources of funding and a solid community base" are some of the reasons why many African groups have been both ineffective and unsustainable. As a result both of their rapid development and the pivotal role they play in facilitating interaction and communication, African-led Pentecostal churches have become dynamic community institutions and one of the foremost signifiers of the presence of Africans in twenty-first century Ireland. This is one of the reasons I have chosen to make them the focus of my research.

Another reason is the near total neglect of this theme in the academic and research sectors in Ireland. Baumann (1995, 1998) has similarly noted the marginalisation of religion in Diaspora Studies, saying it has been subsumed under ethnicity and nationality. While concerted and systematic research on African-led Pentecostal groups in Ireland is only beginning, the research projects that have been conducted on other aspects of African communities were initiated or sponsored by community groups or NGOs and they are mostly descriptive accounts of settlement or surveys of experiences of racism and discrimination. The study conducted by Suzanne Smith and Fidéle Mutwarasibo in 2000 highlighted interesting themes but it is largely exploratory and did not contain analysis of identity construction or intergroup relationships. The project on the needs of African Asylum Seekers published by the African Refugee Network (ARN 1999) documented the pattern of racially-motivated attacks on African asylum seekers. However, it focuses only on asylum seekers. While asylum seekers constitute a sizeable proportion of recent African immigrants to Ireland, a large number of both 'old' and 'new' immigrants are workers, students and spouses of EU/Irish nationals.

In 2001 the Irish section of Amnesty International (Amnesty International 2001) produced data on the types, quantity and frequency of racially-motivated incidents perpetrated against immigrants and members of ethnic minorities. The report succeeded in re-focusing public attention on the plight of ethnic minorities, due mainly to the quantity and quality of statistics and because it was the first large-scale survey of its kind. However, it did not distinguish the experiences of Africans from those of other immigrant or minority ethnic groups. In recent years there have been concerted efforts to reverse the dearth of research on African communities as several post-graduate students in various universities in Ireland, the majority of them Africans, have embarked on research into different but interrelated themes. However, the majority of these studies are still at the preliminary stages and are largely absent from the public domain.

Given this background, this book constitutes the first substantial investigation of Ireland's fast-developing African communities in general but specifically the role of African-led or initiated Pentecostal churches. This privilege came with several challenges. One of the challenges arose from my own determination to produce a substantial piece of work that would not only provide a nuanced and useful insight but also constitute a valid reference for future research on this theme. The other major challenge was the lack of data on African communities in general and these churches in particular. I have had to generate—through multiple investigative techniques—the data I have used in interrogating relevant theories of religion, identity, and 'integration' in order to provide a complex but coherent picture of this emerging phenomenon in the lives of African immigrants in contemporary Ireland.

RELEVANT THEORETICAL FRAMEWORKS

Investigations of African Pentecostal groups and of immigrant religious practices have generally been biased towards Emile Durkheim's functionalism. He theorised religion as "a unified system of beliefs and practices...which unite into a single moral community called a church, all those who adhere to them" (Durkheim, 1965:47). Durkheim further suggested that ritual and participation are essential to religion's unifying role. In his view, religion was not only normal but socially healthy or desirable. Though Durkheim's functionalist interpretation lays the foundation to a theorisation of the sociological nature of religion and remains a useful tool for analysing the relationship between social values and societal integration, it is a uni-focal and ultimately inadequate tool because it overemphasises the role and uses of rituals to the detriment of religious contents and the role of the social actor.

Despite these and other limitations of Durkheim's analysis, the majority of pioneering research into immigrant religious practices in the United States (e.g., Gordon 1964; Glazer and Moynihan 1963; Oscar 1951; Smith 1978), including Will Herberg's (1955) seminal analysis of Protestants, Catholic and Jews, have emphasised the role of religion in facilitating settlement and acculturation or in sustaining particular ethnic and cultural identities. However, the focus as well as the methods have altered in recent decades as researchers like Martin Baumann (1995, 1998) Stephen Hunt (2002a),

Steven Vertovec (2000), Stephen Warner (1998; 2005), Fenggang Yang (1998), Roof and Hodge (1993); Wuthnow (1993); Judith Wittner (1998) and Lori Peek (2005) have highlighted divergent themes including identity and boundary construction/negotiation and the influence of immigration and pre-immigration conditions on the development of immigrant religious institutions (Ebaugh, et al. 2000; Clarke, et al 1990)[2]. The volume edited by Roof (1993) also reflects the increased diversity of themes and methodology.

In the United Kingdom and the rest of Europe pioneering investigations were also heavily slanted towards functionalism as they focused either on the role of immigrant religious practices in facilitating integration and acculturation or in providing a 'safe' place in a racially-biased and hostile immigration environment (for example, see Becher 1995; Calley 1965; Kalilombe 1998, 1997; Hill 1971a, 1971b, 1971c; McRobert 1989; Parry 1993; Pryce 1979; Ramdin 1987). Pentecostal churches dominated and led by 'Blacks' were also constructed as alternatives to 'mainline' churches that refused to welcome these groups of newcomers in their midst (Gerloff 1992). Patrick Kalilombe, a Catholic Bishop from Malawi and former Director of the Centre for Black White Christian Partnership in Birmingham, notes that 'Black Christianity' developed in the United Kingdom "in response to the need for black Christians to make sense of the status of 'ethnic minority' that was imposed on them when they came to Britain" (Kalilombe 1998: 173). He further states that: "The origin and development of Black Christianity in Britain…is preponderantly the result of black people feeling alienated and marginalized in British society, both secular and religious…" (Ibid: 186). Although Kalilombe articulates a nuanced interpretation that, among other things, links 'black Christianity' to the identity politics of that era, his work is located within the realm of functionalism.

This bias towards functionalism is also reflected to various degrees and through multiple themes in research on immigrant religious practices in continental Europe, especially in Germany, The Netherlands and Sweden (Adogame 2003,

2000; Ekué 1998; Ter Haar 1998a; 1998b; Mella 1994). For example, Orlando Mella, who studied Catholic Chilean refugees in Sweden, notes that religion was used by them to "reconstruct a microcosm of the homeland in the host country" in order to counter cultural marginalisation and social isolation (Mella 1994: 114). Similarly, Ter Haar (1998c:159) notes that Pentecostalism equipped African immigrants in the Netherlands with "the spiritual strength and social contacts necessary to survive, and even to begin the long climb up the ladder of social responsibility in a country which, like most parts of Western Europe, has gradually become more hostile to foreigners, particularly when they are people of colour". However, Ter Haar's analysis (1998a, 1998b 1998c) extend beyond functionalism into analysis of self-representation and the representation of self by the 'other'. She challenges the use of the term 'African' to describe these churches when the majority describe themselves as 'international', 'universal' or simply as 'church of Jesus Christ'. She asserts that the use of such terms to describe these churches contributes to their marginalisation or ethnicisation in Europe.

I have made a conscious decision to triangulate theories as well as methods in my investigation of African-led Pentecostal groups in Ireland in order to present a nuanced analysis that incorporates functionalist, critical and substantive interpretations of religion. Inspired by Nicole Toulis's (1997) analysis of Pentecostal Jamaican women in the United Kingdom and Stephen Hunt's (2002a) research on Pentecostal African immigrants, the core of my research eschews functionalism in favour of substantive analysis and I attempt to establish the multiple and complex connections between Pentecostalism and the construction of 'self', 'others' and social reality by African immigrants. The theoretical foundation of my substantive approach is rooted in Max Weber's (1930) contention that the substance or contents of Protestantism served as definers of self and social reality for the Calvinists in seventeenth century Europe. Weber conceptualised religion as a relationship between the actor and a super mundane being, which has implications not only for ethical and moral conduct but also for the actor's understanding of self and situation (Marshall 1982; Weber 1930).

Like Weber, theorists like Clifford Geertz (1966), Peter Berger (1973) and Robert Bellah (1976) have also theorised religion as a meaning-making and meaning-expressing instrument. In his analysis of the transformation of Olaudah Equiano from a slave boy to an articulate anti-slave trade crusader, Paul Gilroy clearly enunciated the role of religious beliefs in the transformation of identities: "The superficial differences of gender and social status, race and caste, marked on the body by the trifling order of man, were...set aside in favour of a relationship with Christ that offered a means to transcend and thereby escape the constraints of mortality and the body-coded order of identification and differentiation" (2000: 119-120). Robert Bellah (1976) similarly argues in *Beyond Beliefs* that religious beliefs provide a framework for social actors to interpret their experiences and construct social realities.

With specific reference to Pentecostalism, Toulis (1997: 210) notes that beliefs offered Jamaican women "an alternative basis for the construction of identity and difference... Rather than define themselves as 'Black' in White society, church members identified themselves as model 'Christians' in an imperfect Christian society." Hunt notes that "Pentecostalism's changing theodicies and value-orientation have more recently come to assist the formation of identity and transitory ethnic constituency" (Hunt 2002a: 148). He calls for "a new paradigm to explain the rise of an innovating expression of Pentecostalism which may be as much to do with identity-building as it is with providing a sectarian form of religious compensation for alienated black minority groups."

While acknowledging that Pentecostalism has served practical, emotional and social purposes for African immigrants, I argue against over-reliance on functionalism in our attempt to understand this latest development on Ireland's socio-cultural and religious landscape. Functionalism in its multiple manifestations, including Karl Marx's critical notion of religion and Stark and Bainbridge's Rational Choice

Theory (Bruce 1993; Chaves 1995; Hamilton 2001; Stark and Bainbridge 1996), may shed some light on how and why the African immigrants who participated in my study have relied on Pentecostalism in a difficult immigration situation, but it does not explain why the majority became Pentecostals in the first place or the links between Pentecostalism and the construction of self-understanding and boundaries/difference. Rather than adopt the problematic and contentious concept of identity (Hall 2000; Woodward 2002) I have re-articulated the concept into clusters of words in line with Rogers Brubaker's (2004) suggestions. Brubaker's theorisation of identity offers far greater conceptual clarity and, in the case of my investigation, it has provided meaningful thematic arrangements for structuring the data arising from ethnographic interviews. The three clusters of words suggested by Brubaker (2004:41) are: 1) Identification and categorization 2) Self-understanding and social location 3) Commonality, connectedness and groupness. These concepts are developed further in chapters seven and eight.

DATA GATHERING

I have triangulated four major investigative techniques to gather data relevant to the themes of my research. These are:

1) Ethnographic interviews involving 18 African Pente-costals drawn from four churches in the Greater Dublin Area
2) A quantitative survey of 144 members drawn from the same churches
3) Ethnographic observations achieved through repeated visits to the four churches in 2001-05. These visits included non-participant observation of various kinds of public and committee meetings.
4) A survey of documents produced by the churches, including pamphlets, posters, recorded sermons, audio-visual recording of sermons and special gatherings, church in-house magazines, mass media reports etc

In analysing the narratives garnered from my interviews, I seek to identify and document specific understandings of 'self' and 'others' and the complex and multiple ways boundaries and differences are constructed. The presentation of the data is always contextualised. I 'interrupt' the narratives in order to provide necessary background information to aid interpretation of the narrators' views. Narratives, like autobiographies and life histories, are neither neutral nor transparent. They are produced in particular contexts and from a particular point of view (Richardson 1990, 1995; Wolf 1992). By interrupting the narratives with my 'lead-ins' and 'lead-outs', I aim to make the reader conscious of this and therefore prevent a sort of 'narratives speak for themselves' interpretation of the data. My approach, in the words of Jayne Ifekwunigwe (1999:60), testifies to "the death of the authoritative ethnographic voice and the rebirth of the collaborative dialogic exchange." My bias towards substantive interpretations does not exclude elements of functionalism from my analysis. The data identify multiple and diverse uses of Pentecostalism by African immigrants to meet material, social and emotional needs. These are discussed mostly in chapter six, but also in chapter seven.

BOOK OUTLINE

In the next chapter I discuss the economic and political changes that have facilitated the metamorphosis of Ireland into an immigrant-receiving nation and highlight the processes and implications of this development. The analysis of relevant immigration and citizenship laws and policies provides necessary background information or context for explaining the reasons for the increased presence of African immigrants in Ireland from the mid-1990s.

Chapter three describes the socio-cultural, economic and political activities of Africans and highlights the pivotal role of African-led Pentecostal churches in facilitating communication and interaction. I aim to demonstrate the contribution of African immigrants to the metamorphosis of Ireland into a multi-ethnic and multicultural country.

Chapter four describes the history and contents of modern Pentecostalism, from its beginning arguably in the United States in 1906, through its journey to and presence in Africa and its 'exportation' to Europe and Ireland through African immigrants. The chapter highlights the controversies that surrounded the origins of Pentecostalism and describes its presence in African countries, first as a religion of the elites and its subsequent spread to other social and economic groups.

Chapters five, six and eight discuss my empirical data while chapter seven examines sociological explanations of religion. Whereas chapter five offers an overview of the history and presence of African-led Pentecostal groups in Ireland, chapter six presents a comparative assessment of the histories, organisation and activities of the four churches I have selected for this study. It also presents the result of the survey of 144 members drawn from the four selected churches. The chapter concludes by providing a brief introduction of the eighteen participants in the ethnographic interviews.

Relying on substantive and meaning-making notions of religion espoused by classical and modern theorists, I argue in chapter seven that religious beliefs can indeed constitute a prism used by adherents to construct self-understanding, stake differences and negotiate boundaries. I review and critique some sociological approaches to religion, especially the functionalist and critical schools of thought, and argue that the proposed link between deprivation and Pentecostalism is, as Hunt (2002b, 2002c) has argued, complex and, in the case African immigrants in Ireland, does not provide a nuanced explanation of their involvement with Pentecostalism. A triangulation of substantive explanations, functionalist interpretations and critical theories is needed to comprehend the complex and multifaceted relationships African immigrants maintain with Pentecostalism.

Chapter eight discusses identity, differences and boundaries, relying on the narratives from the interviews with two main narrators, whose stories I theorise as 'key stories', representing and epitomising the narratives of leaders of African-led Pentecostal churches in the Irish context. I also use quotes from other narrators to further highlight the themes I have chosen to emphasise, after Brubaker (2004): identification and categorization, self-understanding and social location, commonality, connectedness and groupness.

Chapter nine begins by articulating the importance and uses of Pentecostalism for African immigrants in twenty-first century Ireland. It identifies Pentecostal African immigrants' self-understanding and their construction of the 'other', difference and boundaries. The chapter relies on empirical data and theories of immigrant settlement and acculturation (Wirth 1969; Waldinger 1993; Marcuse 1997; Portes and Bach 1985) to arrive at some conclusions regarding the implications of African Pentecostals' self-understanding and boundary construction for their long-term presence and participation in Irish society.

Chapter nine is followed by a postscript where I discuss the research process and some of the major research decisions. Of particular interest here is my reflection on my position as an African researching other Africans and the issues relating to belonging, boundaries and access that were highlighted by my encounters in the field.

Notes

1. The term 'African' is used in this context to describe people from the African continent who are physically or phenotypically different from Caucasians, Asians or Arabs. The reference therefore describes sub-Saharan Africans and excludes 'white' and 'Asian' Africans and North Africans.

2. Two recent publications that best demonstrate the greater diversity in research into immigrant religious practices in recent decades are firstly, a collection of essays by Stephen Warner titled *'A church of Our Own...'* (2005); and secondly, an edited volume by Stephen Warner and Judith Wittner titled, *'Gatherings in Diaspora...'* (1998). The analyses in these publications straddle a variety of themes, approaches and methods.

CHAPTER TWO

IRELAND: FROM EMIGRATION TO IMMIGRATION

In this chapter I discuss the causes, processes and implications of increased migrations to Ireland since the mid-1990s. This is by no means an exhaustive analysis of Ireland's metamorphosis from an immigrant-sending country to a migration destination. Rather, my analysis focuses on specific developments in immigration and citizenship policies and the impact they have had on the migration and settlement patterns of newer African immigrants in the country. The information in this chapter provides necessary background to the analysis of Ireland's African communities that I have presented in the next chapter.

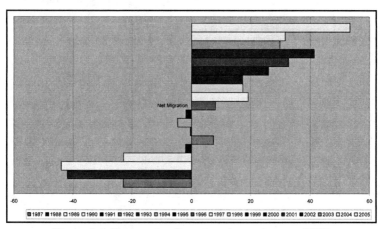

Figure 2.1: Emigration/in-migration estimates: CSO

Until the 1990s, Ireland was a country of intermittent and sometimes massive emigrations (see Figure 2.1). Between 1991 and 1996, migrant in-flows outstripped out-flows by nearly 2,000 but in 2002 the disparity had jumped to 41,300 per year, according to the Population and Migration Estimates published by the Central Statistics Office (www.cso.ie). Seven percent of the 50,500 people that came into the country between April 2002 and April 2003 were nationals of African countries. Following the increase in in-migration provoked by the addition of new members to the European Union, net migration increased from 31,600 in 2004 to 53,400 the following year and to 69,900 in 2006. Immigrants and minority ethnic groups have existed in Ireland long before their pronounced presence in the 1990s and the moral panics that greeted the arrival of increased numbers of asylum seekers at the beginning of this decade. (Goldstone 2002; Keogh 1998; Lentin 2001; Mac Éinrí 2000; McVeigh 1992, 2002). As Ronit Lentin (2001) surmises: "Racism and multi-ethnicity have been a reality in Ireland long before the moral panics created by the arrival of a relatively small number of asylum seekers in the 1990s."

Emigration, especially among young people, has continued even in the years of massive immigration. To illustrate, 59% of the 20,700 persons who emigrated between April 2002 and April 2003 were aged 15-24 years and 40% of them went to countries other than the EU and the USA (CSO 2003). A total of 18,500 persons emigrated from Ireland between April 2003 and April 2004, the lowest since 1987. More than half of them (54%) were between the ages of 15 and 24. However, recent emigrations tend to be non-permanent as many emigrants return after about two or three years. Asia and the Far East have become popular emigration destinations. A prominent feature of the changes in the rates and patterns of immigration to Ireland since the 2002 census is the increased presence of non-European and non-Western immigrants, as Figure 2.2 shows. The other major feature of the changes in immigration is the increased presence of citizens of Eastern European countries since May 2004 when

10 new countries joined the European Union. Migrations from the former communist countries have been dominated by the Poles.

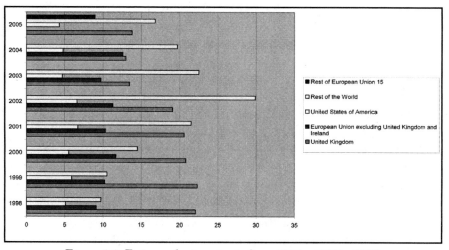

Figure 2.2: Estimated migration inflows 1998—2005—CSO

CATEGORIES OF IMMIGRANTS

The dramatic increases in in-migration and the resultant social and cultural changes took place against the backdrop of a dynamic and fast-growing economy. The 'Celtic Tiger' was itself the result of an economic thrust that encouraged Direct Foreign Investment (FDI) into Ireland, beginning in the late 1950s when the government replaced protection-ist economic policies with more open and internationally competitive ones (Sweeney 1998; Kirby et al 2002). Further incentives for multi-national companies to relocate to Ireland were introduced in the early 1990s, including zero (and later low) export taxes. These measures and the introduction of the Partnership for Prosperity and Fairness (PPF) made Ireland an investment haven for the multinational companies (Mac Éinrí 2001; Sweeney 1998). As these companies relocated their operations to Ireland, the economy experienced real growth that translated into a rapid rise in the GDP, the creation of more jobs, rising wages and a better standard of living. Such was the rate of growth in the economy and in job creation that unemployment rates fell to less than 4% in March 2001 from 15% in 1993 (Beesley 2000d; Brennan 2001). Towards the end of the1990s the prospects of severe labour shortages loomed large. Among other measures, the government reached out to outsiders—non-Irish nationals and Irish emigrants—in order to meet employers' demands for workers. The Department of Trade Enterprise and Employment (DTEE) and FÁS, the state's training and job agency, embarked on recruitment drives mostly in Eastern European countries, South East Asia, China and South Africa. The then Tánaiste (Deputy Prime Minister), Mary Harney, and FÁS officials by-passed sub-Saharan Africa as they travelled to many parts of the world to launch recruitment drives, hence a relatively small number of Africans have been granted permits to work and reside in Ireland.

The post-Second World War recruitment of international labour in Germany set the pattern for the recent and current labour emigrations from countries in the South to those in Western Europe and from East to West. Prior to that era, South-North migrations were mostly from former colonies or dependent territories to dominant centres in Europe (Faist 2000:7; Collinson 1993). The shape of Ireland's recruitment scheme since the 1990s bears some similarities to those of other European countries, especially Germany. Ireland's decision to issue short-term permits/visas resonated with Germany's 'Gastarbeiter' system that was aimed generally at discouraging the long-term presence of immigrant and minority ethnic groups (Bade 2003; Collinson 1993; Rasmussen 1996). Work permits are issued for a short duration, usually for six months or one year but can be renewed.

The working visa/work authorisation scheme was introduced in 2000. Working visas are issued to non-EU/EEA immigrants who require entry visas to Ireland while work authorisations are issued to those who do not require entry visas. Working visas and work authorisations are usually valid for two years or three months in the case of candidate nurses. Workers in these categories are allowed to change their employers within the same skills category after arrival in Ireland as long as they have valid permits to work and reside in the country (www.entemp.ie). Working visa immigrants can apply for family re-unification after three months in the country. Those on work authorisation can come to Ireland with their family since they do not require entry visa.

Since the mid-1990s there have been swift increases in asylum applications although the numbers have fallen in recent years. There were a total of 424 applications in 1995, up from 39 in 1992. This rose dramatically to 1,179 in 1996 and to 7,762 in 1999. In 2000, the number of applicants (including re-applications) stood at 10, 938. It fell slightly to 10,325 in 2001 and rose again to 11,634 in 2002. The total number of applications in 2003 dropped to 7,900. It slipped further to 4,766 in 2004 and to 4323 in 2005, the lowest number since 1998. Nigerians, the largest sub-Saharan African group in Ireland, accounted for the highest number of applicants in 2005 and, for every year since 2000, they have accounted for between 30% and 40% of total applications (ORAC 2006).

In Ireland, asylum applicants can be broadly divided into Geneva Convention applicants and programme refugees. As in most EU countries, programme refugees are a pre-specified number of asylum seekers who have arrived for a specified period as a result of a government decision to waive the requirements of a formal application under the 1951 Geneva Convention. In reality, many programme refugees stay longer or even permanently in the country of asylum. Although they are granted the entitlements of a 'recognised' asylum seeker from the moment they arrive, they are still confronted with problems of social isolation and racism. In the 1990s programme refugees came to Ireland from Bosnia, Croatia and Kosovo. Before that there had been programme refugees from Vietnam and Chile, but none from Africa.

Generally, asylum applications in Ireland are made under the terms of the 1951 United Nations Geneva Convention and the 1967 New York Protocol. Both the Convention (which Ireland signed in November 1956) and the Protocol (Ireland signed in November 1968) have been incorporated into Irish refugee law by means of the 1996 Refugee Act. The Refugee Act has been amended by section 11(1) of the 1999 Immigration Act, section 9 of the 2000 Illegal Immigrant Trafficking Act, and section 7 of the 2003 Immigrant Act. The Refugee Act, which came into effect in November 2000, establishes the Office of the Refugee Application Commissioner (ORAC), which determines asylum applications in the first instance and the Refugee Appeals Tribunal (RAT), which hears appeals against the decisions of the ORAC.

Asylum laws and policies in Ireland have also been influenced by multilateral agreements among member-countries of the European Union. Asylum seekers do not have the right to gainful employment and access to third-level education is problematic. On the 26th of July 1999, the government implemented a 'one-off' decision to allow asylum seekers, including many Africans who had been in the country for up to one year, to work. It refused to extend or repeat the gesture despite pleas from asylum seekers' groups, community and church leaders, as well as employers (Tróicare and ICJP 2002). Until 2000, the majority of asylum seekers were housed in and around the Greater Dublin Area. In December 1999, the government announced a new policy of 'dispersal', which meant that asylum seekers would be assigned to designated accommodation centres all over Ireland.

The implementation of this policy from 2000 has resulted in greater and noticeable presence of African immigrants and African-led Pentecostal churches in smaller cities and towns in far-flung corners of Ireland. Some of these churches were born in state-owned accommodation centres in and outside of the Greater Dublin Area. In mid-2003, about 4,500 asylum seekers were accommodated in 53 direct provision centres in Ireland (FLAC 2003; Haughey 2003a). At the beginning of 2005 there were 6,127 asylum seekers in 63 accommodation centres. The largest centre in Mosney housed 761 people while the one in Athlone had 359 residents. The number fell to 3,874 in January 2006 reflecting both the dramatic reduction in the number of asylum applicants in Ireland and the relocation to private accommodation of immigrant parents of Irish children who have successfully applied for residence permit (Sanctuary 2005; Sanctuary 2006).

Some Africans who came to Ireland as students in the decades before the 1990s have remained in Ireland after they established familial or business relationships. Statistics for this category of immigrants are haphazard and unreliable. Generally, the bulk of foreign students in the past came mostly from North America and Europe, according to the Higher Education Authority (www.hea.ie). In recent years more students are now coming from Asia and Africa. The number of language schools has increased dramatically in the last decade but there are no reliable statistics on the actual number of students. Immigrant students, including those in language schools, are entitled to work for a maximum of 20 hours a week. It is common knowledge that many work full-time with the active connivance of their employers, many of whom often exploit these workers (Haughey 2002a). Introduced at the beginning of this decade as part of the measures to wrestle a slice of the English language market from the United Kingdom, the policy has attracted many immigrant groups to Ireland. As demonstrated in the next chapter, fewer numbers of Africans have arrived in Ireland as students, compared to those that have sought political asylum.

Generally, fewer immigrants have come into Ireland via the family reunification route. This is largely due to the lengthy and strict application procedures. The criteria are non-standardised and the decision processes are not transparent. Though applications are made to the Minister for Justice, the Office of the Refugee Application Commissioner (ORAC) is charged with processing them and with making recommendations to the Minister. The Minister exercises discretionary power in granting or rejecting applications, based on ORAC's recommendations. Between 2001 and the end of 2003, a total of 544 persons were given approval to join their relatives in Ireland. At 227, the number approved in 2002 was the highest, followed by 192 in 2003 (information received from the Department of Justice press office, 2004). A total of 317 new applications were made in 2004. Of the

556 new applications received in 2005, 384 were processed and forwarded to the Minister for approval. In 2005, the highest number of applications was made by Somalis (12%), followed by Nigerians (10%) and the Democratic Republic of Congo (9%) (Sanctuary 2005; Sanctuary 2006)

RESIDENCE PERMITS

Up until early 2003, immigrants, including asylum seekers, who become parents of children/child born in Ireland and therefore an Irish citizen, could also apply for residence permit solely on that basis. Section 2.1 of the Irish constitution, including Article 2 adopted as part of the 1998 Belfast Agreement, grants the right to naturalization to every child born in the island of Ireland (Dooley 2003; The Irish Times 2002). In a famous judgement in what is now known as the 'Fajujonu case', the Irish Supreme Court ruled in 1989 that the children of non-citizens had a constitutional right to the "company, care and parentage" of their parents within a family unit. That ruling effectively compelled the state to grant residence permit to such parents (The Irish Times 2002; Dooley 2003). The number of immigrants relying on this avenue to establish the right of residency grew sharply from the beginning of the twenty-first century after Ireland's stricter immigration and asylum policies made it difficult for immigrants, especially asylum seekers, to establish a presence in the country. Between 1996 and the end of 2001, a total of 4, 859 people were granted rights to remain in Ireland on this basis, while the number of births in 2001 to non-Irish nationals in the Dublin-based Rotunda hospital was reported by the *Irish Times* to be one in five (The Irish Times 2002). As I indicate in the next chapter, the majority of newer African immigrants to Ireland are in the young and child-bearing age. It is therefore not surprising that many of those who gained residence status through this means were Africans who had come into the country either as asylum seekers or migrant workers.

The government's decision to abandon this policy followed another Supreme Court decision on 23 January

2003 in a case involving a family from Nigeria and another from the Czech Republic (The Irish Times 2002; Haughey 2003d). The court ruled that immigrant parents of Irish citizen children and their non-Irish siblings could no longer apply for residence permit solely on that basis. The ruling was applied retroactively to include all parents whose children were born before the court ruling, (excluding those who had been granted residence permit), including those who were awaiting decisions on their applications. In February 2003 when the Minister for Justice issued orders to stop granting residence permits to immigrant parents of Irish citizens, there were 11,493 outstanding applications (Department of Justice 2004). Of these, 9,631 applicants had been or were still in the asylum system and 1,862 were non-asylum related. Many African immigrants were caught up in the quagmire that followed the ministerial directive.

The Coalition Against Deportation of Irish Children (CADIC) spear-headed a campaign to persuade the Minister to have a change of heart over the outstanding applications. Having run, and won (with the support of 78.9 % of the population), a referendum in June 2004 to change Ireland's citizenship entitlement and allow only children born in Ireland whose parents or parent is a citizen to achieve Irish citizenship, the government announced at the end of 2004 a new policy that would allow immigrant parents to reapply for residence permit (O'Brien 2005; Holland 2004b; also see Lentin and McVeigh 2006 for a nuanced analysis). The new policy effectively removed the threats of deportation that had dangled over the heads of these immigrants since February 2003. Under the new policy that came into effect in January 2005, applicants would have to prove, among other things, that they are of good character and that they have the possibility to become self-reliant in two years from the time they are granted residency rights. They are also required to give an undertaking not to invite other members of their family outside of Ireland to live with them. Out of the 17,877 applications received by the Department as of mid-December 2005, 17,660 had been processed. A total of 16,704 persons were granted residency rights and 956 were refused (Sanctuary 2006). It is not clear how many of these are Africans but experiential knowledge and anecdotal evidence suggest that many Africans gained legal residency through this means.

Deportations, which had always been an element of Irish immigration policies, acquired new salience during this time and up till the end of 2005. The majority of the over 550 deportations in 2003 were to countries in Eastern Europe. In 2003 the Garda National Immigration Bureau embarked on the joint chartering of aircrafts with immigration authorities in the United Kingdom and The Netherlands to facilitate deportations to Nigeria, China, Romania, and other countries in Eastern Europe. Whereas 2,866 deportation orders were signed by the Minister for Justice in 2004, only 599 deportations were carried out. The majority of deportations were to Romania (250), Nigeria (77), Moldova (57) and China (18). In 2005, 396 deportations out of the 1,838 orders signed by the Minister were effected. The highest number of deportations were to Nigeria (135), followed by Romania (122) and China (18). A total of 335 people were repatriated 'voluntarily'. Between 1999 and 2005, a total of 12,660 deportation orders were issued, 2,664 deportations were carried out while 2,855 people were repatriated 'voluntarily' (Sanctuary 2005; Sanctuary 2006).

CITIZENSHIP POLICIES AND IMMIGRANT CIVIC ACTIVISM

The most profound change in Irish citizenship law took effect in January 2005. In June 2004 Irish citizens had voted overwhelmingly to repeal Article 9 of the Irish Constitution which grants the right to naturalisation to every child born in the island of Ireland. Since January 2005 immigrants born in Ireland whose parent or parents are not citizens can apply for citizenship if their parent "has, during the period of 4 years immediately preceding the person's birth, been resident in the island of Ireland for a period of not less than 3 years" (Irish Nationality and Citizenship Act 2004). In addition, spouses of Irish citizens and asylum applicants who have attained refugee status can apply for naturalisation after three years. Also, immigrants (excluding asylum seekers and students) who have legally resided in the country for five years are entitled to apply for naturalisation. There is also a provision for applying for leave to remain in the country indefinitely if an immigrant has lived in Ireland for eight years.

The active participation of immigrants in public life is, to a large extent, influenced by the status and conditions of their residency. Anecdotal and experiential knowledge suggests that immigrants with long-term or permanent residence status and those who have Irish citizenship have taken a more confident and committed approach to participation in public life. The picture is a lot more complex than I have painted here. There are immigrants who have been active in public life despite having uncertain or precarious residence status. For others, their civic activism is informed by their pre-immigration education and experience, while others are compelled to tread the path of active civic participation because of the peculiar difficulties they face in Ireland (see Ugba 2005 for a fuller analysis). In relation to politics and electoral participation, there are specific regulations under Irish laws and those will be analysed later in this section. The next section will elucidate the relationship between general immigration policies and immigrant participation in public life.

As documented above, there are different regimes in Ireland for receiving and integrating asylum seekers, foreign workers, students and family reunification migrants. Whereas students, migrant workers and their relatives/dependants have access to all levels of education, asylum seekers have access only to primary and secondary education. In addition, they do not have the right to gainful employment (with the exception of a small number of asylum seekers allowed to work in 2001—see Tróicare/ICJP 2002), secure and private accommodation or to travel out of the country. While these restrictions have barred asylum seekers from participating in some civic activities, many have been engaged in activities mostly aimed at changing these and other restrictive immigration policies and at combating racism. Examples of immigrant-led groups in this respect include the Association of Refugees and Asylum Seekers in Ireland (ARASI), the African Refugee Network (ARN), the Nigerian Support Group (NSG) and the Asylum Seekers Group Ireland (ASGI).

There are no similar restrictions on the participation of immigrant workers in public life. However, there are financial difficulties as well as specific institutional requirements that discourage participation. A recent report by Integrating Ireland, a national network of refugee, asylum seeker and immigrant support groups, identified discriminatory fees, language problems, problems with the recognition of earlier educational achievements and "various social welfare traps and barriers" as some of the obstacles to immigrant participation in education (Integrating Ireland 2005). The report recommended a review of the existing admissions systems to facilitate access to higher education for immigrants who have not gone through the Irish secondary school system.

The civic activities of many foreign workers have been focused mainly on changing discriminatory employment, healthcare and social welfare policies. The paths of many immigrant workers to such activism are usually the trade unions and other kinds of pressure groups. There are no constitutional and institutional barriers to membership of trade unions for foreign workers but immigrant membership of many unions have, until recently, been low because some immigrants were not clear on what their rights in this respect are. Others who were not envisaging a long or permanent presence in the Irish labour market did not feel compelled to join the unions (Ugba 2005).

Religious activism is one area where immigrant participation appears to be most intense and voluntary, less problematic and apparently unhindered by precarious residence status or length of time in Ireland. The most innovative and dramatic changes in Ireland's religious and cultural landscape is not the participation of immigrants in 'mainline' Irish churches but the birth and spread of immigrant-led religious groups—from a variety of Christian churches to several mosques in Dublin and elsewhere. It has been relatively easy for immigrant groups to set up places of worship and to publicly demonstrate their beliefs partly because the institutional requirements are not stringent. For individual immigrants, religion appears to be a convenient and adaptable baggage, which they are able to fold up, transport and unfold, in new circumstances with minimum difficulties.

Immigrants have also been active in media production, particularly in the 'ethnic' media sector (Ugba 2002). The launch of *Metro Eireann* on 17 April 2000 marked a turning point in this respect as it stimulated greater intellectual and public debates on the role of ethnic minority media in Ireland. It also opened the floodgates to the birth of many other publications and provided additional opportunities for immigrant civic participation. The use of new Information and Communication Technologies (ICTs) to enhance participation in public life is becoming widespread. Most immigrant groups have set up websites for publicising their activities and facilitating information interchange.

Political and electoral participation involves specific rules and conditions (see Fanning et al. 2003, 2004 for details). Whereas only Irish citizens can take part in referenda and vote in some kinds of elections, citizens of EU countries can vote only in European and local elections while "every person who is a citizen of Ireland or ordinarily resident in the State and has reached the age of 18 years" can vote and be voted for in local elections (www.environ.ie). Up until the 2004 elections, immigrant participation in the political and electoral processes was low-key. However, about 20 immigrants contested the June 2004 local elections. The two who got elected were Nigerians who had come to Ireland as asylum seekers.

PUBLIC DISCOURSES ON IMMIGRATION

In the late 1990s and early 2000s when Ireland recorded the highest numbers of asylum seekers, insinuations and accusations depicting the majority of asylum seekers as 'bogus' and as 'economic' migrants flooded media and public discourses. Anti-immigration groups and some sections of the media capitalised on the prevailing sense of bewilderment to stir up anti-immigrant sentiments. Groups like the Immigration Control Platform launched campaigns aimed at getting the government to adopt more restrictive and exclusionary policies. While the government professed a commitment to its obligations under the Geneva Convention, some government Ministers made unsubstantiated distinctions between 'genuine' refugees and those they termed as 'bogus', 'economic migrants' or 'welfare scroungers' (Guerin 2002; Cullen 2000).

Racism and racial attacks directed at immigrants rose almost in equal proportion to anti-refugee tirades from official and unofficial quarters (McCarthy and Rafferty, 2002; Haughey 2000b). A parallel development to the rise in racism and racially-biased media discourse is the development of an anti-racism sector that spans governmental and non-governmental initiatives and groups. The National Consultative Committee on Racism and Interculturalism (NCCRI) was established in 1998 to facilitate dialogue between government agencies and non-government organisations (www.nccri.ie) while the Equality Authority, a government-funded body charged with initiating anti-discrimination laws, was established in 1999 (www.equality.ie). The 1998 Employment Equality Act and the 2000 Equal Status Act outlaw discrimination on nine grounds, including gender, race, religion and membership of the Traveller community. The Equality Status Act also established the Equality Tribunal, an independent and quasi-judicial forum that hears or mediates complaints of alleged discrimination under the equality legislation. Its decisions and mediated settlements are legally binding (www.equalitytribunal.ie).

However, Ronit Lentin and Robbie McVeigh (2006) have argued that "the cooption of anti-racism by state(s) and the reformulation of anti-racism as 'integration', 'diversity' and 'interculturalism' mark the end of anti-racism as anti-state racism political action". According to them, "anti-racism based on a 'partnership' model, and including anti-racist organisations fully funded by the Department of Justice—is dominated by white Irish people, often informed by a sense of the colonial past and of anti-Irish racism, all convincing themselves that they are working in partnership with people of colour". Perhaps in acknowledgment of these views, the anti-racism movement has witnessed some transformations in recent years as immigrant groups and members of Ireland's only indigenous ethnic/cultural group—the Travellers—have struggled to assert their voice and place. However, the lack of resources and the fierce competition for the limited funds have often not only stood in the way of collective and effective action but also sometimes placed anti-racism groups on opposite sides while they claim a common goal or vision.

CHAPTER THREE

AFRICAN COMMUNITIES IN IRELAND

INTRODUCTION

The history and characteristics of Ireland's African population fit Khalid Koser's (2003) description of Europe's new African diasporas. He uses the term to capture the newer and more recent transatlantic migrations and settlement of black Africans in the West, distinct from and largely unrelated to the forced shipments of Africans to Europe and the Americas for the purpose of slavery. Although Ireland did not participate in a significant way in earlier post-war overseas recruitments of labour by some European countries or in the influx of former colonial subjects into 'mother-countries', the immigration policies initiated by her at the beginning of the twenty-first century resemble those that had been enacted by countries like Germany and the United Kingdom, which were intended to dissuade the long-term presence of immigrant and minority ethnic groups. This chapter examines the migration and settlement patterns of recent African immigrants and it also analyses inter and intra community relations. However, it begins by discussing the dynamics of recent migrations out of Africa, focussing mostly on Nigeria where the majority of African immigrants in Ireland come from.

DYNAMICS OF RECENT MIGRATIONS OUT OF AFRICA

Migrations out of Africa to Europe and America are not new. However, there have been changes in the numbers of migrants, causes of migration and migration patterns, mostly since the latter half of the twentieth century. From the mid-twentieth century to the 1970s, migrations out of Africa were small-scale and migrants mostly travelled to colonial countries to acquire education or training (Nwajiuba 2005). Nigerians and Ghanaians mostly travelled to the United Kingdom while Senegalese and citizens of the other countries colonised by France went to that country. Migration during this era was non-permanent as most migrants were quick to return to their countries of origin better-equipped and eager to contribute to but also benefit from social and economic opportunities created by decolonisation and national development efforts. The era of decolonisation was one of hope and optimism. Many Africans had interpreted the continent's problem solely in terms of the intervention or presence of the colonisers. The departure of the colonisers, they reasoned, would leave the continent's vast natural resources in the hands of natives who would use them for the betterment of Africa and her peoples. In many ways, the realities failed to match the hopes and expectations. The explanations for this are manifold and complex.

Many analysts (e.g. Chinua Achebe 1983) say that corruption and bad leadership are the major reasons the great African dream never came to reality. In the very first sentence of his 68-page book titled, *The Trouble with Nigeria*, Achebe states categorically that "the trouble with Nigeria is simply and squarely a failure of leadership. There is nothing basically wrong with the Nigerian character. There is nothing wrong with the Nigerian land or climate or water or air or anything else." Achebe examines the flawed 1983 general elections in Nigeria and identifies indiscipline, favouritism and arrogance as some of the other hindrances to progress and development.

Other analysts blame the continent's degeneration into poverty and despair on the dramatic fall in the prices of export goods from the 1980s. For example, the fall in the price of crude oil in the 1980s resulted in drastic reduction in foreign exchange earnings for Nigeria while the fluctuating prices of cocoa pods have drastically affected the economies of Ghana, Cote d'Ivoire and Togo (Adedeji et al 1991). The interventions of international monetary institutions like the World Bank and the International Monetary Funds (IMF) in the economic recovery plans of many African countries have also been blamed for the continent's economic and social ills (Ake 1996). The economic recovery plans imposed on African countries by these institutions resulted, in the majority of cases, in drastic devaluation of the local currency, mass retrenchment of public sector workers, reduction in GDP and high inflation. Nwajiuba (2005) notes that "reduced real earnings through the inflationary impact of devaluation and trade liberalization" contributed to the desertion of agriculture and emigrations from rural to urban centres in Nigeria and to European countries.

Religious and ethnic conflicts in many parts of the continent compounded the problems and resulted in social instability and economic deprivation (DFID 2001). Whereas armed conflicts were always features of the social and political landscapes of Africa, the 1980s and 1990s witnessed dramatic increases in the number of civil wars, inter-country wars and regional conflicts. Those who fled conflict zones found shelter in neighbouring countries or outside of the continent. In the specific case of Nigeria, Carling (2005) notes that the persistence of conflicts and corruption even after the country returned to democratic rule in 1999 "has been a great disillusionment to many Nigerians, thousands of whom have sought asylum in Europe."

As economic conditions worsened and socio-political unrests engulfed many societies, the lofty dreams of many about the continent were punctured and increased numbers of Africans sought salvation outside the continent (Carling 2005; Nwajiuba 2005; Jumare 1997). Since the 1980s, the trafficking of women to various European countries, mostly Italy, for sex trade has become prominent. In addition to the traditional migration destinations of Britain, France and American, several new migration destinations, including, Ireland, Italy, Spain and the Middle East, emerged (Koser

2003: 7-8). Apart from new destination countries, new migration routes also emerged. Whereas the vast majority of migrants before the 1980s exited through air and sea ports, some of the newer migrants crossed land borders into neighbouring countries and many travelled through the perilous North African route via Morocco to Spain. In 2005, an estimated 200,000 Nigerians were legally resident in Europe. The highest number lived in the United Kingdom, followed by Italy, Germany, Spain, and Ireland (2005). The next section discusses the arrival and settlement of increased number of Africans in Ireland.

NEWER AFRICAN IMMIGRANTS IN IRELAND

Media and semi-academic writings (Smith and Mutwasaribo 2000; Cullen 2002, Okamura 2003; Field 2000) about Ireland's African population and comparisons to earlier African immigrant groups have assumed a mostly quantitative dimension. Apart from the census figures and the annual population estimates, the other indicators of the number of in-migrants are asylum and work permit statistics, as I have made clear in chapter one. Generally, immigration to Ireland via the political asylum route was relatively insignificant until the mid-1990s and African asylum seekers did not come to Ireland until the late 1990s. A survey of Africans in the Greater Dublin Area shows that 51% of the respondents had been living in Ireland for between one and four years, 34.8% for less than one year and 14% for between 5 and 10 years. The majority of respondents are in the younger age brackets: 47% were 15 – 25 years old, 29% were between 26 and 35 years and 24% were between 36 and 45. Only one respondent indicated that he was over 46 years old. Most of the Africans who came to Ireland prior to the 1990s were mostly students and a few were spouses of Irish citizens or citizens of other European countries. A combination of events in the African continent (Kabbaj 2003) and the progressive tightening of immigration policies in Europe generally and in Ireland especially, are the reasons increased numbers of Africans have resorted to the asylum route to gain entry into Ireland.

More South Africans than nationals of other African countries have applied and received work permits. A total of 2,273 were issued in 2002, according to the DTEE (2006). This increased to 2468 in 2003. The numbers fell to 2031 in 2004 and to 1833 in 2005. Among sub-Saharan African countries, Nigerians have received the highest number of work permits, though the numbers are very small, as are the numbers for other sub-Saharan Africans. In 2002 Nigerians were granted a total of 87 permits, compared to 84 in 2003. The number fell to 60 in 2004 but rose to 77 in 2005. Nigeria is followed by Ghana, which received 19 permits in 2004 and 18 in 2005. Zambians were granted 12 permits in 2005, up from 4 in 2004. Sudanese received 12 in 2005 and 11 in 2004 while Tanzania received 9 in 2005 and 14 in 2004. The other sub-Saharan African countries received fewer than 10 permits each in 2004 and 2005 (DTEE 2006).

My survey confirms that recent arrivals are asylum seekers and refugees, students and workers on temporary or long-term contracts (Ugba 2004)[1]. Just over 60% of the 182 respondents (from 17 countries in Africa) said they came to Ireland to seek political asylum while 18% indicated they came to study, 13% came to work and over 7% came to join their relatives. The vast majority indicated they had some form of temporary residence or were otherwise uncertain about the future. One-third (or 33 %) of the respondents were asylum seekers, 13% were Irish citizens, 17% were refugees, 14% were students and another 17% simply said they were 'immigrants'.

Despite the fledgling nature of Ireland's African population and its small size, relative to other longer established racialised groups like the Travellers or the more numerous immigrant groups from China and Poland, African immigrants have contributed to the metamorphosis of Ireland into a multiethnic and multicultural nation through their socio-cultural, economic and, of recent, political activities. In the Greater Dublin Area their increased participation in these activities and the disproportionate focus on the anti-social activities of a few Africans by some sections of the media have made Africans visible. Sub-Saharan African immigrants also stand out because of their distinctive physical characteristics or phenotypical features. As Paul Cullen surmised in an article in *The Irish Times*: "Black immigrants simply stand out more than other groups...unlike eastern Europeans, black-skinned immigrants have nowhere to hide in the face of racist behaviour" (Cullen 2002). In a study published in 2000 by the African Cultural Project, Suzanne Smith and Fidéle Mutwarasibo (2000) conclude that "an effective African network" was already in place even though "African communities do not exist". Since that report, African immigrants have formed various groups aimed at expressing their religious, professional, economic, political and national/ethnic interests.

AFRICAN ORGANISATIONS: THE BEGINNINGS OF COMMUNITIES

African-initiated Pentecostal churches are among the most prominent social and cultural institutions established by newer African immigrants in Ireland. Arguably, these churches have become the most prominent testimony to the presence of Africans in Dublin in the twenty-first century (ICC 2003; Cullen 2003; McCann 2000). As far back as August 2000 *Metro Eireann* (2000), Ireland's multicultural newspaper, reported that over 40 'African' churches had been established in the Greater Dublin Area. Any efforts to ascertain the actual number of these churches would have to be repeated frequently, mainly because they have continued to proliferate rapidly as new ones form and splinter groups emerge (Ugba 2003b). These churches are facilitating communication and interaction among their members, providing physical, social and emotional help to the needy, and helping members understand and cope with their situation of voluntary or involuntary exile. Congolese-born Remba Osengo, pastor of Christ Co-Workers Mission, the first of these churches to be established in Ireland, believes that the churches are providing forums for members of the community to organise and consolidate their position and prepare for the challenges of political and other forms of participation in the larger society.

While the churches have flourished and continue to do so, other African groups have waxed and waned. The majority of the groups formed prior to the increased presence of Africans (e.g. Algeria Solidarity Group, Congo Solidarity Group, Irish Mozambique Solidarity, Irish-Sudanese Solidarity Group, Ogoni Solidarity Ireland, the Somali Community) tended to reflect national or ethnic interests, but those formed more recently (e.g. Pan-African Organisation, African Solidarity Centre and AkiDwA – the African Women's Network) have adopted a broader or Pan-African focus. AKiDwA, established in August 2001 by seven women from six different African countries, is devoted specifically to the promotion and protection of the interests of African women, perhaps out of a conviction that the other groups, which are mostly male-dominated, are unsuited and incapable of addressing the unique problems of this category of Africans (www. akidwa.ie).

The emergence of AkiDwA and other special interest groups like the Association of Nigerian Professionals in Ireland, African Refugee Network and the Association of Nigerian Asylum Seekers in Ireland point to the heterogeneous and multifaceted nature of Ireland's African communities. It is a heterogeneity and diversity that is fostered or accentuated not only by different national/ethnic/religious orientations and residence statuses, but also by the gulf between the latest waves of immigrants and the ones who arrived earlier. Although these sorts of diversities and differences can be a source of strength, they can sometimes work against community building and participation. The swift demise of the once thriving Union of Nigerian Citizens Residents in Ireland (UNCRI) illustrates this point.

In the days of lesser migration of Nigerians to Ireland and at a time when the majority of Nigerian immigrants were professionals, students, diplomats and spouses of Irish citizens, UNCRI (I was one of the union's trustees between 1999 and 2000) was for a long time the only representative body for Africans in Ireland. The Union had strong ties with the Nigerian embassy in Dublin and many of its regular meetings and special events were held on the embassy premises. The ambassador attended and, in the majority of cases, sponsored some of its major functions like the end-of-year parties and parties held to mark Nigerian Independence Day anniversaries. Although the Union's close links to the embassy strengthened its financial muscle, it also contributed to its demise.

An early and prominent sign that the Union's growth had become stunted and its demise eminent was that its membership remained static despite the obvious increase in the number of Nigerians in Ireland. The bulk of the new arrivals were asylum seekers and refugees who refused to support or identify with an organisation that had direct links with the Nigerian government. Also, many existing members felt deep animosity towards Nigerian asylum seekers, accusing them of betraying their country and of telling lies in other to secure refugee status in Ireland. It was common at general and executive meetings of the Union in 1999 and 2000 to hear tirades upon tirades directed at Nigerian asylum seekers, with some members even suggesting that they (asylum seekers) were the reasons sections of the Irish society had become hostile and racist towards Nigerians. The few asylum seekers who had attempted to associate with the Union soon withdrew while the non-asylum seekers soon started to complain about the closeness of the Union to the Nigerian embassy. Coupled with these were issues of ethnicity, as members of rival ethnic groups jostled for positions on the executive. By the end of 2002 UNCRI had succumbed to internal divisions and infighting among its diversified membership.

The Association of Nigerian Asylum Seekers in Ireland (ANASI) emerged in place of UNCHRI to cater for the specific needs of Nigerian asylum seekers and refugees. However, as more of its members attained permanent residence status and Irish citizenship, the organisation felt a need to be more inclusive and therefore changed its name to the Nigerian Support Group. More recently, the Yoruba Elders' Council have emerged to promote the interest of Yoruba men and women and the other African ethnic groups, like the Ibos, have similarly formed solidarity groups to cater for their specific interests and, where possible, to present a united opinion on issues in the home-countries. In 2004, the Nigerians in the Diaspora (NIDO), an international organisation with direct links to the Nigerian government, established an office in Dublin. Some of the officials of the defunct UNCHRI have resurfaced in the new group.

Despite what appears to be a highly heterogeneous, or even fractious population, Africans in Ireland prefer a common or unifying identity, perhaps out of a realisation that disunity could only weaken their collective voice and negotiating power in the larger society. Over 82% of the participants in my survey wanted to be identified as an 'African' man/woman, as against 10% who wanted to be identified as a 'Black' man or woman. Only one respondent preferred to be identified by his nationality. In subsequent focus group discussions of the survey results, it emerged that the way members of the community would choose to identify themselves would generally depend on the contexts. While acknowledging the many distinctions and differences among African groups, the focus group participants expressed a preference for the homogenising 'African' label as a strategy both for overcoming those distinctions and for negotiating a place and a voice in Irish society.

AFRICANS IN THE IRISH MEDIA

Active participation in the 'ethnic' media sector is another way African migrants in Ireland have remained visible and also contributed to the evolution of Ireland into a multiethnic society. When *Metro Eireann* hit the newsstands on April 17 2000, it served as a major invitation to the dominant culture to acknowledge and debate diversity. I was one of *Metro Eireann*'s two founding publishers and its first editor. The other publisher is also an African. Though *Metro Eireann* did not set out to specifically promote African interests but to showcase and help establish a multicultural Ireland, the fact that its two pioneering publishers were of African origin meant that its birth signalled a new public presence and role for Africans in Ireland.

Metro Eireann was not the first ethnic minority newspaper in Ireland but its entrance into the media market was pivotal because it signalled a revival of publishing by members of ethnic minority groups (Ugba 2002). For a long time, prior to the birth of *Metro Eireann*, the foray into media production and publishing by minority ethnic groups was restricted mainly to in-house newsletters of particular groups and publications like the *Italia Stampa, L'Chaim Ireland* (published by the Jewish community) and *Voice of the Traveller* directed specifically at members of particular ethnic groups. Members of minority ethnic groups have also made their marks through occasional contributions to mainstream media like *The Irish Times* or *The Irish Independent.* The appointment in April 2001 of Nigerian-born Bisi Adigun and Shalini Sinha, a Canadian citizen of Indian background as presenters of RTE's *Mono*[2], a primetime programme devoted to reporting a multicultural Ireland, represented a milestone in the participation of Africans in national media production (Kelly 2001).

A flurry of publications owned and managed by members of ethnic minority groups, especially those of African origin, debuted beginning from 2000. Some, like *Africans Magazine* published for the first time in August 2001[3], are devoted to serving 'Africans here in Ireland' (www.cmn.ie). Others like *The Street Journal* have tended to focus more on events in the African continent and to promoting a unique African identity. The fledging *Heritage Magazine* appears to want to do both – report events on the continent and portray a socially and culturally active African community in Ireland. In addition to these general interest magazines are some special interest publications, some of them devoted to promoting spirituality, specifically Pentecostal practices among Africans. Other magazines like *Ovation* and *Triumph*, published outside Ireland, including those published in the United

Kingdom and Nigeria, are finding an ever-increasing readership among Africans in Ireland.

ECONOMIC ACTIVITIES

The other aspect of community life that has given visibility to Ireland's African communities is economic activities. Since the first 'African' shop opened on Parnell Street in September 1997 (Freyne 1998), African entrepreneurs have established shops specialising in ethnic foods and hair and body products and those offering immigration advice and internet and telephone services (Spiller 2002; White 2002). In the early days, most of these shops were located mostly in the big cities, for example, on Moore Street and Parnell Street in Dublin's city centre. More recently shops and businesses owned or managed by Africans can be found in smaller cites and towns. In Dublin shops and eateries have been set up on North Circular Road, Phibsboro, South Circular Road, Kilmainham and Inchicore (Cullen 2002). Apart from providing goods for their mostly African clients, the shops double as 'safe places' where many Africans attempt to reconstruct a sense of community life. As Keith Spiller notes: "…people arrive at the shops purely to socialize in the back region, by-passing the front area. The consistent ebb and flow of people into the area creates a sense of people checking in to say hello…the back regions of the African shops on Parnell Street are a site that is comparably similar to a social club or a Mediterranean plaza" (Spiller 2002).

Like most other ethnically-based organisations, businesses owned and managed by Africans have proliferated as more Africans arrive and as a steady rise in unemployment, racially-motivated attacks and institutional discrimination have made ventures into professional and other areas of life difficult (Pollak 1999; Hannon 2003; De Rosa 2000). In my conversations with African shop owners in Dublin, I got the impression that setting up their own businesses was, to some extent, a strategy for overcoming the limitations imposed by institutional and street-level racism. An owner of an Internet shop located in Moore Street complained in 2002 that he was unable to get a job after completing a course in computer applications whereas his Irish counterparts, the majority of whom he said were not as good as himself, got jobs soon after they completed the same course. He attributed his plight to the 'racist attitudes of many employers' and said he set up his Internet shop as a way of proving to himself and to others that he has the capabilities to do it.

Unfortunately, owning and managing their shops has not been the sanctuary from racism and racially-motivated attacks that some shop owners had hoped for. Parnell Street and Moore Street in Dublin, where the socio-cultural and economic activities of Africans are mostly concentrated, were for a long time a hotbed of racial tension involving Africans and their Irish neighbours (McCarthy and Rafferty 2002; Amnesty International 2001). Commenting on the violent and frequent attacks on these shops, *The Sunday Business Post*, in a report on April 23, 2000 notes, "…incidents have included attempted arson, shots being fired at the shop and vandalism. On one occasion…a woman brandishing a knife entered the shop and threatened to 'slash everyone's throats'" (reported in Spiller 2002). Reports in *The Irish Times* (Haughey 2000a, 2000b; Cullen 2002) have also documented a litany of racially motivated assaults on Africans both in the Parnell Street and Moore Street areas and in other parts of the Greater Dublin Area.

POLITICAL PARTICIPATION

Politically, there has been a heightened interest in partisan politics and elections partly as a result of increased mobilisation by groups like African Solidarity Centre and Integrating Ireland. In 2003 the Africa Centre completed a report, *'Positive Politics'* (Fanning et al. 2003), in which it assesses not only the level of political participation by immigrants but also the willingness of the larger society, as represented by the six major political parties, to encourage immigrant participation in the political process. Following the very successful launch of this and a second report (Fanning et al. 2004) by the same group, a flurry of activities took place, including greater media coverage of the views and activities of African political activists. There has also been a greater determination to engage in politics and challenge hegemonic discourses and representation of African immigrants. As Dr Taiwoo Matthew, the Ennis-based immigrant candidate in the June 2004 local elections notes: "…we are not passing through…we are here to stay and we are here to be part of this community…" (Deegan 2004). In June 2004, Dr Matthew and Mr Rotimi Adebari were elected to council seats in Ennis and in Portlaoise, the first Africans to occupy such positions.

EXPERIENCING AND RESISTING RACISM

In November 2000 a Nigerian man was injured in a racially-motivated attack in a taxi company on Parnell Street in Dublin. He was attacked by a man at about 11p.m. and he received treatment at the Mater Hospital for injuries that included facial lacerations and bruising to his head and body. Mr Nasser Diaby, a technical agent with Xerox and an official of the African Refugee Network, had similarly been attacked on Parnell Street (Haughey 2000b). Parnell Street was again the venue of a major clash between Africans and a group of Irish when an African-owned shop was damaged and women and children in the shop were physically assaulted. African shop owners and other African residents in the Greater Dublin Area frequently received verbal racial abuses and hand-scribbled death threats. As one resident put it after the May 2000 attacks: 'I don't know of an African-owned shop that hasn't been attacked' (Haughey 2000a).

A survey conducted by the African Refugees Network (ARN) in 1999 reported that many African asylum seekers and refugees had been the victims of racially-motivated verbal and physical abuse (ARN 1999). In February 1999 *The Irish Times* also reported that 78% of asylum seekers and 95% of African asylum seekers had experienced racially motivated verbal or physical attacks. Some terrified African asylum seekers were too fearful to step out of their flats as a result of repeated attacks. Of the 622 people interviewed in an Amnesty International report, four out of five said they had been the victim of racism, most often on the streets or in shops or pubs. Racism was experienced in banks, schools, churches, buses and taxis, and from councils, housing and tax authorities (Amnesty International 2001). A survey of the racism experiences of Africans in the Greater Dublin Area conducted by Dr. Ronit Lentin and me revealed that verbal abuse (at 73%) was by far the most common type of racially motivated incidents, followed by physical attacks (19%) and denial of service/legitimate request (8%). For about 80% of the respondents, the possibility of experiencing racially motivated attacks was 'very real' or 'real', while another 81% described the 'fear of racially motivated attacks' as one of their greatest worries.[4]

African have, however, not been contended to simply assume the role of passive victims of racist attacks. They have resorted to active protestations. For example, following the May 2000 incident in the Summerhill area in which a young African man was attacked and seriously injured, hundreds of Africans spontaneously engaged in a protest march that took them through some of Dublin's major streets - Parnell Street and O'Connell Street. It was the first time Africans organised and executed a collective action aimed at expressing their displeasure with the rising tide of racism and at what they perceived as government's inaction (McCarthy and Rafferty 2002: 342). Since that march, Africans have participated in and co-sponsored other protests and many African individuals and groups have joined anti-racism groups and coalitions, such as Residents' Against Racism, the Coalition Against Deportation of Irish Children etc.

Many Africans have similarly organised into solidarity groups with the aim of challenging racism and discrimination and of empowering their members, not only to speak out against racially motivated injustices but also to offer guidance on the path to social and economic mobility. The African Refugee Network continues to challenge stereotypes about

African asylum seekers while the now defunct Pan African Organisation (PAO) was for many years engaged in activities aimed at defending the rights and interests of African immigrants. AkiDwA has also been vocal and assertive in demanding rights and greater respect for African women, while the African Centre (I was on the management board of this group for over two years, beginning in 2003) has concentrated on promoting a better image of Africans and the African continent.

Though the size of Ireland's African population is relatively small, the Irish government's immigration policies since the late 1990s have tended to give them disproportionate and mostly negative attention. African immigrants were therefore thrown into the limelight as a result of this attitude and because of mass media pronouncements by state officials and a few members of the judiciary. In 2001 when the Irish government announced its intention to sign re-admission agreements with other governments to facilitate the expulsion of unwanted immigrants, it had Nigerians in mind. As the then minister of justice, Mr John O'Donoghue, told *The Irish Times*: "The re-admission accord would provide a 'structured repatriation procedure' for the return of Nigerians, who are the largest group of asylum-seekers entering the State" (Haughey 2001). The re-admission agreement signed between the Nigerian government and the Irish government in November 2001 (Tróicare and ICJP 2002) has indeed facilitated the deportation of Nigerians, including under-age children.

In 2003 two judges provoked public outrage, especially among anti-racism, immigrant and human rights groups, when they made statements that have variously been described as 'careless rhetoric that encourages racist abuse and harassment' and 'crass racism' (Goldstone 2003; Browne 2003). In the Circuit Court in Castlebar in January 2003, Judge Harvey Kenny, while presiding in the case of Nigerian-born Ms Bukky Abebanjo, charged her with driving without insurance, commenting: "I don't think any Nigerian is obeying the law of the land when it comes to driving...they are all driving around without insurance and the way to stop this is to put you in jail" (Brennock and Haughey 2003). In a separate incident, Judge John Neilan of Longford District Court berated two African women charged with shoplifting offences: "There are people in this State who have worked all of their lives and they don't, in their old-age pension, have the benefits these ladies have... The majority of shopping centres in this District Court area will be putting a ban of access to coloured people if this type of behaviour does not stop" (Brennock and Haughey, 2003). Although both judges subsequently offered public apologies to the Africans concerned, their remarks had succeeded in propelling the African community to the limelight all for the wrong reasons.

In their analysis of the reasons why some sections of Irish society have expressed racism towards African immigrants, McCarthy and Rafferty (2002) argue that racial tensions have been exacerbated because the majority of Africans have settled mainly in deprived areas of the city, which were already experiencing many social ills. In their opinion, conflict between African immigrants and their Irish neighbours in these deprived neighbourhoods is a class, rather than a racial issue: "...many of the young black men arriving in the poor working class areas of Dublin are middle class and more educated than the people of the communities in which they land". Though educated, these "young black men", according to McCarthy and Rafferty, are also machos and oppressors of women who "see the young Dublin uneducated women as white 'slappers' who should be seen and not heard" (McCarthy and Rafferty 2002:364). This argument buys into some of the damaging generalisations and stereotypical images of African men and it fails to ascribe the blame squarely to where it belongs.

Another popular line of argument states that what has been described as racism in the Irish context is in fact nothing but the natural reaction of ordinary Irish people to the novelty of having brown or dark-skinned Africans on Irish soil. The assumption is that racism in the Irish context is transient, a problem that every multicultural society faces in the beginning and that it will disappear as Irish society gets used to the presence of Africans. This line of reason is faulty, not least because the recent immigration of Africans does not represent the first encounters between the Irish and the Africans. As Rolston and Shannon explain, Irish people have encountered brown or dark-skin Africans inside and outside of Ireland "from at least the time of the Vikings" (2002:2).

As participants in the British colonial conquests, the Irish met and interacted with Africans and other peoples of colour. Also, as part of the Catholic religious empire, they travelled to places as far as Nigeria, Sierra Leone, India and the West Indies. Some Africans in Ireland today met and interacted with Irish men and women who had come to African countries as either missionaries, educators or plain pleasure and treasure seekers (Ugba 2003a). In the eighteenth and nineteenth centuries, Dublin, Limerick and some other Irish cities welcomed and hosted black anti-slave trade activists like Olaudah Equiano and Frederick Douglass (Rolston and Shannon, 2002:3) However, the nature of these encounters meant that power relations were always skewed in favour of the Irish, and this has led many Irish people to think of Africans as inferior, a trait that can still be detected in the attitudes of some sections of Irish society to modern-day African immigrants. Rolston and Shannon (2002:88) sum it up: "The Irish had countless opportunities to be reminded of their relative superiority and while that lesson may have remained dormant at various times, it only needed the excuse of immigration to be awakened".

For Irish people who have no direct experience of Africa and Africans through colonialism and missionary enterprises, a constant diet of negative, biased and sometimes untrue Western media reports that rehearse stereotypical lines and images of the continent, have convinced them that no good could come out of Africa. The so-called development and aid agencies have helped to uphold this negative image of the African continent as they fill the mass media with images of sick and dying children as a tactic to convince their Western audience to donate to the cause of charity. Africans in Dublin have also been target of such negative media reports as a section of the media struggles to convince the Irish government and public that the latest waves of migrants from Africa are nothing but opportunists and suckers who are here solely to use and abuse the social welfare system (Cullen 2002).

The difficult times and obstacles connected to the struggles to establish their presence in a new society, it appears, have not changed the determination of many African immigrants to establish a home in Ireland. The various socio-cultural, economic and political activities they are engaged in, some of which have been briefly described in this chapter, can be interpreted as a strategy of survival and of creating safe and permanent places in Irish society. Of the 182 participants in my survey, close to 66% were sure they want to make Ireland their new home, 8% said they would not and 26% were undecided. Josephine Olusola, who used to live in the Greater Dublin Area, seems to have captured the mood of many Africans when, following a racial incident in which she was physically assaulted by a white Irish male, she wrote in *The Irish Times*:

> I am an African woman from Nigeria who likes living in Ireland and have done so for many years…This is my home now, it will remain so for the foreseeable future and I - in my glorious blackness - refuse to accept that it is not my home. I have the right to be here. My house is here, as are my dearest friends and job. I have worked hard to make Dublin home and I will defend my right to remain and call it home - in the face of any hostility. So please stop telling me to go back home. This is my home. (Olusola 2002).

While the reasons many Africans want to make Ireland their new home may be less connected to the reception (or lack of it) they have received from the majority society but to extraneous factors like personal circumstances, the situation in their countries of origin and their investments or stake in Irish society, their position thus supports the view that present-day African migrants in Europe, while maintaining symbolic and practical connections to their countries of origin, generally do not intend to practically and permanently return to Africa (Ter Haar 1998b; Koser 2003; Styan 2003; Riccio 2003; Wa Kabwe and Segatti 2003). As Gerrie ter Haar notes:

> The post-war history of migration in Europe has taught us that physical return on a permanent basis frequently does not take place...the belief that African migrants will return to their homelands as soon as they can possibly do so is contradicted by all available evidence (Ter Haar 1998b: 48).

Kalilombe (1998) similarly notes that many post-war African and Caribbean migrants to the United Kingdom simply refuse to consider the option of returning to their countries of origin despite the hostility, racism and discrimination they face. Rather they choose the path of 'self-defence', mostly in the sense of passive resistance, defiance and 'self-empowerment', seeking and using every opportunity to improve their lot and to change their situation (Kalilombe 1998: 187-192). His analysis has useful lessons for understanding the situation of African immigrants in twenty-first century Dublin. While active resistance has been a less preferred option, individuals and groups are exploring opportunities for self-improvement and empowerment. Pentecostal churches initiated by Africans are a major vehicle for realising the multiple and complex aims of self-improvement, self-empowerment and self-definition.

In the next chapter I undertake a historical and substantive analysis of Pentecostalism, including its presence in Africa and among African immigrants in Europe.

Notes

1. Titled *'Africans in twenty-first century Dublin: A profile and needs analysis'*, the survey began in the spring of 2002 and it consists of a questionnaire survey of 182 Africans from 17 countries living in the Greater Dublin Area, focus group meetings and email discussions. No fewer than 250 Africans from about 25 countries participated in the project, making it the most in-depth and rigorous analysis so

far of the presence of Africans in Ireland. Nigerians accounted for 57 % of the respondents, followed by Sierra Leone (8.9 %) and the Democratic Republic of Congo (4.5 %). A total of 18 nationalities (not countries of origin) are represented in the survey. The respondents are mostly citizens of African countries with the exception of 10 Irish and one Swedish. Of the total respondents, 49.2 % were males and 50.8 % were females

2. RTE (Radio Television Éireann) is Ireland's national radio and television broadcasting authority. The station's decision to introduce Mono and appoint members of minority ethnic groups as the presenters marked a new phase in its public service obligation and a firm acknowledgement that the society it is meant to serve has changed.

3. *Africans magazines* started publishing an electronic version in January 2001. The publishers explained that the decision to publish the print version in August of that year was to bring 'the on-line contents but on a limited scale to people's door' (www.africans-magazine)

4. Titled *'Africans in twenty-first century Dublin: Experiences of racism'*, the project was commissioned by Pan-African Organisation in 2002 and lasted till the summer of 2003. In total, 77 questionnaires were completed, administered mostly in the offices of Pan-Africa Organisation on Moore Street and in business and residential premises in and around Dublin city centre. The respondents came from 12 African countries. More than half of these (or 57.5 %) came from Nigeria, followed by the Democratic Republic of Congo (13.7 %) and Angola (8 %). A total of 16 nationalities, as distinct from countries of origin, were represented in this study. The overwhelming majority were citizens of African countries but there were three Irish and two British. There were 41 males (or 53.2 %) and 34 females (46.8 %).

CHAPTER FOUR

PENTECOSTALISM IN AFRICA AND AMONG AFRICAN IMMIGRANTS

INTRODUCTION

In a period of 100 years, the modern Pentecostal movement has travelled to and taken roots in many corners of the earth. The growth has been accelerated since the second half of the twentieth century and it has resulted not only in increases in the number of adherents but also in the varieties of Pentecostalism (Barrett 1982; Anderson 1999). According to Barrett and Johnson (1999), the number of Pentecostal/Charismatic Christians jumped from 74 million (6% of the world's Christian population) in 1970 to 497m or 27 % of all Christians in 1997. There will be, according to their estimates, 1,140m Pentecostals or 44 % of the world's Christian population, by 2025. *Christian History*, a publication of the US-based *Christianity Today*, estimates that the worldwide Pentecostal membership was growing at a rate of 13 million a year, or 35,000 a day (Christian History 1998: 3). Impressive as the statistical analyses of these growths are, Pentecostalism's major impact is often attributed to its role in reshaping the world's religious landscape and the redefinition of the interfaces between Christianity and the State, on the one hand, and between Christianity and culture, on the other. Such has been the rate, extent and impact of growth that Pentecostalism has been dubbed the "fire from heaven" by Harvey Cox (1996) in his book titled *'Fire From Heaven: The Rise of Pentecostal Spirituality and the Reshaping of Religion in the Twenty-first Century.'*

Assessing the rapid spread and popularity of Pentecostalism, Allan Anderson (1999:19) described it as "the most extraordinary religious phenomena in the world of any time". Whereas the modern day Pentecostal movement originated in the United States, the majority of its adherents and its most phenomenal rates of growth are in South America, Africa and the Caribbean (Anderson 1999; Corten 1999; Corten and Marshall-Fratani 2001; Hollenweger 1972, 1976, 1999; MacRobert 1988). Allan Anderson (1999:20) describes Pentecostalism as "both fundamentally and dominantly a Third World phenomenon" while Iain MacRobert (1988) foresees "a world in which most Christians will probably be in the underdeveloped or developing nations, most will be non-Europeans and most will be of the Pentecostal oral narrative type". Although analysts like Gifford (1992, 2004), Marshall (1993), Marshall-Fratani (1998) and Corten (1999) make some connections between the fast growth of Pentecostalism in some of these places and the deteriorating socio-economic and political conditions, Hollenweger (1999), MacRobert (1988), Anderson (1999) and Kalu (1998, 2003) believe, among other things, that specific Pentecostal teachings and practices which have roots in African culture and spirituality have made the religion attractive to large populations of Africans and African descendants. They also point to the unique ability of Pentecostalism to adapt and respond to local cultures and conditions as another reason for its popularity in the Majority World (or developing countries, as it is often called).

My aim in this chapter is to articulate a historical and substantive account of the main features of Pentecostalism. An analysis of the history, contents and trajectories of Pentecostalism is crucial to a thorough understanding of the various ways individual believers and groups engage with its main tenets and how these beliefs and practices in turn shape the believers' worldviews. I also explore some of the controversies on the origin, beliefs and practices because of their relevance to issues of identity. This discussion differentiates various streams of Pentecostalism. I begin by discussing the controversies surrounding the birth of the worldwide Pentecostal movement. This discourse includes an analysis of salient issues on the spread of Pentecostalism in Africa and among African immigrants in Europe. This is followed by an analysis of the congruence and divergences of Pentecostal beliefs and practices.

In conclusion I highlight other factors that have impacted on the substance and evolution of this religious movement, particularly the relationship between Pentecostalism and African spirituality and how traditional African religious practices might have filtered into Pentecostalism through African slaves in the New World. My analysis is rooted in the views of a variety of scholars, including theologians (e.g. Anderson and Hollenweger), political scientists (e.g. Corten and Marshall-Fratani) and sociologists (e.g. Hunt and Poloma). It also draws on the works of Matthew Ojo, Ogbu Kalu, Gerrie ter Haar and Iain MacRobert. These diverse sources have enabled me to draw sociologically-relevant conclusions in relation to, among other things, the racialisation of early American Pentecostalism and the close links between modern Pentecostalism and 'African' identity and culture. My analysis is illustrated by brief case histories drawn from my interviews with Pentecostal African immigrants in Ireland and they illustrate the different trajectories to Pentecostalism and other issues discussed in this chapter.

ORIGINS: AS IT WAS AT PENTECOST IN THE FIRST CENTURY

Pentecostal believers and analysts have struggled with limited degrees of successes to articulate an acceptable and encompassing definition of Pentecostalism. It is perhaps easier to say who the Pentecostals are than what Pentecostalism is. In my view, Pentecostals are those who profess to be Pentecostals. In other words, people are Pentecostals if they say they are. There are no clear-cut and generally-accepted criteria or standard tests for determining who is a Pentecostal. Outsiders, including writers, analysts and statisticians, have generally relied on the testimony or self-confession of believers or of their leaders or fellow believers. Pentecostals, even in small group settings like the ones that are the subject of this book, do not generally carry official identity cards. Membership of a group is usually established or affirmed by the regularity and levels of involvement in group activities, outward demonstration of fidelity to group beliefs and principles and loyalty to the leadership.

Pentecostalism, on the other hand, is a generic term for a wide variety of Christian practices based on or inspired by the holy ghost experience of the first century Christians, as recorded in the bible book of Acts of the Apostles (Acts 2:1-36.). The account states:

> Now while the day of the [festival of] Pentecost was in progress they were all together at the same place, and suddenly there occurred from heaven a noise just like that of a rushing stiff breeze, and it filled the whole house in which they were sitting. And tongues as if of fire became visible to them and were distributed about, and one sat upon each one of them, and they all became filled with Holy Spirit and started to speak with different tongues, just as the spirit was granting them to make utterance—*New World Translation (NWT) of the Holy Bible.*

According to the interpretation of many Pentecostals, the event that took place in the first century had been foretold by the prophet Joel (2: 28-29) in the Old Testament:

> And after that it must occur that I shall pour out my spirit on every sort of flesh, and your sons and your daughters will certainly prophesy. As for your old men, dreams they will dream. As for your young men, visions they will see. And even on the menservants and on the maidservants in those days I shall pour out my spirit.

DIVERSE PENTECOSTALISMS

Although all Pentecostals cite the above bible passages as the inspiration or the reference for their unique practices,

there is a great divergence of interpretations and application as I hope to demonstrate later in this chapter. Diverse
interpretations and the conscious efforts of some groups to
contextualise or make Pentecostal doctrines respond to and
reflect their unique cultures and socio-political situations
have created a diverse collection of groups and churches
across space and time under the umbrella Pentecostal banner.
As Corten and Marshall-Fratani (2001:7) note, "each society,
each group invests Pentecostalism with its own meanings."
The divergence and differences that exist among the various
groups are doctrinal, methodical, structural as well as racial.
Pentecostal believers, as Anderson (1999) puts it, "range from
the fundamentalist and white middle class 'mega churches'
to indigenous movements in the Third World that have
adapted to their cultural and religious contexts to such an
extent that many western Pentecostals would probably doubt
their qualifications as 'Christian' movements". Evidence of
racially-motivated divisions in the development of African-
led Pentecostalism in Ireland has equally been noticeable, as I
illustrate in chapters five and eight. Some Pentecostal groups
number into the millions while others are little groups of 100
worshippers of even less.

Some analysts (Dempster et al 1999) have pointed to this
flexibility in the way Pentecostalism has been interpreted and
adopted as one of its main attractions and a major explanation
for its rapid spread. For example, Gerlach and Hine (1968,
1970) and Gerloff (1992, 1999) attribute the popularity of
Pentecostalism to it being a 'movement organisation' rather
than a centralised, bureaucratic western institution. This view
is re-iterated by Poloma's (2000:3) description of the Pentecostal movement as "a reticulate (or polycephalous) organization, linked together by a variety of personal, structural and
ideological ties, which is not linear but can be likened to a
cellular organism". She also believes that Pentecostalism has
travelled far and fast because it "travels along pre-existing
daily social relationships such as family, friendship, village
or island community, trade or work companionship, and
shared migration, thus carrying its message like reliable and

comforting luggage". In Ireland, Pentecostalism has travelled along similar routes to reach many Africans as I demonstrate in the next chapter. It has also been evident that African immigrants have found it relatively easy to form Pentecostal groups and join or secede from existing ones. Hollenweger (1972) believes Pentecostalism's rapid spread is due to its 'black roots', which include oral liturgy, narrative theology and witnessing, maximum participation at the level of reflection, prayer and decision making and the inclusion of dreams and visions into personal and public forms of worship. I discuss the interfaces between Pentecostalism and African spirituality later in this chapter.

Walter Hollenweger's seminal publication in which he classifies Pentecostalism into three broad types represents one of the most meaningful attempts to put a form on the many divergences and heterogeneities within this movement. The three types identified by him are: the classical Pentecostals, the Charismatic Renewal Movement also known as Neo-Pentecostal; and the Pentecostal-like 'non-white' indigenous churches, like those in Africa, South America and the Caribbean (Hollenweger 1972: 33-34). The term 'Classical Pentecostalism' is used to described the movement that began in the United States at the beginning of the twentieth century. The history of its beginning is contested as much as its doctrines and practices as I discuss later in this chapter.

The term 'Charismatic Renewal' or 'neo-Pentecostalism' refers to groups mostly but not only within established or mainline churches that adhere to basic Pentecostal teachings, including, in some cases, glossolalia or speaking in tongues, prophesying and divine healing (Hunt, 2002c; Hunt et al 1997) while the category of Pentecostal-like indigenous churches refers to groups in non-western societies that have accept basic Pentecostal doctrines but have consciously mixed them with local or indigenous cultures and traditions (Adogame 2000; Kalu 2003). The Pentecostal-like indigenous churches, unlike classical Pentecostalism and even neo-Pentecostalism, have not been started or influenced substantially by foreign missionaries and although they identify the Bible as the sole source of their beliefs, they consciously include elements of tradition and culture in the way they interpret and manifest these beliefs. As I make clear in this chapter, the classical Pentecostals and neo-Pentecostals mostly do not have affinity to these indigenous churches, which they consider 'spiritistic' and 'satanic'.

Although African indigenous churches (or white-garment churches as some of them are called) have been established by African immigrants in Ireland, they are not included in my research. However, references are made to them, especially in my analysis of Pentecostal self-understanding. This book, therefore, focuses on those African-led or initiated Christian groups that have maintained the traditions of the 'classical' Pentecostals. However, writers like Stephen Hunt (Hunt 2002b, 2002c) and others (Hunt et al 1997; Poloma 1982, 2001) have problematised the dichotomies and differences that are often made between classical Pentecostals and neo-Pentecostals. This study does not cover neo-Pentecostal groups.

Generally, persons from established or 'mainline' churches like Roman Catholics, Methodists or Episcopalians who have embraced classical Pentecostal teachings concerning the Holy Spirit baptism, divine healing and the other doctrines subsumed under the term 'charismata' use the term 'charismatic' to describe themselves. However, churches that have emerged in the Pentecostal traditions independent of, and sometimes in opposition to the established or 'mainline' churches are called classical Pentecostals or simply Pentecostals. Neo-Pentecostals tend not to operate as independent structures and most of their members believe they can bring spiritual revival to mainline churches by remaining within them rather than separating from them and setting up competing bases.

Neo-Pentecostalism has its origin in 1960 and the first evidence of it—an outbreak of tongue speaking—was at an Episcopalian congregation in Van Nuys, California (Hollenweger 1972; Hunt 2002c; Hunt et al 1997; Poloma 1982). Whereas the birth of classical Pentecostalism at the beginning of the twentieth century was interpreted as a reaction to the decline in church memberships and the bureaucratisation of church life, Hunt et al (1997:3) state that "the roots of neo-Pentecostalism lay, not in the state of the mainline churches, but in a response to wider society." Interestingly, Hollenweger (1972:4) notes that the penetration of Pentecostal doctrines into mainline churches in the form of neo-Pentecostalism was facilitated by the ecumenical initiatives of classical Pentecostals, the activities of the Full Gospel Businessmen Fellowship and the separate spiritual regeneration that took place in the Catholic Church in the wake of the Second Vatican Council.

Although Pentecostals and many neo-Pentecostals believe in the baptism of the Holy Spirit as was experienced by first century Christians, they have tended to differ in their interpretation of how this experience is manifested and also on the role of the Holy Spirit in matters relating to divine healing and prophecy (Hunt 2002c; Poloma 1982). As Logan (1975:34, quoted in Hunt 2002c) notes, "modern charismatics tend to emphasize the rational, linguistic character of glossolalia and play down the ecstatic or irrational dimensions of the phenomenon." The two groups also appeared to have maintained different attitudes to wealth, politics and other secular or 'this worldly' affairs (Burgess and McGee 1988). Neo-Pentecostals would appear to be generally more involved in the affairs of this world, including politics and wealth accumulation than classical Pentecostals. Commenting on charismatic evangelicals in South America, Freston (1997) notes that the majority of members were of middle-class background, in contrast to the lower class status of many classical Pentecostals.

However, Hunt (2002:3) notes that the differences between neo-Pentecostals and Pentecostals in North America and Europe had begun to narrow by the 1980s: "...it was not entirely clear what were the distinguishing features of Pentecostalism generally since such doctrines as the Baptism in the Holy Spirit were no longer insisted upon in many strands of the movement". In addition, neo-Pentecostal groups had started to function independent of mainline churches and the movement had started to fragment. As Hunt (2002c: 3) puts it:

> While retaining all the hallmarks of the Pentecostal 'family' the broad movement in the West had undergone considerable evolution and become subject to a remarkable fragmentation, adapting itself to increasing cultural diversity perhaps more so than in any other religion of the world. By the early twenty-first century the movement was identified by its increasing pluralism, enculturation and marketability.

Classical Pentecostals too were no longer shying away from mundane things. In some African countries, particularly in Nigeria and Ghana, classical Pentecostals are increasingly involved in partisan politics and government (Guardian 2003a, 2003b). Indeed, the president of Nigeria from 1999 to 2007, Mr Olusegun Obasanjo and some members of his cabinet were self-professed Pentecostal Christians. During the 2003 general elections, a Pentecostal Christian and former musician, Mr Kris Okotie, was one of the presidential candidates. He again contested during the 2007 presidential elections. His ambitions and attempts have been actively supported by several Pentecostal groups, including the Pentecostal Fellowship of Nigeria (PFN), an umbrella group for Pentecostal churches in the country. Pentecostal African immigrants in Ireland are not averse to politics and some of their leaders foresee a future when the churches would be breeding grounds for political, community and civic leaders.

Apart from politics, the attitude of most Pentecostal groups to wealth accumulation has changed as 'the gospel of wealth and health' (Hollinger 1989) or what Anderson (2000) calls "the capitalistic emphasis on prosperity and success" became popular. Despite the "contradiction, paradox and internal dilemmas" of neo-Pentecostalism (Hunt, et al 1997: 3), Hunt describes it as a latter revival that has helped to renew and sustain the enthusiasm and revival that marked the birth of the modern Pentecostalism movement. As he argues, "Without neo-Pentecostalism, classical Pentecostalism would arguably now be merely another religious denomination. The fresh spiritual experience of largely middle-class neo-Pentecostals, disseminated through religious and secular communication, helped to revive classical Pentecostal beliefs" (2002c: 2).

However, neo-Pentecostalism should not in every case be conceptualised in opposition to or competition with classical Pentecostalism. It has served as the route or bridge to classical Pentecostalism for some believers. Pauline is a mother of two, an African Pentecostal in Dublin and a participant in this research. She was born into a Catholic family in Nigeria and she grew up a devout Catholic. A fellow church member introduced her to a neo-Pentecostal or charismatic group within the church and after participating in the group's activities and listening to the sermons, she decided to be 'born-again', in order to live a dedicated Christian life. Her Catholic church was located far from where she lived and she had to take the bus to the church. On some occasions she could not afford the transport fare, as she was unemployed. Rather than stay at home on those occasions she would go to the Pentecostal church (Redeemed) in the neighbourhood. For some time she dithered between the Catholic Church and Redeemed until she made a decision for the latter. Thus her journey from neo-Pentecostalism to Pentecostalism was completed. In Ireland, she has continued to worship in the Redeemed Christian Church of God. So has her husband who used to attend an indigenous Pentecostal-like church in Nigeria.

Before I engage in a detailed discussion of the beliefs and doctrines of Pentecostalism, I want to shed some light on the controversies that surround its origin, which, among other things, can be attributed to racial segregation as I demonstrate below.

CONTESTED AND CONTENTIOUS BEGINNINGS

This account of the contested beginnings and trajectories of the modern Pentecostal movement relies on the work of

Pentecostal writers like Walter Hollenweger, Iain MacRobert and Allan Anderson. My analysis highlights the racialisation of early American Pentecostalism, signalling the later close links between Pentecostalism and black identity. According to various sources, Pentecostalism was either started in Los Angeles in 1906 by William Joseph Seymour, the self-taught son of a former slave, or it began in 1901 through the efforts of Charles Parham, a racist and anti-Semitic white American, who rigidly enforced segregation in his church (Hollenweger 1972, 1997; Anderson 1999; MacRobert 1988). Parham was a medical school drop-out who became a licensed Methodist preacher at the age of 18. He was a product of the 'Great Awakening' in the United States and he flirted with different Christian groups, including the Quakers—his wife's grandfather was a Quaker. As a result of his contacts with these groups he abandoned the Methodist teaching on eternal torment in favour of annihilation or the instantaneous and complete destruction of unrepentant sinners. He also embraced other doctrines, notably that of sanctification as a second act of grace, that the Methodist hierarchy considered unorthodox or unbiblical. Following disagreements with the Methodist church leadership, Parham left in 1894 and became a travelling preacher (MacRobert 1988:43-47).

Parham's evangelistic works took him to many cities in the US and brought him in contact with more religious groups and viewpoints. His sermons emphasised salvation, sanctification, divine healing, Holy Spirit baptism and the imminent second coming of Jesus Christ. He returned to his base in Topeka, Kansas, where in October 1900 he opened a Bible college. At the college, the Bible served as the basic textbook and its verses were often interpreted literally. Parham emphasised the centrality of the Holy Ghost baptism to the Christian life and taught the students to pray for and seek the baptism experience even though he himself had not received it. In January 1901, Agnes Osma, a congregant in Parham's Bible college, claimed to have received the baptism of the Holy Ghost and to have spoken in tongues (speaking in tongues is discussed later in this chapter).

Others, including Parham himself, subsequently made the same claim (MacRobert 1988:45). But the spiritual revival signalled by the Holy Spirit baptism did not last, as Mac-Robert (1988:46) notes:

> After some interest created by newspaper coverage of the event, followed by unsuccessful attempts to spread the message, Parham and a few of his followers moved to Kansas City where he opened another Bible school. In four months the school was closed and Parham was deserted by all but his wife and sister-in-law. Even Agnes Osma left and repudiated her experience at Bethel.

Parham's ministry experienced a revival after he returned to his original emphasis on divine healing and he established several Apostolic Faith missions and house churches in Kansas, Missouri and Oklahoma. He also opened a Bible college in Houston where much emphasis was laid on the power of the Holy Spirit, prophecies, speaking in tongues and interpretation of tongues (MacRobert 1988:48-59).

William J. Seymour was reported to have associated with Parham's Bible school in Houston. Born in Louisiana in 1870, Seymour developed a keen sense of justice and equity early in life because of the racial violence and institutionalised racism that were features of the society where he grew up. His early religious experience includes membership of a black congregation of the predominantly white Methodist Episcopal Church. But as MacRobert (1988:49) writes:

> As the Methodist Episcopal Church and Methodism in general became more formal and middle class, its concern for racial justice and equality lessened, as did its enthusiasm for holiness. Many black and white working class left what they perceived to be the 'worldly' churches for the Holiness movement. Seymour was one of them.

Seymour was attracted to the ministry of Martin Wells, a white integrationist and also a former disgruntled member of the Methodist Episcopal church, who preached fervently on divine healing and the imminent second coming of Jesus Christ that would bring an apocalyptic end to the world. He became a member of the interracial Evening Light Saints, a group that was expecting a 'Spiritual outpouring' which its members believed would precede the end of the world. Members of the group rejected denominationalism, preached the oneness of believers irrespective of their colour or social status (MacRobert 1988:49-59).

Seymour later became an ordained minister of the Saints, as members of their groups were called and he returned in 1903 to the South to preach the gospel and to search for long lost relatives. He became a minister in the Black Holiness Church of Mrs Lucy Farrow and through her he met Charles Parham. Seymour became interested in Parham's emphasis on speaking in tongues or glossolalia as evidence of the 'third experience' of the baptism of the Holy Spirit, a sign that the end of the world was imminent and as God's means of taking the gospel to unbelievers in foreign lands. He enrolled in Parham's Bible school in Houston, Texas, so as to get acquainted with these teachings and perhaps receive the Holy Ghost experience.

Soon after Seymour left the Bible college as Parham's segregationist policies meant he could only participate in the classes through a door left ajar by Parham. As Nelson (quoted in MacRobert, 1988:51) reported: "At the public evening service Seymour and other blacks sit in the rear and are not allowed to go to the alter for ministration because Parham practises strict segregation". Seymour later left for Los Angeles, at the invitation of a Black Holiness Church, and was appointed the pastor of the church. His sermons emphasised speaking in tongues, divine healing, conversion, sanctification and the second coming of Christ. He soon ran into problems with some members of the congregation who thought of his doctrines as very extreme. Disagreements resulted in divisions and splinter groups emerged.

Seymour moved his little group to a private home in February 1906 and in April of that year a member of the group spoke in tongues for the first time. The experience of that member opened a floodgate as many members started speaking in tongues and Seymour himself later spoke in tongues. Seymour's little group started as an all-black congregation but as MacRobert (1988:53) states, people of other colours and backgrounds soon joined:

> At this time all the congregation were black and the Asbery's home in which they met was in a black residential district. However, during the following three days, crowds gathered and many whites also came as people continued to manifest glossolalia, fall into trances and receive healing. The group quickly became a movement as more and more people came to seek their Pentecost.

As their number grew, they moved out of a private home and rented a disused two-storey wooden chapel built by the African Methodist Episcopal Church in 1888 or, as MacRobert (1988:53) describes it, "a run-down area of town at 312 Azusa Street." Indeed Azusa Street is considered by many analysts (e.g. Anderson 1999; Hollenweger 1972; MacRobert 1988) as the birthplace of the modern worldwide Pentecostal movement. News of the events at Seymour's Azusa Street Mission soon spread through Los Angles and other cities in the US and attracted intense media attention, notably from *The Los Angeles Times*. The Mission also started its own newspaper, *The Apostolic Faith*, which reported the events at the Mission to a wider audience, perhaps in an attempt to counter the mostly sensational and negative reporting in the secular media. Its circulation increased from 5,000 to 50,000 in less than three years.

SPREADING THE MISSION

The mission was reported to have attracted peoples of all colours and racial backgrounds as Seymour taught the followers that the Holy Ghost experience meant more than speaking in tongues and that it should also break down racial and colour barriers—countering the movement's early segregationist tendencies. According to Iain MacRobert (1988:55), the September 1906 issue of *The Apostolic Faith* emphasised the multi-racial character of the congregation: "...multitudes have come. God makes no difference in nationality. Ethiopians, Chinese, Indians, Mexicans, and other nationalities worship together". However, although Seymour's Pentecostal movement grew exponentially and reached over 50 nations, including Britain, India, China, Palestine and Germany within a few years, its non-racial or multi-racial character was quickly dented and lost due to in-fighting, resentment and hostilities from white-dominated middle class church leaders, including Charles Parham.

Although the twentieth century 'Pentecostal fire', marked by holy sprit baptism and speaking in tongues, was sparked in 1901 in a congregation led by Charles Parham, Pentecostalism's revival and journeys to other cities in America and the rest of the world began in 1906 in Seymour's Azusa Street Mission. The missionaries that took the Pentecostal message and ideals to much of America and the rest of the world, including Africa, were bred in Seymour's mission or were influenced by his charisma and vision, according to MacRobert and Hollenweger. Quoting Vinson Synan, MacRobert (1988:8) states: "Directly or indirectly, practically all of the Pentecostal groups in existence can trace their lineage to the Azusa Mission," adding, "it is to Azusa that we must look for the birthplace of twentieth century Pentecostalism".

PENTECOSTALISM'S AFRICAN ROOTS

While the modern Pentecostal Movement originated at the beginning of the twentieth century, some writers (MacRobert 1988; Raboteau 1978, 2001; Wilmore 1983) have argued that the Pentecostal experience itself did not cease after its initial manifestation in the first century only to reappear at the beginning of the twentieth century. Rather it had been sustained by different groups in different places through all of history. Therefore the Pentecostal explosion that started at the beginning of the twentieth century was arguably only a larger scale manifestation of what different groups, including African slaves in America, had practised. As Mac-

Robert (1988:6) puts it: "The twentieth century Pentecostal movement falls into that tradition of enthusiastic, ecstatic and experiential Christianity which has made brief appearances in Church history since the time of the Apostles". For example, Frederick Dale Brunner, according to MacRobert, identified striking similarities between the practices of the Montanists of the second century and those of modern-day Pentecostals. MacRobert and other writers such as Wilmore (1983) and Raboteau (1978, 2001) have also made strong links between the religions that the slaves practised in secret in the plantations and the modern Pentecostal movement, arguing that the religions and spiritualism of slaves from Africa have combined with Christian doctrines and western civilization to produce modern Pentecostalism.

"An adequate comprehension of black Pentecostalism" MacRobert (1988:2-3) argues, "can only be derived from a study of the religion which survived the middle passage in the heart and minds of West Africans and their descendants." He has no doubt that the black interpretation of Christianity, which developed in the crucible of New World slavery "was a syncretism of Western theology and West African religious practice and beliefs". Wilmore (1983:1-5) agrees and he identifies "the quasi-religious, quasi-secular meetings which took place on the plantations, unimpeded by white supervision and under the inspired leadership of the first generation of African priests to be taken in slavery" as the direct antecedents of modern-day Pentecostalism. MacRobert (1988:15) is even more direct: "The religion of slavery was initially an adaptation of African Abosom, Alose, Orisha, Vodun worship or Voodooism which was later overlaid with a veneer of Christianity. Ultimately it became Christian, yet it retained many African elements".

Most African Pentecostals and some writers, notably Edward Franklin Frazier (1964), have challenged this interpretation of modern Pentecostalism. According to Frazier (1964:3), "the manner in which Negroes were captured and enslaved and inducted into the plantation regime tended to loosen all social bonds among them and to destroy the traditional basis of social cohesion". He further argues, "there was hardly a community among the slaves" because the "slave quarters were always under the surveillance of the overseers" (1964:4). Moreover, "the organisation of labour and the system of social control and discipline on the plantation both tended to prevent the development of social cohesion either on the basis of whatever remnants of African culture might have survived or on the basis of the Negroes' role in the plantation economy" (Frazier 1964:3). Frazier argues that most slaves brought to America at the early stages of the slave trade were mostly young males whom he describes as "poor bearers of the cultural heritage of a people" (Frazier 1964: 4).

The condemnation of and opposition of most African Pentecostals to traditional African religion and spirituality, which they often describe as 'the work of darkness', 'Satanism' or 'spiritism', is well documented (Kalu 1998, 2003; Marshall 1993; Olupona 1991; Sanneh 1993; Turner 1979; Westermann 1937). Danielle, a Pentecostal African immigrant from Congo abhors any reference to her beliefs as African:

> I think it's a question of knowledge. Because of lack of knowledge when they see some things they say, 'oh that's African'. They don't realise that even in the Bible King David disrobed himself because he was dancing before God, that the Apostle Paul advised people to pray in loud voice. It's not African, it's written in the Bible. If you don't read the Bible, don't do research, you won't realise that God enjoys people who are exuberant in the expression of love to him.

Charles, another Pentecostal African immigrant who took part in my study, has preached in many African-led Pentecostal churches in and outside of Dublin on the churches' invitation. He would even honour an invitation to preach in a Catholic church because 'it is the sick that need a physician' but he would not preach in an indigenous Pentecostal-like church (or a white-garment church) because he considers them to be 'Satanic'. Pauline, already mentioned in this chapter, was already a born-again Christian when she met and married her husband, then a member of an African indigenous church. Before she committed to the marriage, she made sure they came to an agreement that she would not switch over to his church and that their children would not be raised in his church. Such was the disdain she had for indigenous African churches. In Ireland her husband has converted to her Pentecostal church. Asked why she would not convert to her husband's former church, she retorted: "Light can never be overcome by darkness. I can't leave the light and go into darkness. Never".

However, both Raboteau and Wilmore have adopted a sort of middle of the road position, arguing that the African native religious practices that the slaves mixed with Christian teachings and Western civilization have not remained unchanged or authentically African. According to Wilmore (1983:18), "...the faith that evolved from the coming together of diverse influences was...distinctly different from its two major contributors". Raboteau concurs: "...the religions of Africa have not been merely preserved as static 'Africanisms' or as archaic 'retentions'". In his view, "African styles of worship, forms of ritual, systems of beliefs, and fundamental perspectives have remained vital...not because they were preserved in a 'pure' orthodoxy but because they were transformed. Adaptability, based upon respect for spiritual power wherever it originated, accounted for the openness of African religions to syncretism with other religious traditions and for the continuity of a distinctively African religious consciousness". Joseph Washington similarly describes 'Black folks religion', the other name used for Pentecostalism by many earlier writers, as a fusion of "traditional African religions, Western civilization, and Christianity" (Washington 1984:20). In Ireland, many Pentecostal African immigrants deny this fusion although a few admit that Africans practise Pentecostalism differently from non-African Pentecostals.

PENTECOSTALISM IN AFRICA

It is relevant to briefly examine the history of Pentecostalism in Africa since the groups that are the subjects of this study have strong historical, organisational and doctrinal connections to groups in Africa. The arrival and spread of Pentecostalism in Africa is less clouded in controversies than the history of its beginning. Classical Pentecostalism was introduced to West Africa in the early twentieth century mostly through the efforts of African-American Pentecostal missionaries who arrived in the region with zeal to spread the gospel in their ancestral land. In western Nigeria the Faith Tabernacle and the Apostolic Church were some of the earliest Pentecostal churches, while in eastern Nigeria the Assemblies of God came from the United States into a much more stable religious environment. Gerrie ter Haar (1994: 224) reports that Assemblies of God, the first Pentecostal church in Ghana, was established in 1931 by two missionaries also from the United States. According to Ojo (1988a and 1988b), other Pentecostal churches came to Nigeria mostly from the USA in the 1940s and 1950s. Many of these churches incubated in university campuses, mostly in the 1970s, where students and lecturers played leading roles in propagating their doctrines both within and outside university campuses. During this period of its early development in Nigeria and the West African coast, Pentecostalism was dominated mostly by intellectuals and students (Ter Haar 1994; Ojo 1988a, 1988b). African students who had returned from the United States and the United Kingdom played a leading role in spreading the Pentecostal ideals. Pentecostal and charismatic revivals became more widespread in Nigeria in the 1970s and 1980s as the number of universities and other tertiary institutions increased (Ojo 1988a and 1988b).

Using university campuses as their organisational base, many Pentecostal groups launched evangelistic outreaches to towns and villages, first to places around the universities but later to most parts of the country. In 1973, the Nigerian government set up the National Youth Service Corp (NYSC). The programme required fresh university graduates to spend one year working for some stipends in parts of the country other than their own locality or the locality where they attended university. Pentecostals and evangelicals who participated in the scheme used it as an opportunity to take the message to the most distant parts of the country, including the predominantly Muslim North. Commenting on the growth and evangelistic activities of these churches, Anderson (2000) notes:

> ...many new churches use electronic musical instruments, publish their own literature and run their own Bible training centres for preachers, both men and women, to further propagate their message. These movements encourage the planting of new independent churches and make use of schoolrooms, cinemas, community halls and even hotel conference rooms for their revival meetings. Church leaders sometimes travel the continent and inter-continentally, and some produce glossy booklets and broadcast radio and television programmes.

One of the implications of universities and elite institutions serving as breeding grounds for Pentecostalism in Africa was its concentration in the urban centres. Gifford (1992), Anderson (2000) and Ter Haar (1994) note the influence of foreign missionaries and tele-evangelist, mostly from the United States, on the growth and development of the Pentecostal movement in West Africa. However, their impact was mostly felt in the urban centres because the lack of electricity and other social infrastructure meant that rural dwellers had little or no access to their messages.

SOCIO-POLITICAL AND ECONOMIC CONTEXTS OF THE SPREAD OF PENTECOSTALISM

Apart from winning converts through aggressive forms of evangelism, analysts (e.g. Gifford 2004; Ter Haar 1994; Hunt and Lightly 2001; Larbi 2001; Marshall-Fratani 2001) affirm that the growth of Pentecostal churches in many African countries from the 1980s has been facilitated by the degenerating economic conditions and the consequent decay in social infrastructure and services. High unemployment, rising cost of basic necessities, including foodstuff, and the depletion of the middle class were direct consequences of drastic economic changes connected to the Structural Adjustment Programmes inspired or imposed by international financial institutions like the World Bank and the International Monetary Fund (IMF) in the 1980s and 1990s (Kabbaj 2003; Olukushi 1993). Writers like Nigerian renowned novelist Chinua Achebe (1983) and Larbi (2001) have also blamed bad leadership and corruption for the economic conditions in Nigeria and Ghana in the past three decades.

In the case of Nigeria's mono-product economy, fluctuations in the price of crude oil, mostly in the 1980s, bad management and a growing debt burden compounded the problems. When General Ibrahim Babangida shot his way to power in 1985 he rejected the IMF-inspired Structural Adjustment Programme but he imposed sets of stringent measures aimed at broadening the production base of the economy and streamlining public expenditures. Despite these and other measures adopted by his and subsequent governments in Nigeria, the social and economic conditions continued to deteriorate. At the beginning of the twenty-first century, Nigeria was still classified as a low-income and a developing country by the World Bank. Larbi's account of the situation in Ghana in the 1980s and 1990s supports Gifford's (2004) proposition that bad governance has equally been a major obstacle to development in that country. In Nigeria, social and political unrests have added to the problems and caused hardships for the majority of citizens. Whereas inter-communal and religiously-motivated conflicts were always features of the social landscape, in recent times armed youths from oil-producing areas have repeatedly engaged in armed and forceful agitations for a greater share of revenues from oil.

Gifford (2004) suggests that economic hardships and failing social services are major reasons for the rise of Pentecostal churches in Ghana that have placed great emphasis on physical redemption, financial success and victory over poverty. His comparative analysis examines major Pentecostal churches in Greater Accra, including such well-known ones as the International Central Gospel Church founded by Mensa Otabil and the Action Chapel International led by Duncan Williams. While acknowledging the differences among them, Gifford states that all the churches preach the importance of success, which they consider a Christian's birthright. He relies on extensive empirical observations and quotations from church leaders to claim that these churches entertain a similar perception on wealth and how it should be acquired and utilised by Christians. He argues that the attitude of the leaders of these churches to wealth accumulation conform to the broad traditions of faith gospel, which originated in the United States. He, however, criticises the emphasis on 'deliverance' that fails to equally emphasise the role of individual responsibility or an attitude to wealth accumulation that does not encourage productivity. Gifford surmises that the over-emphasis on wealth accumulation and individual success were some of the major differences between latter generations of Pentecostal churches and the Pentecostal and charismatic churches established before the 1980s. Similarly, Hunt and Lightly (2001) note that the earlier Pentecostal churches in Nigeria emphasised "strict personal ethics" and they also preached "a retreat from the world and its material possessions and practices". For this reason, they became known as 'holiness' or 'righteousness' churches. Both Larbi and Gifford agree that the popularity of the newer Pentecostal churches in Ghana was in large part due to their teachings on wealth accumulation, individual success and deliverance.

Analysts of the Nigerian situation have reached similar conclusions. For example, Ojo (1988a: 186) notes that "the social and political life of the country in the 1970s provided the appropriate context for the social message of the charismatics". It is his view that the rapid spread of charismatic/Pentecostal teachings in Nigeria during this period was because the new movements "offered more avenues for expressing the Christian faith in more meaningful manner relevant to the condition and circumstances of independent Nigeria" (1988:175). Circumstances in independent Nigeria changed from optimism and relative affluence to despair, poverty and hopelessness within two decades, as I have described above.

As healthcare delivery deteriorated, Pentecostal preachers responded with messages that promised complete healing for the body as well as the soul (Dublisch and Michalowski 1987). They also promised salvation from other problems. As Ojo (1988a) noted: "...in the area of healing and miracles, the charismatic organisations often promise success in any undertaking—in securing employment or accommodation, in the banishment of fear, among other things. The restlessness accompanying city life and the need to find 'salvation' out of its tensions invariably swell the congregations..." Although Ojo's contention appears to buttress the functionalist approach, a deeper analysis of his concept of contextualisation refocuses attention on other reasons for the growth of Pentecostalism in West Africa and it harmonises with Anderson's (2000) suggestion that "a sympathetic approach to local culture and the retention of certain cultural practices are undoubtedly major reasons for their attraction, especially for those millions overwhelmed by urbanisation..."

The history and growth of Pentecostalism in Anglophone West Africa, as illustrated by the situation in Nigeria and the developments in Ghana, suggests that some of its earliest adopters and major proponents were the intellectual elites (university teachers and students) and middle-class professionals. Some leaders of the early Pentecostal and evangelical groups in university campuses in Nigeria later became church leaders with large followings. Examples are Mr W.F. Kumuyi, a former mathematics lecturer in the university of Lagos, who founded the Deeper Christian Life Ministry, one of the earliest and largest Pentecostal groups in Nigeria and Mr Enoch Adeboye, also a former lecturer in the same university and founder of Redeem Christian Church of God, the largest African-led Pentecostal group in Ireland and probably in Europe and America.

As Anderson (2000) argues that these churches "initially tended to have a younger, more formally educated and

consequently more westernized leadership and membership, including young professionals and middle class urban
Africans." Although the demographic picture has changed
over the years to include people of different social and economic backgrounds, the available evidence (Corten and
Marshall-Fratani 2001; Gifford 2004; Hackett 1987; Larbi
2001; Marshall 1993; Marshall-Fratani 1998; Ugba 2006b)
suggests that the elites have retained a large presence both
in the movement in Africa and among Pentecostal African
immigrants in Europe. For example, Mrs Oluwa, a Nigerian lawyer and a Pentecostal leader who participated in my
research, recalls seeing or meeting prominent people at her
first Pentecostal meetings in Nigeria. She told me:

> I saw ex-governors there, I saw people of importance,
> people that I know in the society—major-generals—
> dancing as if their position did not matter to them...
> the pastor happened to be a lawyer and I'm a lawyer. I
> was in practice in Nigeria then, the guy too was prac-
> ticing as a lawyer and I knew that he was very success-
> ful. He had a very big practice. I knew him very well.

As suggested in this quotation, Pentecostalism in Nigeria
and indeed in most of Africa has not been the exclusive preserve of economically and socially deprived persons. This has
implications for my analysis of membership of the groups
in Ireland in the next chapter. The majority of members
are educated to tertiary level and they would not consider
themselves deprived, although there is a case for arguing that
their immigrant status and the racism and ostracism from
the dominant society constitute a disadvantage that could
hinder upward mobility.

AFRICAN-LED PENTECOSTALISM IN EUROPE

The arrival in Europe of Pentecostal groups led by
Africans represents another dimension to the long quest
by what Afe Adogame has called 'African New Religious
Movements' for space in the 'global spiritual marketplace'

(Adogame 2003). Churches led by African immigrants first made their appearance in Britain in the 1920s. The first ones were not strictly Pentecostal but Evangelical. For example, the African Churches Mission (ACM) was established in Liverpool in 1922. The group led by Daniel Ekaete from Calabar in Nigeria, was the initiative of churches in West Africa and they provided the financial backbone. (Adogame 2003:28). In the 1960s, indigenous Pentecostal-like churches such as the Church of the Lord-Aladura, the Cherubim and Seraphim, and the Celestial Church of God were established in Britain mostly through the efforts of African students. Over the years the socio-demographic characteristics of these churches have changed as the numbers and categories of African immigrants in Europe have increased.

The classical Pentecostal groups are the latest African Christian initiatives in Europe (Ter Haar, 1998a, 1998b 1998c; Adogame 2001). Some, like the Redeemed Christian Church of God and Deeper Christian Life Church, started in Britain in the 1970s and 1980s as overseas branches of established groups in Nigeria or other African countries. Others had their beginning in Europe through disgruntled former members of existing groups or charismatic converts claiming to have received a special commission to either preach the gospel in a secular Europe or to heal the mentally, emotionally and physically sick. Those groups with parent bodies in Africa have continued to maintain that tie while some of the groups that started in Europe have established branches in countries in Africa. Since the ownership and management structures of Pentecostal groups in Europe are similar to those that have emerged in Ireland, I reserve the analysis of these aspects for my discussion of the situation in Ireland.

It was not long before African immigrants in continental Europe started copying the examples set by their counterparts in Britain. In Germany, the numbers of African-led churches have risen since the 1970s as more Africans came into the country to study, work, or seek political asylum. Many churches are based in big cities like Hamburg, Cologne and Berlin, which have experienced a longer presence of Africans

(Ter Haar 1998b; Ekué 1998). Gerrie ter Haar (1998c:153-171) has documented the presence and activities of many African Christian congregations, especially those formed by immigrants from Ghana, in the Netherlands. Most of the groups were formed in the 1990s and are located in or near urban centres where a large percentage of African immigrants live and work. As far back as 1997 African immigrants had established as many as 40 Christian groups in Amsterdam alone. Membership of these churches and participation in their activities, Ter Haar (1998c:159) notes, equip African immigrants with "the spiritual strength and social contacts necessary to survive, and even to begin the long climb up the ladder of social responsibility in a country which, like most parts of Western Europe, has gradually become more hostile to foreigners, particularly when they are people of colour". Ireland, it seems, is the latest attempt in this quest by African-initiated religious groups for a space in the global spiritual market. The history, trajectories and implications of the presence of these groups in Ireland is discussed in the next chapter.

ONE FAITH, MANY BELIEFS

Pentecostalism is doctrinally not homogeneous or even consistent. It is not uncommon for members of the same Pentecostal group to hold different interpretations of core Bible teachings. Whereas this can be a source of friction and rebellion, as illustrated by past and present developments among Pentecostal groups in many places, it has enabled Pentecostalism to accommodate a diverse membership and respond to the specific desires of individuals and groups. In this section, I analyse the Holy Spirit baptism and glossolalia or speaking in tongues as Pentecostals' key beliefs but also as examples of doctrines that have received multiple and con-flicting interpretations. In examining those beliefs and prac-tices that unify Pentecostals, I focus on the notion of 'rebirth' or 'born-again'. I argue that a thorough analysis of this experience as professed by believers is central to an under-standing of the transformational qualities and capabilities of Pentecostalism. My analysis is illustrated by quotes from interviews with some of the participants in my research.

Pentecostals are differentiated from most Christian groups by, among many other things, the emphasis they place on the role of the Holy Spirit in all aspects of their lives. They say the Holy Spirit empowers them to speak in tongues, to live a life of magical reality in which they heal the sick, surmount obstacles and defeat enemies; it enables them to foresee and plan for the future, to rectify present and past errors, to receive visions, prophecies and dreams, to hear the voice of God, thwart the plans of Satan, engage in enthusiastic and deeply emotional prayers and worship in public or private. The Holy Spirit connects the past, the present and the future, the sacred with the mundane, the personal with the group, the seen with the unseen and the spoken with the unspoken. For many Pentecostal African immigrants in Ireland, the Christian life and the knowledge of God is mostly about power and experience. For example, Danielle (already mentioned in this chapter) and her Congolese husband say they received specific instructions from God in a dream concerning their journey to Ireland:

> I knew we would go to a country where there are white people and where they are speaking a language I had never heard about. That was all I knew. It was only when we arrived in Ireland that I realised, through listening to TG4 (Ireland's Gaelic language television), the full meaning of my dream. You see, the things of God are mysterious. I realised that this language (Gaelic) was the language I heard in my dream.

Samuel, Danielle's husband, believes that the essence of the Christian life is to be connected to God, to hear from him and to experience the power that He gives through his Holy Spirit. Samuel has many stories, including raising a dead person, which he says demonstrate the power of God in his life or in the lives of other people after he offered supplication to God on their behalf. Sam says he hears audibly from God and from the Devil but he is able to distinguish one from the other and does not confuse the messages. Citing references and instances from the Bible, he says true Christians should be able to hear from God:

> I believe that everybody can do it. If you pray in the name of Jesus Christ, the lord will give you the power. It is the same thing as having the Holy Spirit. If you have the Holy Spirit, you'll hear when God speaks. If I can hear the voice of the devil, why not the voice of God?

Danielle and Samuel are not alone in making these claims. Mrs Oluwa says her prayers have helped women with birth complications who were seconds away from a Caesarean operation. Pauline prays in Ireland and her sister in Nigeria experiences a relief from her pains and headaches. Blessing, Pauline, Charles and a host of others pray daily to God to intervene in Ireland's immigration debacle and to help them establish legal residency. Most Pentecostal African immigrants in Ireland believe that the Holy Spirit and prayers can restore true Christianity in Ireland. They observe weeks and months of prayers and fasting as part of their supplication to God in connection with this desire.

The Holy Spirit baptism is often the second major stage in the Pentecostal journey for most believers, the first being the act of spiritual rebirth. Some believers have experienced this baptism by consciously praying for it, it happened to others in a group setting during prayers, while others have received it as a pastor or church leader prayed for them. For some the experience was as dramatic as the Apostle Paul's encounter with Jesus Christ on the way to Damascus, as recorded in the book of Acts of the Apostles, while for others it is a silent and serene experience. Most believers claim that the initial and most important sign of the baptism is speaking in tongues but other have argued that baptism in the Holy Spirit should manifest in increased display of love to others (Hollenweger, 1972:330-331). Still for others speaking in tongues is simply not the most essential feature of the Christian identity.

Mr Ola is a Nigerian lawyer and an official of the Christ Apostolic Church. Neither he nor his Irish wife speaks in tongues. He says that speaking in tongues is not what identifies a Christian: "...the Bible says some are gifted to speak in tongues. But if you can't speak in tongues, that doesn't mean you're not a Christian, it's just a gift, a gift of speaking in tongues, just like any other gift". But Mr Esan, leader of the Gospel Faith Mission, says all Christians ought to and should speak in tongues: "We speak in tongues because it is one of the promises of God for believers. Every believer must be able to do that. I'm not saying that if you don't do that you are not a believer but that is the promise our lord Jesus Christ has given to us."

These divergences are part of the long-running controversies surrounding Holy Spirit baptism and speaking in tongues, two important doctrines of the Pentecostal faith. However, Walter Hollenweger states that the controversies have often taken a racial colouration. For example, the Apostolic Faith Mission in South Africa could not accept speaking in tongues as the sole sign of baptism in the Holy Spirit because some African-initiated or indigenous churches in that country also practise speaking in tongues. To distinguish themselves or their version of speaking in tongues from that practised by the indigenous churches, the Apostolic Faith Mission opted to recognise speaking in tongues as an initial sign but not the only sign of Holy Spirit baptism. "All who are baptised in the spirit must speak in tongues, but not all who speak in tongues have been filled with the Holy Spirit" (Hollenweger, 1972:330-331).

As Hollenweger (1972: 342) explains, speaking in tongues could be an initial physical sign of the baptism of the Holy Spirit or one of the gifts of the holy spirits. Pentecostals make a distinction between public speaking in tongues during group worship and prayers and private speaking in tongues, which Hollenweger (1972:342) describes as "a non-intellectual prayer and praise too deep for words", in reference to the Bible book of Romans 8:26. According to First Corinthians 14:27, public speaking in tongues must always be interpreted. However, Hollenweger says that public speaking in tongues can sometimes cross into private speaking in tongues when a congregation of worshippers direct their utterances to God, not for the edification of others and no interpretation is given. Hollenweger, a former Pentecostal pastor and the first Professor of Mission at University of Birmingham and Selly Oak Colleges, describes the experience of Holy Spirit baptism as a librating and dis-inhibiting one that integrates "emotional and sometimes even erotic urges". In his view, the baptism is of "fundamental importance" for the course of life of the believers who have experienced it genuinely. He notes there are also baptisms that are "forced and strained" in the setting of the psychological group pressure of a Pentecostal meeting.

Although the apostle Paul speaks of speaking in tongues as groaning too deep for words in the Book of Romans, analysis of the initial Pentecost experience of the first century Christians shows that they spoke in the language of men, foreign languages which they had not learnt. The Bible's account says that the multitudes that had gathered in Jerusalem from other countries including countries in Africa, could hear the disciples speaking in their (the listeners') native languages. Among Pentecostal African immigrants in Ireland, speaking in tongues during public worship is restricted to non-intelligible groans. As Hollenweger (197:342) states: "The question whether real languages are used in speaking in tongues can only be clarified when there are sufficient tape recordings of speaking in tongues available. Pentecostals hesitate to make themselves available for such experiments."

Whereas some writers have described speaking in tongues as fake and of limited or even no use, others say it is an outlet for people who are denied other outlets of speaking in society. Despite the criticisms and reservations, Hollenweger says that speaking in tongues has a wholesome effect on those who practise it and that there are no scientific reasons to dismiss it as a pathological form of expression. According to him, "…man needs the possibility of meditation and the relaxation of tension, and these are not limited to intellectual forms. For some people art fulfils this function, for others, speaking in tongues; and those who can unload their mental burdens in both ways are not so rare as commonly supposed" (Hollenweger, 1972:344).

Despite these controversies and divergence of views, classical Pentecostals are unified by what Poloma (2000: 5-7) describes as "a particular Christian world-view that reverts to a non-European epistemology from the European one that has dominated Christianity for centuries". In other words, Pentecostals have not only relocated the geographical centre of Christianity from its European axis to many centres around the world, they have redefined the understanding of specific Christian teachings/practices, mostly by grounding them in non-European social and cultural practices. They have established ways of ascertaining or validating the Christian experience different from the long-established ones that are saturated by European values and cultures (Kalu 1998, 2003; Ter Haar 2003; Cox 2003).

There are other traits and practices that are common to most or even all Pentecostal groups. Most Pentecostals believe in the Bible as God-inspired and they adhere to a literal interpretation of it. The Bible has relevance for their everyday conducts and experiences and it serves as a practical manual for life's processes. As many African Pentecostals would say, 'the Bible is the living word of God'. Margaret Poloma (2000:6) puts it like this: "The Word of the Scriptures and the Spirit of the living God are in dialogical relationship, playing incessantly within and among individuals as well as within the larger world."

In the world of the Pentecostal, the natural interacts seamlessly with the supernatural and the lines that divide the transcendence from the ordinary and the sacred from the profane are sometimes blurred. Communications and interactions are carried on through dreams, visions and trance. These out-of-body experiences are very often embedded in the public and personal worship of many Pentecostals. Theirs is a world, as Poloma (2000: 6) puts it, "of miracles and mystery, where healings, prophecy and divine serendipity are woven into the fabric of everyday life." Pentecostal pastor and writer Jackie David Johns describes the entire Pentecostal experience as God-centred (Johns 1999: 70-84). Nothing happens outside of God or without his knowledge and even direct or indirect intervention. God intervenes in all situations to reward or punish or merely to have his purpose accomplished.

The Pentecostals' longing for and explanation of divine healing and prophecies is based on their interpretation of many Bible texts, mostly those contained in the gospels but also in the Old Testament. Some of the ones commonly cited by African Pentecostals in Ireland include Mark 16: 17-18, Isaiah 53:4, and Hebrews 13:8. Mark 16:17-18 reads: "these signs will accompany those believing: By the use of my name they will expel demons, they will speak with tongues, and with their hands they will pick up serpents, and if they drink anything deadly it will not hurt them at all. They will lay their hands upon sick persons, and these will become well" (Holy Bible- NWT). Isaiah 53:4 reads, "Truly our sicknesses were what he himself carried; and as for our pains, he bore them," while Hebrews 13:8 states that, "Jesus Christ is the same yesterday and today, and forever". Citing these verses and a host of others, Pentecostals assert that divine healing, receiving and interpreting visions, prophecies and dreams are proofs that Jesus Christ is their Lord and the Holy Spirit their companion. However, the interpretations given to these verses by various Pentecostal groups and the very practice of divine healing, prophecies and visions have also been shrouded in controversies for many decades.

Hollenweger notes, "whenever the Pentecostal movement has taken on organisational forms, spontaneous prophecy which goes beyond exhortation for edification has necessarily been rejected as 'Satan deceiving and misdirecting simple souls" (Hollenweger, 1972:345). He further asserts that genuine prophecies in the biblical traditions appear to be absent in the Pentecostal movement because "biblical prophecy contains more than the edificatory exhortation known as prophecy in the Pentecostal movement at the present day" and he notes that failed attempts of healing through prayers have resulted in public criticisms and mistrust, charges of negligence, murders and even imprisonment (Hollenweger, 1972: 368-69). He relates the story of August Waltke, a Pentecostal leader sentenced to six months' imprisonment in 1955 for manslaughter by criminal negligence after a believer he attempted to cure of diabetes through prayers died. The victim, a 16-year-old boy named Rolf Kober, had expressed an explicit desire to reject hospital treatment and to die if Waltke's prayers could not cure him. More recently, it was revealed, during the much-publicised case of Victoria Crumbie in the United Kingdom, that her Aunt and official guardian had sought assistance in Pentecostal churches to exorcise demons out of little Victoria. The aunt and her lover were convicted of Victoria's murder.

As Hollenweger comments, "the attitude of individual Pentecostal groups to the healing of the sick by prayer in general, and to the healing evangelists in particular, varies a great deal" (Hollenweger 1972:357). While older groups, some of whom once enthusiastically defended healing by prayer, now discourage and disapprove of the practice, more recent and more enthusiastic groups tend to support it. Even from among the Pentecostal ranks, critical voices have expressed doubts about the authenticity of widely publicised healing ministries and the motives of many healing evangelists. They have been accused of egotism, arrogant behaviour and of placing overriding emphasis on bodily healing to the detriment of spiritual healing and equating material prosperity to sound spiritual health or piety. Hollenweger (1972:375) notes:

> ...the healing evangelists proclaim that it is the will of God—with or without the help of doctors—to heal the sick...The healing evangelist lives in a constant dialogue with angels and demons, the Holy Spirit and the spirits of diseases from abyss...If the healing of a sick person does not take place, this can be the result of one of ten, fifteen or twenty reasons why prayers are not heard (unbelief, sin etc., on the part of the person seeking healing).

Despite the controversies and criticisms surrounding divine healing, Hollenweger states that "the connection between salvation and healing cannot simply be denied", adding that it is a testimony to the reality and relevance of healing through prayers that the Bible contains many accounts of miracles performed by Jesus. He also conceives of healing through prayer as "an effective form of support, and in some cases a substitute, for medical healing" and calls for "a useful dialogue between medical science and the Pentecostal practice of healing by prayer" (Hollenweger 1972: 370). Believers who lack money to afford medical care or have no confidence in Western medicine often seek healing through prayer. Hollenweger says the practice of divine healing has remained popular particularly among Africans because "the scientific treatment of illness as practised by Europeans is unacceptable to many Africans...European medicine seems to them to be a new and worse magic" (Hollenweger, 1972: 360). Added to this is the deplorable state of healthcare facilities and institutions in many African countries. Whereas the belief in healing through prayers translated into the rejection of modern medicine among many groups in the past, most groups these days accept medicine while still professing to believe in healing through prayers.

Charles, a Pentecostal African immigrant and a participant in my research, believes in divine healing. He has experienced healing through prayers and prayed for others to receive it. But he says he does not oppose Western medicine and that he would encourage fellow believers to avail of it where they need to:

> Whether I decide to pray about sickness or take medicine depends on my intuition, how I feel about the situation. If I see that it's something spiritual, I wouldn't go for medicine but assuming that I've a headache I would pray and I would still take medication believing that medication complements prayers. But if it's a thing I know faith would do I would stand on faith.

Unlike Charles, Danielle and her husband Sam would not readily accept medication except in extreme cases. Danielle refers to the instance in the Acts of the Apostle where the Apostle Paul survives snakebite without medical help. Citing Mark 15:17-18, she describes the power to effect divine healing as one that every believer should possess: "It is a power that is given to those who believe in Jesus Christ. You can use it in every day life and in all situations. No sickness is bigger than God. You have the authority of the believer." Along with the doctrine of divine healing is the belief that even dead people can and have been resurrected. Hollenweger notes that accounts of raising the dead—both successful and unsuccessful—are not rare in the Pentecostal movement. He tells the story of Laura Johnson Grubb, "an evangelist of the Assemblies of God, who has risen from the dead". As evidence of her unique experiences in the land of the dead, she touts a death certificate signed by her doctor. As with healing through prayer, accounts of raising the dead have been discredited even by practising Pentecostals (Hollenweger, 1972: 360).

The concept of spiritual re-birth or 'born-again' is the last of the unifying traits or practices that I examine in this chapter. As Corten and Marshall-Fratani remark: "The experience of getting born-again reproduces itself in an almost identical form across the world" (Corten and Marshall-Fratani, 2001:11). Every Pentecostal, even those born and brought up in Pentecostal families, claims this experience marked the beginning of a personal and intimate relationship with God. For examples, Aremu and Godswill, pastors and heads of branches of the Redeemed Christian Church in Dublin, were both raised by Pentecostal parents. For Aremu, his Pentecostal upbringing did not make him a born-again Christian. He attended church services only when he had important decisions to make or on New Year's Eve. His narrow escape from a motorcycle accident and the conversion or spiritual re-birth of his closest friend in 1995 got him thinking about the meaning of life. The following year he felt a deep conviction in his heart to "give" his life to Jesus, to cultivate a more personal relationship with God and serve him wholeheartedly. It was the beginning of his Pentecostal journey. Godswill's story is similar:

> I grew up to know my father to be a born-again Christian. Before I left home, he founded a church called Message Assembly. But at a point in my Christian life I discovered that apart from being born in a Christian family, there is a time you personally make up your mind that you want to live for God. I came to the realisation that serving God is a personal thing, that it's not a collective thing... at a point I had an encounter. I mean, a man of God was preaching and it really touched my heart and I started feeling sorry for myself. I felt sorry for myself because I had failed to grasp the extent of the pains and suffering Jesus went through for me. He went so far and so much just to give me peace and salvation. The word salvation now started to mean a different thing to me, so much that I felt like crying, I just felt that I should give something back to someone that has shown so much love to me...I gave my life to Christ.

Pauline was a Catholic and then a member of neo-Pentecostal group within the church before she made her transition to Pentecostalism. Mrs Oluwa was a devout and active member of a mainline church but she "gave" her life to Christ after she attended a Pentecostal service at the invitation of her husband and, like Godswill, was cut to the heart when she heard the sermon about Jesus and the ransom sacrifice. Mr James Esan's parents were "idol worshippers" and his father had 33 wives. Mr Esan joined a church as a young boy and later switched to a Pentecostal one:

> I had been attending a church for over ten years before I became a born-again Christian. I was going to a Pentecostal church for over 10 years before I became a born-again Christian. I got born again in 1994—I know that was the year I gave my life to Christ.

Pentecostals are fairly uniform in their description and interpretation of the significance of the experience of re-birth. They say it is a prerequisite for salvation, that those who must escape the destruction that awaits this ungodly world and go to heaven to be with Jesus Christ must undergo spiritual re-birth. They identify the encounter between Jesus and Nicodemus, as recorded in the gospel of John, as the basis of this unique interpretation. That accounts reads:

> Now there was a man of the Pharisees, Nic·o·de´mus was his name, a ruler of the Jews. This one came to him in the night and said to him: "Rabbi, we know that you as a teacher have come from God; for no one can perform these signs that you perform unless God is with him." In answer Jesus said to him: "Most truly I say to you, Unless anyone is born again, he cannot see the kingdom of God." Nicodemus said to him: "How can a man be born when he is old? He cannot enter into the womb of his mother a second time and be born, can he?" Jesus answered: "Most truly I say to you, unless anyone is born from water and spirit, he cannot enter into the kingdom of God. What has been born from the flesh is flesh, and what has been born from the spirit is spirit. Do not marvel because I told you, YOU people must be born again (John 3:1-7). *New World Translation.*

Pentecostal interpretation of this experience tends to include not only a deeper commitment to God but also a rupture with the past and many aspects of the present. They develop new scripture-centred interpretations of their present, past and future and of their relationship to the 'others'. The person who has undergone spiritual rebirth is a "new creation" who has forsaken 'worldly' or fleshly habits like drinking alcohol, smoking, visits to discos/pubs, sexual relations outside or before wedlock, quarrelling, fighting, resentment and enmity. The human race is one and fellow Pentecostals, especially members of the same group, are considered brothers and sisters. Ethnic, social and racial differences should pale into insignificance, replaced by love for humanity and concern for the ungodly. To buttress their point, Pentecostals would often quote the Apostle Paul: "Consequently if anyone is in union with Christ, he is a new creation; the old things passed away, look! new things have come into existence" *(2Corinthian 5:17)*. Godswill had to "sort out"himself after he became born-again. He says:

> You see, giving your life to Christ must cost you something. I had to give up my girlfriend. I stopped going to parties. I loved music so much. I had a huge collection, getting the latest releases, keeping abreast with the latest dance-steps. I had to give them up. That was very painful, that was the really painful one, not the girlfriend. I didn't think I could survive without my music, secular music.

Corten and Marshall-Fratani (2001), however contest the Pentecostal interpretation of re-birth that emphasise rupture with the past. Conversion, they argue, does not imply "a straightforward trajectory in which the individual is liberated from an imagined collective history and moves to a monolithic form of 'modern' individuality. Rather, it offers believers a plurality of "technologies of the self". My empirical research among Pentecostal African immigrants demonstrate that the re-birth experience and the Pentecostal identity do not necessarily replace or obliterate other identities and relationships but rather it makes additional relationships and identities or new ways of thinking about oneself and the 'other' possible. In chapter seven and in the 'key' stories in chapter eight, I expatiate on this point. I problematise my informers' self-definition and the dichotomies between the 'old' life and the 'new' and between the self and the 'others'.

HEALTH AND WEALTH GOSPEL

Whereas early Pentecostal groups conceived of 'conversion' or 'new beginning' as a "radical transformation of the self through rupture with a sinful past", Corten and Marshall-Fratani argue that many recent groups have placed emphasis on the mundane, especially on the acquisition of health and wealth: "Salvation is now resolutely this-worldly, and the evidence of a new life has become as much material as spiritual. Moral rigour and strict personal ethics have not been superseded, yet the notion of transformation has been broadened to include the possibility of material change in everyday life" (Corten and Marshall-Fratani 2001: 6-7).

Health and Wealth Gospel, also called 'Prosperity Gospel' or 'Faith Gospel', has been a prominent feature of particular brands of Pentecostalism from the 1960s (Dublisch and Michalowski 1987). Hollinger (1991) reckons that the movement began in the United States during the post-Second World War spiritual revival when increased emphasis was also placed on other qualities of Charismata like speaking in tongues, the inerrancy of the scriptures and the power of the Holy Sprit that empowered believers to perform and receive physical, emotional and spiritual healing. As Coleman (2004) notes: "After the Second World War, the teachings of American Protestant revivalism became even more closely intertwined with commodity logic."

Rev. Kenneth Hagin who in 1974 established the Rhema Bible Training Centre in Tulsa, Oklahoma, became a key figure of the post-war spiritual renewal movement and a foremost proponent of Prosperity Gospel. He is often called the founder of the Faith Movement both because his ministry and teachings emphasised spiritual and material/physical redemption but also because of his direct and indirect influence on many of the early prosperity preachers in Africa, South America and North America. Some of these preachers were either trained in his Bible college or had access to his publications and television programmes while others saw him as a role model largely because of his massive media and public presence.

Another major player in the post-War Faith movement in the United States was Dr Oral Robert. In 1954 the charismatic preacher invented the 'Blessing-Pact' that promised anyone who pledged $100 to his ministry a refund if the person did not receive at least an equivalent sum back as a gift from an unexpected source within one year of giving to Oral Robert (Barron 1987: 62-3). In the 1970s, he invented the concept of 'seed faith', based on the biblical idea that sowing precedes harvest or that those who wish to reap bountifully must sow generously. He invited the public to sow by donating money to his ministry. Coleman notes that proponents of Faith Gospel "have created highly organized commercial networks which ostensibly exist in the public arena but are in fact patronized primarily by those who have already embraced the Faith Gospel." Some preachers from Africa, South America and the Caribbean, while professing to reject cultural imperialism, have established their own Bible training schools, but as Coleman (2004) notes, they "invite American Faith preachers to their conferences and/ or sell Faith products." In just over thirty years, the Faith Movement has spread to most parts of the world but mainly to countries in the Majority World, also called Third World.

According to Barron (1987), Faith theology in the West combines Pentecostal healing revivalism with nineteenth-century American New Thought Metaphysics which states that the Divine Truth cannot be fully comprehended by the conscious mind. This assertion suggests that Faith theology is rooted in existing practices such as glossolalia or speaking in tongues, divine healing and participation in emotionally-charged prayers, singing and dancing. Coleman (2004) expatiates on the implications of these activities for the Faith theology: "These activities are all informed by the conviction that, through dominion over consciousness, one may fully develop the potential of one's innate spirituality. By giving tongue, that is, by making the utterances known as 'positive confessions', the believer externalizes the power of the inner, spiritual self and therefore gains power over physical reality."

Coleman's analysis of The Word of Life group founded by Ulf Ekman in 1983 on the outskirts of Uppsala, Sweden, articulates some of the major criticisms that have been levelled against Faith Ministries in different parts of the world. Ekman, who became known as "God's capitalist" in the Swedish media, and the members of his group were called "a network of hucksters involved in the systematic fleecing of susceptible dupes" (Coleman 2004). They were also accused by opponents and critics of "the systematic brainwashing of potential recruits." In the case of Pentecostal churches in Nigeria, Marshall (1993: 218) notes that "the aggressive pursuit of material support from members in the guise of the doctrine of prosperity has sparked some controversy...about the venality of leaders."

Inevitably, analysis of 'Health and Wealth' theology has involved explorations of the connections Weber (1930) made between the work and consumption ethics of the Calvinists in eighteenth century Europe and the development of modern capitalism in parts of Europe. Like the Calvinists, many of today's proponents of 'Health and Wealth' gospel consider material wealth a sign of God's approval. However, Weber's analysis places emphasis on production, rather than consumption and the Calvinists abhorred the attachment to wealth and conspicuous consumption that have been associated with preachers of Health and Wealth gospel. As Coleman surmises, their "aesthetic of excess in the redistribution of material and other resources might appear to be an ideological world away from Weber's Calvinists." He adds: "In the contemporary group, a sense of being in touch with the transcendent emerges not from denial of commodified expressions of generic spirituality but from the ability relentlessly to deploy such expressions in ways that suggest mobility, the transcendence of distance, and 'reception' by multiple, even imagined, others".

Critics (e.g. Brouwer et al 1996) of the Faith Movement see it as a strategy for propagating the American capitalist culture, but others (e.g. Martin 2002; Anderson 2000; Anderson and Hollenweger 1999) have focussed on the peculiar and complex manifestations and adaptations of the broad prosperity teachings in local circumstances. For example, Martin (2002) states that the prosperity teaching of the Faith Movement appeals to many groups in Africa and the Caribbean because it correlates with their notion of the intersection of the mundane with the sacred and of the spiritual world with the material. Gifford (2004), on the hand, documents significant variations in the application of this doctrine by the main Pentecostal churches in Ghana. He notes that the emphasis on black identity, self-confidence

and self-empowerment by some groups in that country contradict the apolitical stand and focus on individual salvation
of the Faith Movement in the United States.

In Nigeria the economic down-turn and the chaotic
social and political environment of the 1980s provided a
fertile ground for the spread of 'Health and Wealth' gospel.
Commenting on these developments, Marshall (1993: 222)
notes that they "had profound effects on the social conditions legitimating accumulation, status and wealth." Whereas
many of the Pentecostal churches that began before this era
of economic and social deprivation placed emphasis on holiness and retreat from the world of materialism and immo-
ralities, the newer generation of churches interpreted material
success both as a sign of God's favour and a component of the
salvation package designed by God himself. Salvation and the
rebirth experience acquired an overly materialist interpretation or enunciation as Marshall (1983: 229-230): reports:

> The power to succeed and be prospered is seen as
> being given to those living exemplary born-again lives
> through the power of Jesus and material gains must be
> distributed according to His rules. Those who aspire to
> riches and social status are taught that only through
> adherence to born-again doctrine, prayer, hard work,
> and generosity in giving (of time if they don't have
> money) will they likewise be 'prospered'. Those who
> do not live a 'true life in Christ' gain wealth through
> contact, consciously or not, with evil forces, and will
> likewise be ruined by them.

Both in Nigeria and Ghana, prosperity teaching also
manifested in the greater emphasis on divine healing. For
example, Larbi (2001) notes that the theologies of Pentecostal churches in Ghana during the 1980s were dominated by
increased emphasis on physical healing and deliverance from
demonic oppression in order to pave the way for material
and spiritual prosperity. Many Pentecostal churches, particularly the Church of Pentecost, established prayer camps
dotted around the country where the faithful and needy
came together to prayer about all sorts of problems, includ-

ing health-related ones. Although he agrees that the economic hardship of that era provided a fertile ground for the message of prosperity preachers he asserts that the concept of divine healing as preached by Pentecostals conforms with indigenous African worldview of spirituality causality.

Gerrie ter Haar (1994: 226) similarly states that although "Pentecostal doctrine leaves no room for the incorporation of traditional African spiritual beings or other entities…its theology accommodates certain African traditional beliefs, such as those concerning witchcraft or evil spirits, in the sense that it will explicitly address these as manifestations of evil which can be overcome through the power of Christ." Gifford (1994: 516) concurs: "The faith gospel is an American doctrine…yet much of Africa's traditional religion is concerned with fertility, health and plenty." This intersection between Pentecostalism and African indigenous beliefs provides an additional explanation of the popularity of Pentecostal teachings on health, wealth and divine healing.

Other analysts also believe that economic deprivation and socio-political problems were not the only reasons health and wealth gospel became popular in Africa. For example, Matthew Ojo (1988a: 184) states that Pentecostal churches in Nigeria gave "heightened and specialised interpretations" of common Pentecostal teachings and defined them in "sometimes special and peculiar ways." According to him, the activities and growth of these churches represent "the contextualisation of a form of Christian spirituality which, while taking it roots from external models, has become an indigenous growth." His opinion is similar to that of Larbi (2001: 298) who acknowledged the influence of American tele-evangelism on the proponents of Health and Wealth gospel in Ghana but states that the groups are nonetheless indigenous innovations.

In Europe, Pentecostal groups formed by African immigrants are either off-shoots or proponents of the Health and Wealth gospel in the African continent or have been influenced by them. In the case of African-led groups in the United Kingdom, Hunt and Lightly (2001:107) notes that they have been shaped by "developments in West Africa" and "an adaptation to Western society." While the theology and the worldview of these churches express "the experiences of Nigerians in their country of origin," they are equally "in many respects world-accommodating and embrace a theology that is inclined to follow the contours of Western culture." Hunt and Lightly (2001: 107) concluded that the doctrines and practices of these churches in the United Kingdom "reflect means of coping with, and responding to, adverse circumstances while at the same time, translated into the British setting, they subsequently assist their immigrant black membership in adapting to a secondary range of social conditions."

Among Pentecostal African immigrants in Ireland, Health and Wealth Gospel is manifested in diverse and complex ways but it is observable mostly in the over-emphasis on the material circumstances of their lives. The future they wish for in prayers and songs is not a trouble-free world in heaven but a permanent and settled life in Ireland. Prayer requests and public worship sessions are dominated by issues connected with work and residence permit, visa and passport application, employment and financial worries. But as a respondent, Mr Ola, states:

> Our purpose is to go to heaven. God knows that and we don't have to come here and remind Him every day. We do pray about heaven because that is our goal. However, we have other goals too. How can we serve God comfortably and carry out His will if we are not settled? God knows that we need the stability and the means if we are to accomplish the mission He has given to us.

Leaflets and posters advertising the presence and services of the churches often promise solution to a variety of problems, including the ones I have mentioned above. Church members dress in fanciful clothes both to reflect attachment to African traditions but sometimes to showcase material prosperity. Some pastors and church leaders say their mission is to help empower church members spiritually but also materially. During service, they often invite members to accept the challenge self-improvement which, they say, leads to material and spiritual prosperity, happiness and societal recognition. The concept of 'sowing with God' is also prevalent in some churches. Members are requested to sow by giving to God through the church or pastor. Those who sow abundantly will reap abundantly, the church leaders tell the adherents. Sometimes, church members are asked to list specific needs and to present them to God either through the pastor or by raising the piece of paper towards heaven as the pastor offers prayers. Other signs of the Health and Wealth doctrines are discussed in the next two chapters.

Among African Pentecostals in Dublin, salvation or rebirth is conceived in terms of a new and strengthened relationship with God and it is also the means to upward mobility and personal success. Ireland's precarious socio-political environment has meant that emphasis has been laid on personal security, survival and prosperity. The point is made clearer in the next chapter where I discuss African Pentecostals in Ireland.

CHAPTER FIVE

THE SEARCH FOR COLOURLESS SOULS

INTRODUCTION

In this chapter I examine the origin and spread of African-led Pentecostal groups in Ireland. My analysis relies on data from ethnographic observations, in-depth interviews and a survey of 144 members drawn from four churches in the Greater Dublin Area. The groups are Christ Apostolic Church (CAC), Redeemed Christian Church of God (RCCG), the Mountain of Fire and Miracle Ministry (MFMM) and the Gospel Faith Mission (GFM). Detailed background information about these groups, including the history of their formation, is discussed in the next chapter. In addition to ethnographic observation and in-depth interviews, I have garnered data for this chapter by analysing secondary documents like in-house magazines, leaflets and posters produced by the churches and recorded sermons. My aim is to provide insight into the causes and course of growth of these churches in Ireland. I also aim to describe their modus operandi, activities, organisation, aspiration and relationship with one another and with other groups in Irish society.

The presence and spread of Pentecostalism among Africans in Ireland has taken place against the backdrop of the increased presence, since the mid-1990s, of African immigrants in the country (Ugba 2007b, 2006a, 2006b, 2003b). The majority of Africans, who have arrived in Ireland since the mid-1990s, are Christians. Of the 182 respondents in a survey of Africans in the Greater Dublin Area, 72% indicated they were 'Christians' while close to 26% said they were

Muslims (Ugba 2004).[1] Only one respondent indicated he or she was neither a Christian nor a Muslim. The survey results re-emphasise the primacy of religious participation among African immigrants but they also remind us of the dearth of research on immigrant religious participation in Ireland, especially on non-Christian faiths.

Whereas this book focuses on African Pentecostals, experiential knowledge and the results of the 2002 and 2006 censuses suggest that the participation of African immigrants in Christian initiatives in Ireland extends beyond Pentecostalism. Some Africans belong to mainstream Christian groups like Roman Catholicism, Methodism, Presbyterianism and the Church of Ireland. A growing number are Jehovah's Witnesses. Other Africans are members of 'white-garment' churches, as they are popularly called in Nigeria because their members wear white cassocks for services. Churches like the Eternal Sacred Order of Cherubim and Seraphim and the Celestial Church of Christ Worldwide belong to this category. As I indicate in chapter four, the relationship between African Pentecostals and members of the 'white-garment' churches is one of mutual antagonism and rejection. The relationship between Pentecostals and members of 'mainstream' Irish churches, on the other hand, is more complex and, as I argue later in this and the next chapter, this relationship is further complicated by African church leaders' avowed mission to proselytise and thus change the racial and cultural profile of their membership.

THE SPREAD OF AFRICAN-LED PENTECOSTAL GROUPS

Although the activities of African-led Pentecostal groups did not come to public and media attention until about 2000, empirical investigations and interviews with various respondents suggest that the first of these groups was set up in Dublin in 1996 by Congolese-born Remba Osengo, who had migrated to Ireland that same year. Since then many African-led Pentecostal groups have been established, first in the Greater Dublin Area and later in other parts of Ireland. The diffusion of these groups to regions outside of the Greater Dublin Area is connected in large part to Irish government policy of 'dispersing' asylum seekers all over Ireland initiated in 2001. The majority of asylum seekers were located in the Greater Dublin Area before this policy came into effect (Tróicare/ICJP 2002). The number of African-led Pentecostal groups established outside of the Greater Dublin Area has increased substantially as 'dispersed' asylum seekers and other Africans form new groups and set up outreach posts for the Dublin-based groups. The spread of these groups is also a deliberate strategy by church leaders to take their message to more people since the vast majority of them believe that they are on a mission ordained by God to spread the gospel in the whole of Ireland before judgment day arrives. As Aremu, a Minister and church leader in Redeem, says:

> Right now we believe God is leading us to pray for a spiritual revival in Ireland. We've organised special prayer sessions, we've been praying every day for 60 days. We've done it every day for one month. We're doing it from October to November. We pray every day... I would really love to see that people in the Irish society experience the power of the Holy Spirit. Ireland is a Christian nation but the bible says, 'by their fruits you'll know them'. You don't measure Christianity by what they say; you measure it by the fruits they show. And as I look around there seem to be so many fruits that do not look like Christian fruits. But it starts from us. You can't give out what you don't have. So that is what God is leading us to do, to pray for this land, for this country. And we've been doing that.

The Redeemed Christian Church of God is acknowledged by my interviewees as the largest and the most widespread African-led Pentecostal church in Ireland. Registered in 1998, the church had close to 40 branches in Ireland at the end of 2004. The other large and prominent African-led Pentecostal churches include the Mountain of Fire and Miracles Ministry (MFMM), the Christ Apostolic Church (CAC), the Gospel Faith Mission International (GFM),

Christ Co-Workers in Mission (CCM), Hope and Glory Ministries (HGM) and Christ Ambassadors Ministries. In the absence of an official census, the exact numbers of these churches and the total population of worshippers have been a matter of guess-estimates and media speculations.

As far back as 2001, *Metro Eireann* reported that over 40 of these churches had been established in the Greater Dublin Area (Metro Eireann 2001). A report by the Irish Council of Churches in February 2003 estimated the number of African immigrants in what it called 'Black Majority churches' to be over 10,000 (ICC 2003), while the Moderator of the Presbyterian Church of Ireland, Dr Ivan McKay, estimated the number to be 30,000 in 2004 (McGarry 2004). Information published by the Company Registration Office (CRO) on its website buttresses the fact that many groups have been established since the late 1990s, although it does not specify the exact number and types of churches. Most churches are registered as companies limited by guarantee and a few have attained charity status.

MAIN DEMOGRAPHIC FEATURES

Demographically, African-led Pentecostal churches are a microcosm of the larger African community and the demographic profile of one church tends not to differ considerably from that of the other. Generally there are more women than men and a large number of children in any group. The large presence of children is not surprising since over 75% of those who participated in my survey said they have children. More than 72% are married although the spouses of some were still in their home-countries or outside of Ireland. An overwhelming 93% are married to fellow Africans. Among those married to non-Africans, more than 83% were males. In the majority (85%) of cases, husband and wife belong to the same Christian group but over 60% of the 15% who said their spouses were not members of their groups were women. This could perhaps indicate that women are less successful in convincing their husbands to join their groups or that men are generally less inclined towards this kind of religiosity.

Mr Esan believes women have shown a greater tendency towards spirituality dating back to the days when Christ walked the earth: "If you look at the scriptures you'll find that many places that our lord Jesus Christ went to, women went there".

Half of the respondents in my survey identified themselves as Immigrants. They comprise work permit holders and those who have gained residence status by other means including parentage of child/children born in Ireland. About 15% were Irish citizens or citizens of an EU country while close to 24% were asylum seekers. Just over 7% were refugees while 4% said they were students. Although educational and professional attainments are quite high, the unemployment rate, at 31%, is also high. More than 8 of 10 have third-level educational qualifications and the occupational profile includes medical and veterinary doctors, nurses, accountants, computer specialists, teachers, diplomats, engineers, medical technicians and writers. There are no significant differences in the educational attainments of males and females but the employment rate was higher among males while the 10 respondents who said they were full-time parents were females. About 70% of those who described themselves as students were females.

TYPES OF AFRICAN-LED PENTECOSTAL GROUPS IN IRELAND

African-led Pentecostal groups in Ireland can be categorised into three main groups according to their historical background and the transnational links they maintain. A further distinction can also be made based on how the churches understand or interpret their roles in the lives of their members and in the larger society. On the basis of history, the first category of churches are those established by African immigrants with no support from or links, at least in the initial stages, with groups in Africa or elsewhere. Examples of such churches include Christ Co-Workers in Mission and the Gospel Faith Mission. Immigrants who have taken such initiatives are usually experienced Pentecostals who had been active members of Pentecostal groups in their home-countries and have had some experience of leadership. The majority came to Ireland to seek political asylum and the period before they gained refugee status, when the Irish government prevented them from gainful employment and formal education, provided ample opportunity and the incentives for spiritual devotion and activism.

For example, the Pentecostal journey of Mr James Esan, the pastor/leader of Gospel Faith Mission (GFM), began in Nigeria in 1994 when, according to him, he experienced a spiritual rebirth. After he arrived in Ireland in 1998 to seek political asylum, he worshipped for a brief period with Graces Mission, a Dublin-based Irish-led Pentecostal church. Mr Esan, however, left to start a prayer group in his living room because "…their way of worship was quite different from the way we pray in Africa". Initially, his group comprised of five members but that soon blossomed into a large group and by mid-2005 they had established two other groups in Ireland and one in London. After years of squatting and sharing substandard premises, the Dublin branch relocated, in 2004, to premises it purchased for about half a million euros. As at the end of 2004, between 250 and 300 people were attending Sunday services in its newly refurbished and modern hall.

Once they have established their base, churches in this category are quick to seek national and international links with other Pentecostals. For example, GFM has established links with churches in the United Kingdom and Nigeria. Mr Esan said such links with longer-established Pentecostal groups are necessary because they serve as sources of spiritual guidance. Mr Esan makes frequent trips to the United Kingdom for consultation and training. Like Mr Esan, Mr Osengo also associated with the Graces Mission before he established Christ Co-Workers in Mission in 1996.

The second group of African-led Pentecostal churches in Ireland are those established by disgruntled members of existing African-led Pentecostal churches. For example, pastor Adewumi had been the pastor of Christ Apostolic

Church (CAC) before he started his own group—Christ
Glory Ministries—and his church is located not far from
his former one. Usually a disgruntled leader who leaves to
form a new group takes some members of the congregation
with him. They do not see themselves as rebels or disgruntled
fellows but persons called by God to fulfil a different and
often greater mission from that being fulfilled by the group
they have deserted. On the surface, those who stay appear
not to harbour resentment against those who leave and
those who leave still see those they forsook as members of
one large family of God's children. For example, Adewumi
still receives invitations to special programmes organised by
the CAC although there is no evidence he has honoured the
invitations. However, Emmanuel, who took over the leadership of CAC after Adewumi deserted, said Adewumi's exit
had debilitating effects on the church and left many members
unsure of the future of the church. Schisms of this nature were
rampant in the history of the modern Pentecostal movement
(see chapter four) and they have been features of the growth
of Pentecostalism in many parts of the world (Hollenweger
1976, 1999; MacRobert 1988; Cox 1996; Anderson 1999).

The third category comprises churches like the Christ
Apostolic Church, Redeem Christian Church of God and
the Mountain of Fire and Miracle Ministry, which have their
parent-bodies in Africa. They were started either by trained
pastors sent by the parent-bodies or by ordinary members
of the church who, when they arrived in Ireland, found no
other Christian group that suited their style and expectations. Spiritual and material support for these churches came
directly from the parent-bodies or their European headquarters in the United Kingdom in the beginning. Such support
includes the exchange of personnel and training of pastors
and other church officials.

The beginning of the Christ Apostolic Church (CAC),
for example, is traceable to a series of dinner evenings at a
central Dublin hotel organised by the visiting Nigerian
founder of the church. Invitations to these meetings were
mostly displayed in refugee hostels, African shops and busi-

nesses and in other places frequented by Africans. Mr Ola Ellori, a Nigerian-trained lawyer and a CAC official, had his first encounter with the group at one of these dinners. His initial information about the dinner was through a leaflet that had been displayed in the lobby of the refugee hostel where he lived. He was persuaded to attend by a colleague who had attended a previous dinner. At the dinner Ellori met and chatted with the visiting Nigerian minister. He was impressed by the style and content of the programme, the opportunity to interact with other Africans and by a prediction by the visiting minister that he (Ellori) would marry an Irish woman, gain legal residency and have a successful business: "Afterwards, I said to myself this is more of my thing, the way of worship was very much like the way we worshipped back home. I made up my mind that I was going to be a member after that first meeting…"

REASONS FOR GROWTH

Apart from the desire to re-live the past and recreate the kind of Christian activities they had experienced in their home-country, there are other reasons African immigrants flock to these churches. The majority of members have had some experience of Pentecostalism before they arrived in Ireland. For them, Pentecostal worship or services correspond with their firmly-held notion of experiential knowledge of and relationship with the Supreme Being. That, after all, was the reason they forsook or discounted all prior religious experience or the religion of their parents and became born-again. In other words, some members of these churches came to Ireland armed with the notion that nothing else apart from Pentecostalism is good enough. It is therefore not surprising that they search for Pentecostal churches once they have arrived or that they do not feel satisfied and comfortable in any other group they might have joined.

Whereas this reason explains their devotion to Pentecostalism, it does not necessarily explain their attachment to groups led and mostly populated by black Africans. In Ireland many of them have chosen to associate with African-led Pentecostal groups, rather than ones led by native Irish persons, because the former represent the kind of Pentecostal practices and settings they were accustomed to. For example, a respondent who flirted with an Irish-dominated Pentecostal church and a few African-led ones explains the reasons he eventually joined CAC where he is now an official:

> I found CAC to be a church that could give me the same type of things that I was enjoying back at home...the first day I stepped into the church I was able to witness the things I was enjoying back at home and after about four Sundays, I came to the conclusion that this might be a suitable church that will give me the same kind of atmosphere that I long for in a service to God...so, it wasn't a mistake, it was just a choice that I made to join the church... you see we cannot separate the sentiments of Africans from our way of worship because our custom plays a big part in our worship... You see, if you look at where we are coming from, we have to battle with many problems; we have to think of witches and wizards, and all of those things. And if you have a deliverance from any of these problems, the way you will worship God or give thanks will be a lot different from somebody who can live on credit cards.

Another reason African immigrants embrace these churches is the direct connections between the contents of service or worship and the socio-political conditions of their existence in Ireland. Themes in songs, prayers and sermons make direct reference to their situation of voluntary or involuntary exile and they become the basis of hope and optimism as the views of Blessing (quoted below) illustrate. Whereas Africans Pentecostals proclaim that their most cherished desire is to be with Christ in heaven, the activities in these churches appear to be mostly this-worldly or mundane. They focus especially on how to survive in an increasingly difficult social and political climate.

Quite apart from their devotional affiliations, some members see the church as a place of refuge from the problems, hostilities and rejection they face in Irish society. For others, the church does not serve as a mere place of refuge or a distraction from the realities but as a channel for receiving real solutions to various kinds of problems. Blessing, a mother of three, was awaiting decision on her application for residence permit when we first met. Her two younger children were born in Ireland and her application for residence permit was made on this basis. But after the government abolished the policy in February 2003, she and about 11,500 others were caught in an immigration quagmire. In her moments of anxieties and uncertainties the church provided support and assurance:

> Since I came into this country, it has been one problem or the other. Today, the government will say 'we're not giving you paper', tomorrow they will say 'we're giving you'. In times like these when I get to the church there are some messages that I hear that will help me to keep calm, that will give me some encouragement. Through these messages I can see that God is still there for me. In this country, there is nobody there for you except God.

For some members, particularly those holding prominent positions, their involvement in these churches is a way of compensating for the lack of recognition or the diminished social status that they experience in Ireland. Many members, including pastors and top officials, had enjoyed societal respect and recognition as successful professionals or businesspersons before they came to Ireland as asylum seekers. Official and public attitudes to asylum seekers and most categories of African immigrants are a far cry from the respect and recognition they had been accustomed to. Several studies (Amnesty International 2001; ARN 1999; Ugba 2004) have documented the racism and discrimination experienced by asylum seekers and other categories of immigrants in Ireland. African-led Pentecostal churches, for many members, are the only place in Irish society where they can experience the sense of self-fulfilment, importance and relevance they had experienced in their home countries. Emmanuel is an asylum seeker and an official of CAC who had practised as an estate surveyor and worked as a banker before he came to Ireland. He believes: "People want to go to a place where they will be appreciated, they want to be understood and they want to feel that they are important and relevant".

In the case of female members, the pastor of GFM, Mr Esan, said that women have found the churches to be a source of solace, comfort and succour in the face of the domestic problems they face. Some female respondents describe how membership of the church or the intervention of the pastor saved their marriage, helped them through a period when their children or husband was sick or in inculcating strong moral values in their children in the absence of their husband or a father figure. Mrs Tokunbo Oluwa, who took care of her five children on her own before her husband joined her, said the task was made easier because of strong moral guidance in the bible:

> You know, the Irish society, with all its permissiveness and immoralities, is not an easy place to raise children. At 16, children are supposed to be free to do what they like. But the Christian values that I've taught my children since infancy have made them amenable to my advice and instructions. If not for these Christian principles, things would have been a lot harder. I know of many Africans that have lost their children, their children are with the Social Welfare authorities, they are living in hostels because they revolted against their parents. So it takes the grace of God to bring up children in the Western world.

Mr Ellori believes single mothers and women living apart from their husbands find strong social network and emotional support in the church. While she waited for her husband to join her in Ireland, Pauline immersed herself in church activities and enlisted the prayers of the pastors and those of fellow worshippers for a speedy and safe reunion with her husband. She found companionship and acceptance in the church at a time of extreme loneliness at home and rejection by the larger society. During a special service at the church the speaker foretold that the prayers of one women in the church who had been "waiting on the lord" for her husband to join her had been answered and that the husband would soon join her. Pauline concluded that the prophecy referred to her although many other women in the group were in a similar situation. About a week after the prophecy was uttered her husband arrived from Nigeria through The Netherlands on a fake passport and after two failed attempts.

Pauline's story is the story of many women members of African-led Pentecostal groups and the direct consequence of a citizenship policy (abolished in January 2005 as a result of the June 2004 Citizenship Referendum) that conferred automatic citizenship on every child, including children of immigrants, born in Ireland. Until then, the parents of such children could apply for residence permit solely on the basis of having child/children born in Ireland (as discussed in chapter two). Once the parent of the citizen child has established legal residence, he/she could apply for his/her spouse to join them. In practice, the application process was not easy and it certainly did not produce quick results, especially as more immigrants took to this route to gain citizenship and residence permit. Long delays, recalcitrant state officials and red-tape stood in the way of quick results. The frustrations and uncertainties increased when the government announced in early 2003 that it was abandoning the policy of granting residence permits solely on the basis of parentage of a child born in Ireland. The government did not say what it wanted to do about the outstanding applications and the long wait that followed tested the patience and tenacity of many immigrants, including members of these churches.

In prayers, songs, and ordinary conversations, the church members spoke of their wish to be freed of these immigration problems. These desires also became recurrent themes in Sunday and mid-week worship sessions and in night prayer vigils. The women and men caught in this immigration quagmire found not only friendship and spiritual guidance in the church but also professional advice. Church members who could not afford high legal fees relied on free advice from legal professionals within the church. Both Ellori and Mrs Oluwa recall making many representations to the Department of Justice on behalf of church members. In January 2005 the government implemented a new policy that paved the way for those caught in this immigration debacle to apply for residence permit under certain conditions (see chapter two for a detailed discussion). For many African Pentecostals, the new policy was God's direct intervention and the answer to their prayers.

EVANGELISTIC ACTIVITIES

Like Mr Ellori, nearly 79% of the 70 respondents who said they became members of their groups after they arrived in Ireland, either received their initial information through family members/friends or were influenced by them; 17% were contacted directly by officials of the church while 3% received their initial information through posters/leaflets displayed in public places. Posters and leaflets produced by the church appeal to people's sense of insecurity, fear, uncertainties, hope and expectations. They promise physical, emotional and spiritual redemption and solution to a wide array of problems including depression, sudden death, jinxes, anxieties and unemployment. The use of the mass media to spread their message and to invite interested enquiries is still very limited although some newspapers like *Metro Eireann*, *Street Journal* and *Africans* (all published by Africans) regularly feature articles by church leaders. For many years CAC has placed advertisements in *Metro Eireann* informing readers of the venue, days and times of its activities. Coverage of the activities of these churches in the mainstream media is limited and the few and occasional reports have constructed them mainly as exotic display of national/ethnic cultures and solidarity forums (McCan 2000; Haughey 2002; McGarry 2004).

Door-to-door and street evangelism is not popular among Pentecostal African immigrants in Ireland. Rather they rely mostly on word-of-mouth and on members to invite and convince their friends or relatives. It is a strategy that has yielded results because 48.6 % of the 144 members who participated in my survey said they became members of their groups after they arrived in Ireland. Although some church leaders believe that street evangelism is a more effective means to reach a greater and more diversified audience, they are hindered by the fear of a hostile reception from the Irish public and the lack of knowledge of what is permissible under the law. Aremu, a church leader, told me that his group abandoned attempts to preach and distribute leaflets at the Huston train station in Dublin after the management threatened to invite the Gardai (police) and arrest them. That incident, according to Aremu, ended their efforts to take their message to public places: "We didn't know we could not distribute tracts there. I want to preach the gospel; I don't want to go to jail. So we've been a bit wiser since then."

MANAGEMENT AND ADMINISTRATION

There are striking similarities in the beliefs, activities, demographic profile and administrative methods of African-led Pentecostal churches in Ireland. As I explain later in this chapter, the churches are populated predominantly by black Africans who have migrated to Ireland since the mid-1990s and the gender, age, occupational and educational profiles of their membership closely resemble those of the larger African communities (Ugba 2004). All the churches have one spiritual head (the pastor), who is usually a full-time paid employee of the church. The smaller churches and branches of the big churches do not have paid pastors. They usually have persons who combine pastoral duties with secular pursuits. The majority of pastors are persons with long and substantial experience of Pentecostalism. The pastors of the four churches that this analysis focuses on are married and have children. Their wives are also officials of the church and are usually the coordinators of the women's group, the Choir or the Sunday school. The pastors are university-educated and had at one time been successful professionals or businessmen. They command the respect and admiration of church members who in some cases refer to them as 'the man of God' or 'the servant of God'.

The pastor relies on other appointed but unpaid officials and management committees to govern the church. In most churches the pastor is the final authority on all matters but particularly spiritual ones. Most pastors have offices in the church and they are usually in the office or within the church's premises six days a week, including weekends. Office hours can sometimes drag on till late in the night. All pastors tell stories of having been called out in the middle of the night or early hours of the morning to attend to the needs of a sick or desperate member. Pastoral duties extend beyond spiritual matters to offering advice or assistance on mundane needs. On the days when there are no group meetings or worship sessions, the pastors attend to administrative matters, have private audiences with church members, offer prayers and advice and prepare sermons, talks and lessons. Most pastors set aside one day every week to visit church members in their houses or sick members in hospital. Pastors also visit the homes of church members to perform naming ceremonies or christenings or to participate in wedding anniversaries and birthday celebrations.

A few churches have paid administrators or secretaries who are usually part-time employees. According to the pastors, the churches rely on voluntary donations, offerings and tithes for finances. Members are invited to donate or make offering at least once at each of the three meetings that the churches hold every week. Members are also required to pay 10 % of their gross earnings every week or month. During public talks and sermons a great emphasis is placed on the need for members not only to meet their financial obligations but to go beyond them. In some churches, members go in a queue to the pulpit to drop their offerings and tithes into the collection basket. This strategy ensures compliance, as most members feel uncomfortable to remain in their seats while others file past them. Usually, the pastor or another official of the church stands near to the collection basket, shakes the hands of the givers and mutters words of prayers, thanks or praise.

Church groups or committees contribute to the effective management of the church and they also offer opportunities for participation and inclusion. The church hierarchies have used membership of committees as instrument for securing loyalty, commitment and cohesion. Some churches have as many as 10 committees and groups. They include finance committee, project committee, elders' committee, choir, women's forum or group, men's forum or group, prayer group, evangelism group, hospitality committee, hospital visitation group, management committee, executive committee etc.

Close to 52% of the respondents in my survey said they hold a position or an office in their group. The percentage of women holding positions or offices was slightly higher than men. This could be because women tend to be more devoted or simply because some activities, for example membership of the choir, are mostly dominated by women. The majority of office holders are married. Usually committee and group members have a greater sense of belonging and responsibility than non-members. They are selected on the basis of their spiritual qualification and maturity and demonstrated zeal, including regular attendance at church activities. Daniel, for example, said he had to develop a respectful and courteous attitude towards people after he was appointed the protocol officer in his church. He said he was a proud and arrogant man before his appointment. Appointment to an office is a privilege most members aspire to.

CHURCH ACTIVITIES

All the churches have three regular public meetings each week. They include a Worship Service on Sundays, usually from mid or late morning till late afternoon, a Bible Study on Wednesdays, from about 7pm to 9pm and a Prayer Meeting at about the same time but on Fridays. The fact that most churches have their meetings on the same days and times minimises the opportunities to belong to more than one group at the same time or to participate in the activities of different groups simultaneously. Other meetings held regularly but less frequently include all-night prayers (usually monthly), women's prayer group, Love Feasts and evangelistic seminars and conferences. Groups and committees also meet but their meetings are open to members only.

A typical Sunday service begins with a Sunday School, where adults, youths and children meet in groups of about 10 or 15 and are taught lessons from the bible by a Sunday School teacher. The end of the Sunday School marks the beginning of the actual service, which includes prayers, songs, special numbers (or songs rendered by an individual), testimonies, prophecies, announcements, tithes and offerings, altar call (or invitation to new members or visitors to stand up or come forward to be born-again and be prayed for) and the sermon, usually given by the pastor or an official designated by him or her. Prayers as well as songs and the sermon are loud, animated and emotional. They are also very participatory involving speaking in tongues and enthusiastic response from the audience. The general atmosphere during Sunday worship is festive and different from Wednesday bible study or Friday prayer meetings. Most members, especially children and women, dress in African attires on Sundays unlike other days when they are more likely to dress less formally. In some churches children are fed biscuits and soft drinks on Sundays and on special occasions. In CAC a female member sells Moin Moin or baked beans and rice prepared in that unique Nigerian way soon after the service on Sunday. The after-service banter, eating and drinking can sometimes last for an hour or more.

Most churches have special thanksgiving services either on the first or last Sunday of the month. During the thanksgiving members take turn in publicly proclaiming the "goodness of the lord" as they relate specific ways God has spared them of a major problem or helped them out of one. The problems are usually connected to finance, marriage, childlessness, bereavement, unemployment, witchcraft, depression, residence and work permit, citizenship application and illness. These testimonies usually begin and end with special songs sang by the individual member and some offering or donation, usually money. They usually also include specific acknowledgement of the contribution of the pastor or some other official of the church to finding a solution to the problem. It is usual for testimonies to start with or to include sentences like: "I'm here to thank God and my pastor for..." or "My God and the members of this church have been very good to me and I'm standing here today to show my appreciation..." At the GFM and in some other churches Thanksgiving Sundays usually end with food and drinks.

The testimonies are also an instrument for widening participation and for promoting cohesion and a sense of belonging. They are unique and major opportunities for 'ordinary' members to take control of the pulpit and the attention of the entire congregation. The bond of unity and oneness are re-enforced and strengthened as they share experiences and as they identify and show appreciation for the specific ways members and officials of the church have supported them in their trials and tribulations. Testimonies have also become an instrument used by church leaders to demonstrate the superiority of their particular group and to show that their group enjoys God's favour and approval. As Emmanuel, the leader of CAC, said during a thanksgiving session: "The many goodness of God shows that his hand is upon us in this church. It shows that he is present here, he is in our midst. In fact, God is a citizen of this church". Churches that have many and amazing testimonies tend to attract more worshippers.

The themes that dominate the testimonies are often also common in the sermons and prayers. They paint a picture of worries, anxieties, expectations and hope. During the prayer meetings on Fridays, members often request the prayers and support of the group in connection with specific problems. It is also not uncommon for a member of the group to offer direct advice or solution to another member's problem in the form of a 'prophecy' or 'Word of Knowledge'. Pauline told of an incident during an all-night prayer session when the visiting minister 'prophesised' that the prayer of a childless couple in the group for a child had been answered by God but that the couple would have to make love before or by 12am that night for the prophecy to come true. On the order of the resident pastor the couple left the gathering immediately and went home. According to Pauline, within a year of that dramatic event the couple had a baby.

INTER-GROUP RELATIONSHIP: UNITY IN DIVERSITY?

As the historical accounts I have rendered in chapter four showed, divisions and disagreements in Pentecostal groups are often the result of personality clashes, struggle for power and position and differing interpretations of doctrines (Anderson 1999; Cox 1996; Hollenwenger 1976). Disagreements and splinter groups have frequently also been the result of racially-based differences and outright racism (Hollenwenger 1999; MacRobert 1988). Inter-group mobility is relatively easy since splinter groups usually retain the core Pentecostal teachings, especially regarding speaking in tongues, spiritual rebirth, Christianity as God-centred and mostly experiential and the direct experience of God's power in all areas of life. The four groups covered in this study adhere to these fundamental Pentecostal teachings although members of each group or even of the same group have slightly different interpretations of some of them.

For example, Mr Esan of GFM believes that "all born-again children of God ought to and should speak in tongues" but Ellori of CAC says it is important but not necessary or essential to speak in tongues. Charles would only take medicines as a last resort, Pauline would take medicine and pray at the same time, while Mr Esan believes he has been healed "by the stripes of Jesus" and therefore he needs no medicine. Ellori pays 10% of his income to the church but his wife, an Irish lady and a member of the same group, does not. The leader of MFMM discourages female members of the group from wearing long pants to the church's services but the leader of a branch of RCCG believes that what matters most is the inner person, not the outward attire.

Although these and other differences may appear subtle, they have deep implications for group cohesion and inter-group relationships. Group loyalty and Inter-group mobility can also be explained by these differences. Convinced of their own uniqueness despite a general adherence to fundamental Pentecostal doctrines, each group has tended to position itself differently mostly by emphasising what it believes it does better or more effectively than the other groups. For example the members of CAC talk of their group as a place of intense and efficient prayers or, as one interviewee puts it, 'a prayer power-house'. The RCCG emphasises music and joyous praise while MFM prioritises holiness and righteous living. The GFM sees itself as a dynamic group that is focused solely on 'winning souls for Christ'.

A former member of RCCG says he left the group because its leadership had started to tolerate 'every kind of behaviour' from the members and accepting 'all kinds of people' into its fold simply because it wants to increase its membership. When one member of MFM discusses some other African-led Pentecostal groups, he uses the language that Pentecostals use when they discuss non-Pentecostal religious groups. He believes that many pastors are refusing to teach their members about righteous living and devotion to God because they are afraid of losing them. Rather they pamper them by saying the things the members want to hear. He also believes that some Africans with neither the pastoral training nor a clear spiritual vision have assumed leadership of some groups in Ireland. According to him, the hollowness and fakery of such pastors would in time be revealed: "Some feel they can do the job because they have the money or material base or because they speak good English. But ask them who ordained them; are they ordained? If a man is not ordained and does not have a spiritual vision, he will mess up".

But these differences have not hampered cooperation and inter-group initiatives. From time to time some groups have come together and rallied around a common cause while the leaders and members of one group are often invited to major events organised by other groups. For example, the CAC invites other church leaders and members to its yearly 'Jesus Festival' and when the GFM and a branch of RCCG inaugurated their new places of worship invitations to the events were extended to the leaders and members of other churches. The CAC has invited pastors of other African-led Pentecostal groups to preach in some of its services. The RCCG mostly relies on its vast numbers of ministers and the leader of one branch is often invited to speak at another branch.

Aside from these bi-lateral initiatives, the majority of African-led Pentecostal groups joined together in 2003 to organise a mass evangelism meeting at the RDS, a popular venue in Dublin for large exhibitions, show jumping events, musical events and international meetings. Some Irish-led Pentecostal groups also participated in this event. The preparations for and successful organisation of that meeting, which was attended by many Pentecostal leaders from Africa, paved the way for the birth of Joy in the Nation, an association of African-led Pentecostal churches in Ireland. The aim of the association is to promote unity and cooperation among the members. However, it is also a forum for settling disputes among members, for promoting discipline and mapping out strategies of cooperation and interaction with non-Pentecostal Christian groups, the government and the larger Irish society.

RELATIONSHIP WITH IRISH-LED CHURCHES

Another trait common to African-led Pentecostal churches in Ireland is their attitude to and relationship with non-Pentecostal Christian groups, especially mainline churches like the Catholics, the Methodists, the Church of Ireland and the Presbyterians. Whereas some of them have benefited from the kindness and support of these mainline churches, Pentecostal groups led by Africans see themselves as very different and distinct from these churches. They believe these churches have embraced doctrines and practices that have no basis in the bible and that the lives of the majority of their members do not give evidence of adherence to bible principles. Pastor Eze of MFM puts it like this:

> As a born-again Christian, my life should be based on the bible. When people see me they should know that I live by the bible…this is not common in the Catholic Church. They just go through catechism and the Simple Prayer book. The Catholics have their own bible called Apocrypha. The body of Christian organisations recognises only 66 books with 40 authors but the Catholic bible has additional books like Maccabees.

Emmanuel, an official of CAC, said he felt "as if I wasn't a Christian" the only time he went to a Catholic church in Ireland. He describes the "cold reception" he received and the reluctance of fellow worshippers to sit on the same row with him.

Most Pentecostals believe these churches are 'spiritually dead' or in 'spiritual darkness' even though they generally like to disguise these resentments or attitude. Mr Esan, for example, believes that the mainline churches in Ireland are finding it difficult to recruit new members and halt their dwindling membership because they are out of touch with the realities and their services are boring, uninspiring and irrelevant to the lives of the congregants. But this disdain of or opposition to these churches has not stopped some African-led Pentecostal groups from maintaining a relationship of convenience with them.

In the case of the GFM, a Catholic church had at one time provided it with accommodation. This cooperation soon evaporated when the priest discovered that members of his church had started taking a positive interest in the boisterous activities of GFM. According to Mr Esan, the priest asked them to leave after complaining that the GFM could in time draw away the members of his church. Accommodation sharing arrangements between other African-led Pentecostal churches and Irish mainline churches have also broken down because of other reasons including complaints that Africans are too loud when they sing or pray and their services often last longer than scheduled. However, despite this unevenness in their interaction, some African-led Pentecostal groups still maintain this very ambivalent relationship with Irish mainline churches, having no connections with them in spiritual matters but relying on them, if they need to, for material support.

Although I have not explored Pentecostal churches led or mostly populated by native Irish in this book, the relationships between African-led Pentecostal churches and these churches are articulated by my interviewees or respondents mostly in the context of discussing the history/activities of their own churches or when they discuss their individual Pentecostal journey/experience in Ireland. For example, Mr Odukoya acknowledges that the Redeem Christian Church of God received advice and guidance from the Victory Christian Centre, an Irish-led Pentecostal Church, on how to register the church. Mr Esan, like a few other respondents, flirted with Irish-led Pentecostal churches before they relocated to those managed and mostly populated by Africans.

Although Pentecostal African immigrants mostly portray groups as universal or accommodating of all people, irrespective of ethnic, racial or social background, the defection of some of them from Irish-led groups to those led by Africans suggest that there are differences and preferences. Mr Esan admits that he relocated to an African-led church because the 'way' they prayed in the Irish-led church differed from the way 'we pray in Africa'. By 'the way we pray', Mr Esan could have been referring to the method of prayer or the substance. The themes of prayers, songs, and sermons in African-led churches, some of which I have highlighted in this and other chapters, are most unlikely to feature prominently in congregations of Irish Pentecostals. In Mr Esan's analysis, Irish-led churches are interpreted as the 'other'. He uses 'we' to describe 'African' Pentecostalism while 'they' describes Irish-led ones. His analysis introduces another layer of difference or particularism into the supposed universalism of Pentecostalism. Mr Esan's encounter with 'Irish' Pentecostals has been as important for self-definition and entrenchment of boundaries as the encounter with non-Pentecostal 'others'. This point is re-emphasised in the concluding chapter

RELATIONSHIP WITH THE MAJORITY SOCIETY

The attitude of African Pentecostals to Irish mainline churches mirrors, in some ways, their attitude to the social habits and culture of the larger Irish society. They detest many major social trends and habits of the majority society but they are dependent in important ways on the institutions of state and society. African Pentecostals are opposed to alcohol consumption (in whatever quantity), visits to pubs for social reasons, sex before and outside of marriage, homosexuality, attendance at non-Christian music events and the use of expletives or unwholesome language. Given that many of these ideas and practices are wide-spread in the dominant culture, African Pentecostals in Ireland can rightly be said to be living in a parallel social and moral universe. However, it is a universe that is connected to and even dependent on the majority society in many significant ways. Some members point to these interfaces or links between their world and the Irish society to buttress the point that the parallel moral and social universe they inhabit will not prevent their integration into the dominant society. Remi, a medical laboratory technician and a member of CAC, believes:

> There is no way our involvement with the church will cut us off from the immediate day-to-day environment or prevent us from getting involved in the wider society. Even if we're in the church 24 hours a day, seven days a week, we still have to live in a neighbourhood, shop and work with people from other ethnic groups. We find ways to get involved in the system and work within it, otherwise we'll not survive.

Emmanuel believes church membership, rather than hindering integration, is helping to prepare African immigrants for the long and arduous task of integration. In the church believers are able to gain confidence and the right attitude to face the larger society. The leader of Christ Co-Workers in Mission, supports this view and he says the church is providing a conducive environment for African immigrants to devise and implement strategies of social and economic mobility and political participation. Remba foresees a future when the churches will offer political direction to the entire African communities in Ireland and constitute a breeding ground for civic and political activities.

IRISH MEMBERS: THE STRANGERS WITHIN

The native Irish members of African-led Pentecostal groups are few and they are mainly spouses, partners, friends or acquaintances of African members. Their presence in these churches tends to be intermittent and short-lived. However, there have been a few cases where some native Irish persons visited these churches out of curiosity or in search of solutions to personal problems. Aremu, leader of a branch of RCCG, relates the story of an Irishman who walked into their church seeking help for his depression. According to his account, the man was "bent over, in physical pain and dark in the face." He experienced some relief, according to Aremu, after he and other church officials prayed for him but two days later the man telephoned Aremu to tell him he was about to kill himself. Aremu responded swiftly by driving to the man's house where he prayed for him and offered practical advice, including an invitation to participate regularly in the church's weekly activities. Aremu said the man has attended the church's services regularly since then and that his condition has improved considerably. The majority of church members were yet to get accustomed to the man's presence in their midst and a few have actually asked Aremu if he was really sure of the man's true identity and intentions.

The Irish or non-African members of African-dominated Pentecostal churches are the outsiders or strangers within. They tend to be less boisterous and emotional during services and they also appear to exchange lesser pre- and post-service banter with other members. Although a few of them are familiar with the songs and routine of service and even dress in native African attires, their full integration remains problematic. In the case of his Irish wife, Mr Ellori says with a hint of anger and frustration in his voice that fellow worshippers still "keep her aside" despite the fact she has attended the church in the four years they had been married and even gyrates to the music during service. Mr Ellori blamed "ignorance" and "feelings of insecurity" for the aloofness of most church members towards non-African members. Some churches, however, have native Irish persons in the upper echelons. For example, an Irish person is one of the seven trustees of GFM while an Irish person is on the project committee of one of the branches of RCCG.

REVERSE MISSION AND END-TIME PROPHETS

The majority of church leaders and pastors I interviewed say their intention is to take the message about God's Kingdom and judgment to the Irish public and to ultimately change the racial and cultural profile of their membership. They are quick to say that their message is for people of all races and most of their activities and public communications are geared towards promoting this image of inclusiveness. The names of most churches include words like 'international' or 'worldwide'. Leaflets and posters produced by them employ racially neutral symbols like the dove and well-known ones like the bible and the crucifix. Some have even produced posters that include African and Caucasian faces in their attempt to assert their de-racialised credentials and attract native Irish persons. Most church leaders and some members firmly believe they are part of God's plan to re-introduce the gospel to Europeans, the very people who brought it to Africa about two centuries ago. The idea of reverse-mission and the conviction that the time to accomplish this work is short before God's judgment arrives motivate the activities of many African-Pentecostal groups.

However, there remains a debilitating lack of consensus among church leaders and members on how to achieve racial inclusiveness and multi-ethnicity. Whereas Aremu and Godswill, pastors of RCCG, believe that African Pentecostals would need to modify aspects of their activities to make them culturally sensitive and acceptable to members of Irish society, the pastor of FGM, Mr Esan, says that racial bias is the real reason Irish people have distanced themselves from the initiatives of African-led Pentecostal groups. The Irish, he said, have been reluctant to accept that God could use 'Africans' to initiate a spiritual revival in Ireland:

> God can use any people irrespective of their colour. The problem is that they (Irish people) have not accepted that God is using the Africans. We'll not give up. The fact is that God has brought us Africans here to bring spiritual revival to Ireland. It will happen if they accept."

But Makinde, a leader of RCCG and a former university lecturer, believes African Pentecostal churches are, at these initial stages, sowing the seeds that will blossom into a major spiritual revival in Ireland and much of Europe. He compares the efforts of African Christians in twenty-first century Ireland to those of European missionaries who introduced Christianity to Africa about two centuries ago and says that time and a major spiritual revival occasioned by God himself are needed for their efforts to succeed and for the cultural and racial profiles of these churches to change:

> Little by little, we'll get there. What will get the work done is the revival, which only God can bring. Revival is not a matter of culture or colour; it's a matter for God's Holy Spirit. The Spirit changes people's hearts. When the heart is changed, everything assumes different dynamics or dimension. It doesn't matter what colour people have. Souls don't have colours. The situation will change and we'll have native Irish people in the church.

Most pastors and leaders I interviewed share Makinde's vision of an Ireland dominated by Pentecostals, and many are quick to declare their presence and activities as a plan of God which he foreordained since the beginning of creation. They speak of the imminence of God's judgment and the destruction of the ungodly. It is only fair and just and very much in the nature of God to warn people of all nations about the impending judgement and give them the opportunity to escape eternal torment in hellfire. Pentecostal African immigrants believe they are the instruments of God to pass the message to the Irish nation. By faithfully discharging this duty they are absolving themselves of any blame or guilt for the destruction that surely awaits the unrepentant. As Mr Esan puts it: "The blood will not be upon us if they don't accept the message."

Makinde says: "We're investing here because it is the kingdom of God that we're investing in. We're believing in the harvest of souls. We're going to see souls saved and we're going to see people born into the kingdom". Charles, an itinerant preacher who has flirted with four African Pentecostal churches, believes the harvest of Irish souls will happen only when the management and administration of these churches pass on to Irish-born Africans or the second and subsequent generations of African immigrants. He is scathing of the low leadership skills and the poor social and evangelistic abilities of many pastors. The present generation and leaders, he said, are mostly inflexible and they lack the vital skills to implement a trans-racial transmission of their messages.

Some interviewees agreed that the focus of these churches would change when they are dominated and led by subsequent generations of Africans who are most unlikely to face the peculiar economic, socio-political and racial problems confronted by the first and second generations. According to them, the prospects of a multi-racial and multi-cultural membership will be brighter when the focus, aspirations and culture of these churches come to resemble those of the larger society. As I explain in the concluding chapter of this book, this view is problematic because it oversimplifies a complex phenomenon and it is not supported by experiences from the United Kingdom and continental Europe where these kinds of churches have remained on the periphery of society even after many decades (Adogame 2000; Ter Haar 1998a, 1998b; Gerloff 1999). What, however, is beyond doubt at this stage in the history of the development of these churches in Ireland is that the very features that make them distinct and attractive to many African immigrants are also some of the major barriers to the inclusion of other ethnic or national groups, especially the Irish.

The next chapter profiles the four churches I investigated and it also presents the survey results and background information on the qualitative interviewees.

Note
1.   Background information about this research has been provided in the footnotes in chapter three.

CHAPTER SIX

PROFILING IRELAND'S AFRICAN PENTECOSTALS

INTRODUCTION

Relying on data from in-depth interviews, non-participant observation, a survey and secondary documents, this chapter profiles the four African-led Pentecostal churches selected for this study and it also presents relevant background information on the participants in the qualitative interviews. The participants both in the survey and in the qualitative interviews were drawn from the Redeemed Christian Church of God (RCCG), Christ Apostolic Church (CAC), the Gospel Faith Mission (GFM), and the Mountain of Fire and Miracle (MFM). In the postscript I have discussed the reasons for and processes of selecting these churches. The profile, presented as case histories in this chapter, examines the history and organisation of these churches, the circumstances of their birth and their self-definition and aspirations. The data from the survey of 144 members identify the major demographic trends as well as those features that are common to the four churches while the notes on the interviewees provide the contexts for interpreting the narratives in chapter eight.

The profile buttresses my contention in chapter five that the inspiration to set up these churches came either from Pentecostal churches in Africa eager to gain or expand their foothold in Europe or from African immigrants who had had substantial experience of Pentecostalism before they came to Ireland. Initial resources for groups with transnational connections were sourced from those churches in Africa or their European representatives mostly in London but the churches without such ties generated resources from their members. All the churches were set up in the late 1990s or early 2000s and they were located initially in north inner city Dublin, where the majority of recent African immigrants are based, for a variety of reasons, including the relatively cheaper accommodation and proximity to job sites and offices. Although some churches have relocated from the city centre to other parts of the Greater Dublin Area, the halls and venues vacated by them are being speedily re-occupied by newer African-led churches. There appears to be a unity of purpose or common goal with the majority of churches claiming evangelism and the conversion of souls as their main mission. However, individual churches tend to define their relationships with their members and the larger society differently. The self-perception of the individual churches, in some cases, translates into a negative perception of one another, resulting at times in deep-seated differences, resentment and mutual hostility. The survey indicates that the majority of members are educated to tertiary level and that they have been in Ireland for less than 10 years. Many are in precarious immigration and unemployment circumstances, despite their high educational achievements. Evangelistic activities are carried out informally, mostly through church members who are encouraged to invite their relatives and friends to the activities of the churches.

In the next section I present the four case histories, beginning with the Redeemed Christian Church of God, the largest and most wide-spread African-led Pentecostal church in Ireland.

THE REDEEMED CHRISTIAN CHURCH OF GOD

The Redeemed Christian Church of God (also known as Redeem) is the biggest and the fastest-growing African-led Pentecostal church in Ireland. It was the first to be established by Nigerians but the second by Africans, after Christ Co-workers Ministry set up by Congolese-born Mr Remba Osengo in 1996. Redeem started as a small group in 1997 at number 5, Mary's Abbey, in north inner city Dublin. Its founder and pioneering pastor was Ms Grace Okorinde, a Nigerian who had been an ordained minister of the church in her home-country. She has since relocated to the United States. Mr Godswill Odukoya, a pioneering official of the church who now heads its branch in Sword, got his initial invitation to the church from Ms Okorinde. He describes the church's small beginnings:

> When I started attending the church, it was a very small place. They had no drums. In the beginning I was playing the samba, the local drum. But I told the pastor, 'look I'm very good on the set drums. If you get the real drums I'll be playing them for the church'. We got the drums and the whole service changed. It became livelier and more people came in. We started growing at a very rapid pace.

Many respondents described Ms Okorinde as an itinerant preacher and ambassador of Redeem who, prior to coming to Ireland, had also established branches of the church in countries like Italy and Germany. According to Mr Odukoya: "Sister Grace was mightily blessed. She was very gifted with the ability to organise and manage people. It would appear she had a special calling to plant churches. She worked tirelessly when our church in Dublin started". When Ms Okorinde relocated to the United States in 2000, Mr Odukoya was made the temporary head of the church until an ordained minister, was dispatched from the Nigerian headquarters. In its formative years, Redeem received advice and guidance from Victory Christian Centre, an Irish-led Pentecostal group. Mr Odukoya describes the sort of help they received: "We got a lot of help on how to go about the registration of the church from Pastor Schiller. He gave us the name of a solicitor who happened to be a born-again Christian as well."

Churches under the Redeem fold, like the majority of African-led Pentecostal churches, are registered as companies limited by guarantee and some have acquired a charity status. The financial and material support needed to start the first Redeem church in Ireland came from Nigeria. The first branch has since attained financial independence and it has supported the establishment of other branches in Ireland. Like all branches of Redeem, it relies mostly on offerings, donations and tithes from members. Financial and material support for the establishment of some other branches in Ireland was provided by branches of Redeem in Nigeria and in the United Kingdom. Such links and inter-dependence have placed Redeem in a strong material position and given it the ability to set up churches faster than other African-led Pentecostal churches.

Mr Makinde, the second substantive pastor of the first branch of Redeem in Ireland, later relocated to Moore Lane in the heart of Dublin's city centre and handed the management of the church in Mary's Abbey to Mr Daniel, an ordained pastor of the church who had been living in the United Kingdom. The establishment of the branch in Moore Lane marked the beginning of the expansion of Redeem in Ireland. At the beginning of 2005, the church had close to 40 churches in Ireland and an estimated 3000 members. An official of the church says, "one of the principles of the Redeem Church is to carry as many people as possible to heaven. We have to make disciples." Mr Makinde believes that the church members are serving as God's instrument for proclaiming the gospel to the Irish nation before the end of this world. He believes that their presence and purpose in Ireland "is a grand design of God, which he has known from the foundation of the earth". Mr Makinde says the church or its leaders are not motivated by financial gain and that their central focus is to win souls for the kingdom of God. Towards the realisation of this purpose, the church has established a bible school where it instructs church ministers and leaders on all aspects of church management, evangelism and Christian conduct. Mr Odukoya, a graduate of this school, says all ordained officials of the church must attend the school:

> When the Bible School started all the pastors were
> made to go through the training and we passed out
> with a diploma in theology. I went through it. We
> had lecturers from the United States. Now they're
> beginning to source some lecturers locally. We
> now have some Irish lecturers. There are about ten
> modules—God-head, counselling, child evangelism,
> church administration and some other ones. Most of
> my lecturers were practising pastors who would share
> from their personal experiences."

Despite the cooperation and inter-dependence among
the branches of Redeem, each church has its own administrative and financial arrangements. The churches are, however,
grouped into two administrative districts (or Areas) headed
by Mr Makinde and Mr Daniel. Although the district leaders
are consulted from time to time by the parishes or individual
churches, they have no direct input into the management
and financial affairs of these churches. All the branches of
Redeem in Ireland have similar weekly activities, consisting
of worship sessions on Sundays, mid-week Bible Study and
Prayer Meetings on Fridays. Once a month there is a special
'night vigil', prayer sessions that last for four or five hours
beginning at midnight. English language is the medium of
communication during services in all the churches but it is
usual for church members to communicate in native languages or dialects outside of official services.

THE CHRIST APOSTOLIC CHURCH

The Christ Apostolic Church is based on Rutland Place
in Dublin's north city centre. It is the first of four branches
of the Church in Ireland. Its international headquarter is
located in Ibadan, Nigeria. The other branches of the church
in Ireland are in Cork, Galway and Dundalk. In Europe, there
are branches in Britain, Greece and Germany. The church
also maintains a presence in Canada and in the United States
of America where it has at least two branches, making it an
African and European-based church rather than a North
American one.

The Dublin branch registered an attendance of between 30 and 40 worshippers in the first months when it commenced services in April 2000. The birth of CAC in Ireland is traceable to a series of dinner evenings named 'Dinner with Jesus' organised by its visiting Nigerian founder, Dr S.K. Abiara, at a Dublin city centre hotel. The church began against the backdrop of the increased presence of African immigrants in Ireland and at a time when some other African-led Pentecostal groups were also setting up bases. Mr Emmanuel Efuntayo, a senior official of the church who had also acted as its pastor, said it was necessary to provide spiritual guidance and emotional and material support for members of African communities. Though the church exists to meet the interests of all groups in society, it serves a special purpose for Africans. According to him:

> Africans and other immigrants come to the church to socialise because they don't go to the pub. They feel socially excluded in the pubs. That is why they put on their head gears, put on nice dresses when they come to the church. It's like a big day out for them. Socialising is an important component of the service, of the worship… in the church, Africans are able to fellowship, meet with other Africans who have similar problems, people they can trust. So fellowship is number one. People want other people they can fellowship with, share their problems with, they want people who can give them encouragement, probably because they're coming from the same background…in the church they feel socially included.

Apart from providing a community of support and assistance, CAC also sees itself as a place of prayers, where members 'pray their way out of problems'. As Mr Efuntayo put it:

> Our own competence is prayers. We pray with passion. That is not the culture in Redeem or in any of the other churches. I'm not saying they don't pray. They do and they also preach the word. But in CAC we believe in praying with passion and in getting results.

Judging by the rapid pace at which African-led Pentecostal churches were being planted, it was evident from 2000 that Ireland had become a special target of African Pentecostal ministers. Some ministers like the CAC founder were directly and physically involved in the struggle to establish a presence in Ireland, while others mobilise their members and officials in other countries in Europe, mostly the United Kingdom, to relocate to Ireland. The initial invitations to join these churches were targeted mostly at members of Ireland's fast-growing African communities. For example, leaflets advertising 'Dinner with Jesus' were displayed in refugee hostels, African shops and other places frequented by Africans. Those who responded to the invitation were people who had either been members of CAC in their home-countries or those invited by friends and members of the church. Persons coping with the uncertainty and traumas of being strangers in a strange land and those seeking help with family problems also responded. By the end of 2002 a combined total of about 500 worshippers from the Greater Dublin Area and the suburbs were attending two separate Sunday worship sessions, one in Yoruba and the other in English, at the church's premises in Dublin. The first session begins at 10am and ends at about 12pm and the second lasts from 1pm to about 3pm. As soon as CAC started flourishing, a pastor was transferred from Greece to manage it.

A full-time pastor is the administrative and spiritual head of the Church. He is accountable to a Central Executive Committee consisting of all the officials of the church and to the church's regional administrative head office in London. His wife, known as the Lady Evangelist by the members, is also a full-time but unpaid minister of the Church. The officials of the church include an accountant, a treasurer and a secretary. The major source of revenue is the weekly offerings and donations by the members. Members are also required to contribute 10% of their incomes.

Apart from the worship sessions on Sundays, the members also meet on Wednesdays, from 6pm to 8pm, for a bible study session and on Friday, from 6pm to 8pm, for prayers. Once a month, there is a special prayer session from about 11pm to 5am. At other times during the week and at weekends, activities like choir practice, counselling and meetings of the different groups and committees are held in the church premises. The activities in a typical Sunday worship session can be divided into songs, prayers, sermon, offering and announcements. Typically, the announcements will give details of the church's activities for the benefit of new members and visitors and of social activities involving the members. Announcements relating to naming ceremonies, birthdays, weddings, wedding anniversaries, and new births are commonplace.

The other channels of information, communication and interaction are the various groups and sub-committees and informal meetings and chats before the worship sessions kick off and after they have ended. The Pastor is also a pivotal source and channel of information. Members with special needs and requests meet with him before and after worship sessions and at other times of the week. He also visits the members in their homes to offer prayer, advice and solidarity. The CAC has gone through two major crises after two pastors resigned or deserted the church to start their own churches. On each of these occasions, a senior minister was appointed to act as pastor until a replacement was sent from outside of Ireland. In 2004 a new pastor was sent from the United States after the substantive pastor deserted.

THE GOSPEL FAITH MISSION

Unlike CAC or Redeem, the Gospel Faith Mission (GFM) was not set up by a representative of an existing church group in Africa or elsewhere and it did not receive direct financial or material support from any group. Its pastor and one of the five founding members, Mr James Olu Esan arrived in Ireland in 1998 to seek political asylum. In Nigeria he had been a businessman, buying and selling cocoa pods. He grew up in a family that adhered to African Traditional Religion. As he puts it: "My parents were idol worshippers. We worshipped idols". His introduction to Christianity began in the 1980s but, according to his own account, his personal relationship with God began in 1994 when he experienced spiritual re-birth: "I became a born-again Christian in 1994. I had been attending a church for over 10 years before I became a born-again Christian. I got born again in 1994—that was the year I gave my life to Christ." His parents have since also converted to Pentecostalism and they have made their family house in Nigeria available for their group's weekly meetings. When Mr Esan arrived in Ireland, he attended services at the Dublin-based Graces Mission, an Irish-led Pentecostal group, before he decided to set up a prayer group in his sitting room in 1999. According to him: "We decided to form the group because the way they worshipped in the church we were attending was quite different from the way we pray in Africa."

Their little group soon blossomed and Mr Esan's sitting room could no longer accommodate the ever-increasing worshippers. After two months they relocated to a rented basement on Dorset Street in north city Dublin. There they shared the property with other users, some of whom would organised all-night parties and leave the place a complete mess. Mr Esan and members of his group were often saddled with the task of cleaning the mess so they could have their meeting in a tidy and dignified environment. The group relocated six months later to a Catholic Church on Aungier Street in Dublin's south city after their membership swelled again and the rented basement became too small to accommodate them. But the relationship with the church was short-lived. Mr Esan explains:

> The priest of the church, the Irish church, complained that members of his congregation were getting attracted to what we were doing, they were taking positive interest in our worship. Because of that the priest asked us to vacate the place. He said we could in time draw away members of his congregation if we continued to use his church auditorium.

The group relocated to a nearby YMCA building but relocated soon afterwards to a terraced house located near

Parnell Square in north inner city Dublin, where it held its services for about two years before it purchased a disused warehouse on the South side of Dublin. In late 2004, it moved its activities to this newly refurbished place of worship and invited officials and members of other African-led Pentecostal churches to a colourful opening ceremony.

GFM is registered as a company limited by guarantee and it has also acquired a charitable status. The church is self-financing, relying on offerings, tithes and donations from members. Whereas Mr Esan is the senior pastor and the only paid official of the church, there are other appointed ministers and leaders who assist with administration or governance. Mr Esan's wife is in charge of the Choir and Sunday School. The church has seven groups or departments—children, ushering, the choir, prayer, evangelism, youths and Sunday School. Each department has a head. Members of the groups or departments are called 'church workers'. The church also has a board of trustees consisting of seven members. One of them is a native Irish man. The board is concerned with corporate strategies while the ministers attend to spiritual matters. The church's executive committee, consisting of all the officials, is in charge of administrative matters.

Mr Esan said the church exists to win souls for the kingdom of God and to bring spiritual revival to Ireland:

> My primary goal is to make sure that more souls are won for the kingdom every day. I just want to see that spiritual revival is brought back to Ireland…I am after the souls, all sorts of souls - Africans, Irish—the colour doesn't matter. I want more souls for the kingdom of God. Every other thing could be added but my primary goal is to see that more souls come to the Lord through our ministry. That includes every people, not just Africans.

The Gospel Faith Mission has established branches in Navan and in Carlow and this has helped to reduce overcrowding at its Dublin branch. Although the church has attempted street evangelism, Mr Esan said that "about 80 %" of new people joining the church every month are invited by members. He posits GFM as a dynamic church that has gained recognition and many new members in recent years because it preaches truth. The number of worshippers has continued to increase, according to him, because people are fed up with the 'lies' and 'human philosophies' that are being propagated in the other churches:

> People are actually hungry for the truth. The truth is that if you preach the gospel, if you preach the gospel of our lord Jesus Christ, there will be an increase. But if you preach human philosophies it may affect the growth of the church...We are preaching the gospel of our lord Jesus Christ and I sincerely believe that that is actually what people are looking for today. That is why they are coming to us. They are fed up with lies.

Members of GFM meet for worship on Sundays, from 12 to 2.30pm, bible studies on Wednesdays, 6 to 8pm and, prayer meetings, on Fridays, from 6 to 8pm. On the last Friday of the month, they have five hours of prayers, from 12 midnight to 5am. On the last Sunday of the month, the church holds a dedication and thanksgiving service and at the end of the year it organises a social gathering. The dedication and thanksgiving services are also occasions for social interaction and merriments. Members bring drinks (non-alcoholic) and prepared food to the church and for two or more hours after the church services have ended they would still be eating and drinking in the church premises.

THE MOUNTAIN OF FIRE AND MIRACLES MINISTRIES

The headquarters of the Mountain of Fire and Miracles Ministries are located in Lagos, Nigeria. The church had three branches in Ireland at the end of 2004. The first was established on May 24, 1998, by Dr Peter Eze, a veterinary doctor, who had been living in London. Raised in a family that adhered to Catholicism, Dr Eze abandoned the religion of his parents in 1990 when he became a born-again Christian. In 1994 he migrated from Christ Pentecostal Ministry to the Mountain of Fire and Miracles. On the history of the church in Ireland, Dr Eze says:

> I came as a vet doctor to London. In London, I got involved in the ministry again. After working with the pastor who has left us now, I was posted to Ireland. I have been in Ireland since 1998…I started the church. I'm the pioneering resident pastor.

Dr Eze describes the task of setting up the church as "challenging". The challenges included trying to convince people to believe in his vision and brand of Pentecostalism: "They said I was so harsh…that I talked a lot about holiness but I remained who I am. I refused to change." The London branch of the church offered material and spiritual guidance to the one in Ireland in the beginning:

> In the beginning we received some financial assistance from the London church. We received money to pay the rent for the hall we hired for meetings. We also got money to buy instruments and to do a few other things. We didn't have to pay back because it was a gift, a help that they rendered to us. Now we in Dublin are assisting some of the branches that have just been set up in Ireland.

For a few years, Dr Eze combined the duties of managing the church with secular employment as a computer network technician with Smartforce. Registered as a charity, the church relies on offerings, tithes and donations from members for its finances. Increased membership and income put the church on a more solid financial position and Dr Eze gave up his secular employment to concentrate on managing the church. Apart from him, the church also employs a paid administrator and some unpaid volunteers. Although his wife is the head of the church's Sunday School Department, she is not a paid official of the church.

The church, which is now located on Prussia Street in north Dublin city centre, held it first meetings in 5 Gardiner Road, in north Dublin city centre. There were 15 members in the beginning. The group rented its meeting hall from the

Presbyterian Church. In December 1999, it relocated to its present location and it hopes to acquire dedicated premises in the near future. At the end of 2004, about 300 families or 500 members belonged to the church's Dublin branch. The church has established branches in Lucan, Galway, Drogheda, Navan, and Dundalk.

As the first and the most senior minister of the church in Ireland, Dr Eze oversees the management of the Dublin branch, coordinates the activities of all the branches and liaises with the London branches and Nigerian headquarters. He describes the relationship between him and the pastors in the Irish branches as cordial and mutually beneficial:

> We work hand-in-hand. It's a family. The church is not mine. It does not even belong to our General Overseer who is the founder. It's a church of God. Sometimes misunderstandings might arise but we're able to resolve them. Even the apostles had misunderstandings among themselves.

He meets with the other pastors on the last Wednesday of the month to receive reports and to discuss collective strategies. Dr Eze, who writes a column on Christianity in the *Street Journal,* a monthly newspaper aimed at Ireland's African population, said members of the church have attempted to reach out to native Irish people by distributing invitation leaflets and by engaging in street evangelism. He also describes the monthly newspaper as "a very good instrument of evangelism".

Dr Eze says the main mission of MFM is to nurture God-fearing Christians who strive after holiness. "Holiness within and without is our aim. As children of God, we must aim to be clean, to be holy". He says the Catholic Church and some African-led Pentecostal churches have not placed great emphasis on righteous living and holiness as MFM has. According to him, some leaders of African-populated Pentecostal churches in Ireland are charlatans and opportunists who are ill-prepared and morally unsuitable to either lead congregations of 'true' Christians lead or provide spiritual guidance:

> I know that there are a few genuine churches among the many churches that have sprung up in recent years but there are also rebels and impostors. Some people are working for personal gains or to fill their own pockets. But time will sort out the genuine from the fake. There are some that are preying on people; they prey on people's problems... It is deadly. It's wickedness...many have jumped or gate-crashed into the ministry. They feel they can do the job because they have the money or material base or because they speak good English. But they have not been properly trained and they are not ordained. If a man is not ordained and does not have a spiritual covering, he will mess up. It's only a matter of time.

In the next section I discuss the results of my survey of 144 members of these churches.

SOCIO-DEMOGRAPHIC CHARACTERISTICS OF CHURCH MEMBERSHIP

I conducted this survey mainly to elicit basic socio-demographic information on members of these churches. Such information could not be obtained from secondary sources because there is no existing detailed research on the presence and activities of African-led Pentecostal churches in Ireland. Detailed information on the research techniques and decisions are contained in the postscript, where I discuss methodology and investigative techniques.

Members of the Redeemed Christians Church of God account for about 46% of the 144 persons who participated in this survey. Members of the Mountain of Fire and Miracles account for 33.3%, Christ Apostolic Church accounts for 13.2% and members of the Gospel Faith Mission constitute about 8%. Although these percentages do not mirror the exact relative numerical strengths of these churches, experiential knowledge, anecdotal sources and information gathered from secondary sources confirm that the Redeemed is the most populous, followed by MFM, CAC and GFM respectively. On average, the respondents have been members of their groups for approximately five years. However, it must be acknowledged that the situation is still evolving and that the populations and proportions of these groups are most likely to change in future.

Out of the 144 respondents, 77 (or 54%) were female. This reflects the gender balance in all the churches where the population of women is higher in all cases. Among the married respondents, 84% said their spouses were members of the same church, suggesting that families maintain a large presence in these churches. More females (17% compared to 7% male) have spouses who did not belong to their church. This could mean that men are generally not inclined towards this kind of religiosity or that women are less successful in convincing their spouses to join their churches.

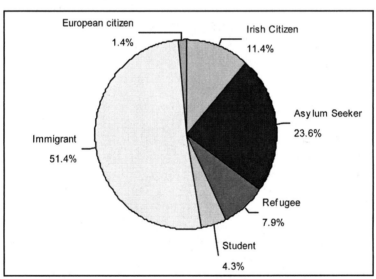

Figure 6.1: Residence Status of African Pentecostals

More than half of the respondents (51%) described themselves as immigrants. Included in this category are migrant workers and those—including students and asylum seekers—that have acquired residence permit after they gave birth to children in Ireland. Asylum seekers are the second highest category, accounting for about 24%. This is followed by those who described themselves as citizens of Ireland or EU member-states. They accounted for close to 13% (see figure 6.1 above).

More than three of four respondents were married, over 24% were single and those who were separated, divorced or widowed were less than five percent. The vast majority (92.4%) are married to fellow Africans. The men are more likely to get married to non-Africans. Whereas 70 % females said their spouses were Africans, only 64 percent of male had African spouses. More than three-quarters (76%) of the 144 respondents have children. More female (79% compared to 70% male) said they have children. Although it is tempting to make a direct connection between having children and the quest for residence permit, it must be noted that the majority of respondents are in the child-bearing age. The average age of the respondents is 32.4. It is worth noting that Africans traditionally place great importance on children and family. Some respondents had been living in Dublin for as many as seven or eight years while others had been there for about six months. The average length of time the respondents have been living in Dublin is 3.3 years.

More than 42% said they became members of their churches after they arrived in Ireland. This, however, does not imply that they were not Pentecostals before they arrived in Ireland. Some were Pentecostals who had associated with different churches than the ones they have joined in Ireland. The fact that the respondents had been living in Dublin for an average of 3.3 years and they have been members of their churches for an average of approximately five years, lends credence to my contention that some had been Pentecostals before they arrived in Ireland. The vast majority (82%) of those who became members of their groups in Ireland got initial information about the group from family and friends or were influenced by them. The other means used by the churches to contact potential members are direct approach by church officials (15%) and through posters/leaflets (2.6%).

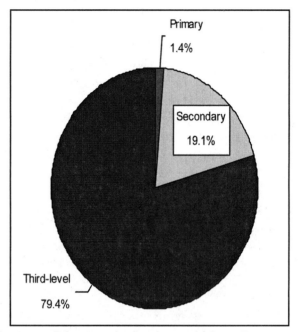

Figure 6.2: Educational attainments of African Pentecostals

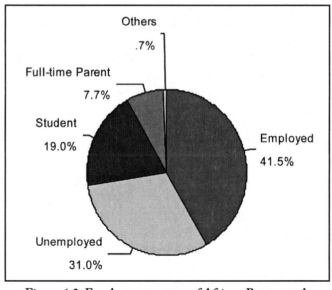

Figure 6.3: Employment status of African Pentecostals

Almost eight out of 10 respondents (or 79.4%) have third-level qualifications, 19.1% have secondary qualifications and those with primary qualifications constitute 1.4% (see figure 6.2). The categories of professions include medicine, social care, nursing, teaching, journalism, computing, engineering, software designing, law and veterinary medicine. There are no significant differences in the educational and professional achievements of males and females.

However, the unemployment rate is high despite the high levels of educational and professional accomplishments. More than one-third (or 31%) said they were unemployed while 7.7% said they were full-time parents (see figure 6.3). The females appear to be more affected by unemployment. Whereas 56% of males were employed, only 44% of females were. Seven out of ten of those who described themselves as students were females and all the full-time parents were females.

The majority of respondents do not belong to ethnic associations, implying that their primary allegiance belongs to their churches. Female church members are most likely to be affiliated with social and ethnic organisations. Whereas 29% of females said they are members of ethnic associations, only 16% of men were members. Equal percentage of male and female said they were workers or office holders in the church. Overall, half of the 144 respondents said they were office holders (perhaps due to the greater willingness of office holders to participate in the study). More than 51% of them were female. As I explain in chapter five, membership of subgroups and participation in their activities, apart from its role in effective administration, is a means of ensuring inclusiveness and a sense of joint ownership. It is also a way of engendering a sense of responsibility in members. Office holders are expected to be exemplary in their behaviour and to uphold the collective positive image.

The privilege to hold an office appears to be connected to the degree of involvement in group activities, marital status and parentage. For example, all those who indicated they participated in meetings or group activities five or

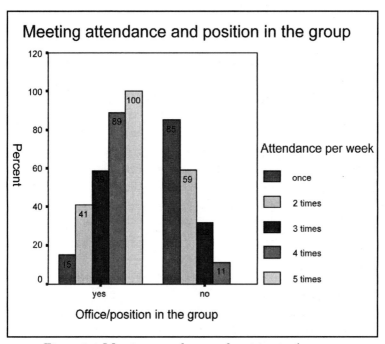

Figure 6.4: Meeting attendance and position in the group

more times a week were office holders. Among those who participated in group activities four times a week, 89% were office holders. This fell to 59% for those who participated three times, 41% for members who participated two times and 15% for those who participated once a week (see figure 7.4). Similarly, members who are single are less likely to be entrusted with position of responsibility than those who are married or separated. Whereas 51% of married respondents were office holders, 37% percent of single members held offices. Similarly, parents are most likely to be entrusted with positions of responsibility in the church than non-parents.

QUALITATIVE INTERVIEWEES

Although my analysis of the history and organisation of these churches relies mostly on interviews I conducted with pastors and church officials, my interviewees also include members who are neither pastors nor high-ranking church officials. Of the 18 persons I interviewed, eight were pastors or acting as pastors, five were church officials while five were ordinary members, although many interviewees insisted there were no ordinary members because they are all important and equal before God. In this concluding section, I present background information, which I hope would help to put into context some of the views expressed on identity and difference in chapter eight. The biographies of the interviewees tell a collective story of a relatively recent migrant subgroup at the early stages of defining its identity and place in twenty-first century Ireland.

All the interviewees arrived in Ireland in the second half of the 1990s and they had been living in Ireland for less than 10 years. While some had been members of their groups in Ireland for seven years, others had been in Ireland for only two years. The majority of my respondents came to Ireland to seek political asylum and from the onset they envisaged a long or permanent stay. One interviewee came in as a migrant worker, another got a permit to work as a pastor or missionary while another came on a tourist visa, had a child and became a legal resident. Some of those who came as asylum seekers became legal residents after they became parents of Irish citizens—see chapter two for analysis of immigration and citizenship policies.

Six interviewees were still waiting for decisions on their application for residence permit. Four of these made their applications on the basis of parentage of Irish citizens but they were caught in the immigration quagmire that I discuss in chapter two. One had lived in Ireland for about six years, having entered as a student. His application for residence permit was on the basis that he had lived in Ireland continuously for over five years. The sixth had applied to remain in Ireland on humanitarian grounds after his application for political asylum failed. One interviewee who came into the country as an asylum seeker had gained legal residency by marrying an Irishwoman and he was in the process of applying for Irish citizenship. The relatively short time all interviewees had been in Ireland and the precarious or uncertain residence status of some suggest they were at a phase in their immigration journey when they still harboured fresh memories of home while being preoccupied with charting paths of existence and survival in a new environment. Church membership, for some, became a means of accomplishing the two paradoxical aims.

All the interviewees were married but three were living apart from their spouses. Among the three living apart from their spouses was a female with five children who, like the other two, was awaiting a decision on an application for entry visa she had made on behalf of her spouse. In their struggle to establish their presence and families in Ireland, they relied on the support, advice and prayers of fellow worshippers. All my interviewees, except one, had post-secondary qualifications. Two of them were lawyers, one was a veterinary doctor, another was an engineer, while another was a medical laboratory technician. Most were gainfully employed, three of them as full-time pastors. Of the seven who were officially unemployed, five did not have work permits.

The majority of interviewees had been members of other religious groups before they converted to Pentecostalism. Two interviewees were raised by Pentecostal parents. But they equally insisted that the re-birth experience was necessary as it marked the beginning of their personal walk with God and their full-fledged admission into the Pentecostal fold. Two of those who became Pentecostals in Ireland were influenced by their wives while another was persuaded to attend his first Pentecostal meeting by a friend.

This profile reveals commonalities and differences among the church groups and the qualitative interviewees, providing wider contexts for interpreting the history and activities of these Christian groups. The next chapter explores the inter-relationships between religious beliefs and self conception/ the articulation of difference/sameness, focussing mainly on Pentecostal African immigrants in Ireland.

CHAPTER SEVEN

RELIGION AND IDENTITY

INTRODUCTION

'When I gave my life to Jesus Christ, it was a new beginning'
-A Lawyer and African Pentecostal in Dublin

The notion of a 'new beginning' or new personality is central to the self-perception of Pentecostal African immigrants in Ireland. Although the vast majority have Christian background, having been introduced to bible doctrines and customs very early in life, they use the term 'new beginning' to describe not their initial contact with or acceptance of Christian beliefs but rather their acceptance of and devotion to the unique Pentecostal interpretation of the bible which emphasises 'experience and practice' (Anderson 1999; Hollenwenger, 1972, 1999). Though born into a 'Christian family', Aremu said that the re-birth experience marked the beginning of his experience of God: "After I got born-again, my relationship with God became experiential, it wasn't just a fact but something I felt and experienced. I didn't require further prove of who God is or what he represents. I became convinced in my heart, in my inner being, from inside me." The act of spiritual re-birth or 'born-again' marks the beginning of the 'new beginning' as it makes available to the believer a new prism for looking both at self and at 'others'. Although my respondents' accounts of the process and implications of the rebirth experience differ from one person to another, they all emphasise its transformational qualities. In all the accounts spiritual re-birth inevitably led to a new and radically different understanding of self, of 'others', of situation and of hope and aspirations, much like the Calvinists that Max Weber (1930) writes about.

In theorising the relationship between the beliefs of the Calvinists and the rise of modern capitalism, Weber asserts that the self-conception/social orientation of those seventeenth century believers was influenced by specific Calvinist teachings or doctrines. His theory constitutes a different approach to explanation of religion because it emphasises the substance of religion and it suggests that orientation towards or believe in a super mundane being can have direct implications for the mundane. This idea forms the major theoretical plank of my research of Ireland's Pentecostal African immigrants. It is also the basis of 'meaning-making' notions of religion espoused by Clifford Geertz (1966), Peter Berger (1973) and Paul Gilroy (2000). In the case of my respondents, I argue that Pentecostal doctrines constitute the major, but by no means the only, prism for defining themselves, their situation and the 'others'.

Put differently, I contest the 'essentialist' qualities implied in my respondents' definition of self and argue that identity is conceptually and experientially more fluid, fractured and multi-dimensional than their self-definition admits. This is even more so in a situation of voluntary and involuntary exile like the one Pentecostal African immigrants in Ireland are experiencing. Though African Pentecostals in Ireland portray Pentecostalism as their essential and only window on the world and the only mirror for self-analysis and projection, I contend that they in fact have other windows and mirrors, smaller and less significant they might be, through which they define themselves and define the 'other'. I also argue, based on identity theories (Barth 1969; Woodward 2002, 2004) that stress the definition of 'self' by the 'other' or, as Woodward (2004: 7) puts it, 'the perceptions of others', that it is important to consider the definition of my respondents by the majority Irish society in order to comprehend a fuller understanding of their identity and location in twenty-first century Ireland. Popular and media discourses in Ireland suggest that there are conflicts or tensions between the way African Pentecostals define themselves and how they are defined by the 'other'—see analysis of racism experiences in chapter three. It is important to explore the dimensions and implications of these conflicts, as I have done in the concluding chapter of this book, in order to arrive at a more nuanced assessment of the future and place of Pentecostal African immigrants in Ireland.

Though Weber (1978, 1930) did not offer a comprehensive definition of religion, an analysis of his writings suggests that he conceptualised religion as a relationship between a social actor and a super mundane being which has implications for the ethical and moral conduct of the actor. Following Weber, theorists like Robert Bellah (1976), Clifford Geertz (1966) and Peter Berger (1973) also conceived of religion as a meaning-making and meaning-expressing instrument, as I demonstrate later in this chapter. In his analysis of the transformation of Olaudah Equiano from a slave boy to an articulate anti-slave trade crusader, Paul Gilroy (2000: 119-120) describes the role of religious beliefs in the transformation of self and social location: "The superficial differences of gender and social status, race and caste, marked on the body by the trifling order of man, were...set aside in favour of a relationship with Christ that offered a means to transcend and thereby escape the constraints of mortality and the body-coded order of identification and differentiation".

My analysis of the practices of Africa Pentecostals in Ireland is rooted in the substantive understanding of religion as a meaning making system proffered by Weber and these other theorists, as against either the functionalist explanations championed by Emile Durkheim (1965) and Parsons (1968); the rational choice theory of Stark and Bainbridge (1996) or the secularisation theory (Berger 1967, Wilson 1966; Luckman 1967). Christiano et al (2002) assert that the debates on the interrelationship between sociology and religion have been shaped by the Durkheimian and the

Weberian approaches. These are known respectively as the functionalist and substantive approaches.

In the functionalist approach, religion is conceived of chiefly in terms of the functions it performs for society and individual believers while the substantive approach places emphasis on the contents of religion and the implications of the believer's attachment to the contents and to the transcendental or the Supreme Being. Although I will return to this theme later in this chapter, it is worth emphasising at this stage that public and media perception of Ireland's Pentecostal African immigrants has mostly harmonised with or reflected the functionalist interpretations while their self-description have mostly reflected the substantive approach. Put differently, whereas African Pentecostals often talk about what they have become as a result both of their new relationship with God and of following specific bible teachings, media and public discourses mostly concentrate on the social relevance of these groups to individual believers and to community formation.

In the next sections I begin by applying a Marxist analysis of religion. I then present a brief but general survey of other functionalist perspectives both to contextualise the substantive approach enunciated by Max Weber and other theorists and to demonstrate why the functionalist theories are inadequate for explaining the beliefs and practices of Ireland's Pentecostal African immigrants. Thereafter I examine these beliefs and practices in the light of substantive theories and conclude the chapter by examining the identity and self-definition of my respondents in the light of Rogers Brubaker's (2004) conceptualisation of identity.

SOCIOLOGISTS ON RELIGION

Marxist Approach

The sub-field of sociology of religion has since the birth of the discipline of sociology enjoyed a visible and prominent place. Classical social theorists like Karl Marx, Max Weber and Emile Durkheim developed interesting but mostly divergent views of religion. Though some of their ideas are insufficient, perhaps unhelpful, for a critical understanding of religious dynamics at the beginning of the twenty-first century, most analyses of religious practices still use them as a starting point. Karl Marx did not offer a general theory of religion probably because it was never his intention to explain religion as an autonomous cultural or social reality. His study of religion relates to his main quest for solutions to the problem of political oppression and social inequality. Marx saw religion as a secondary phenomenon that is provoked or maintained under certain social and economic conditions. The notions of alienation and exploitation, two concepts that dominate his theory of social stratifications, shaped his views on religion. As Norma Birnbaum (1973:12) notes, Marx posits religion as "a spiritual response to a condition of alienation." Media reports (Cullen 2002; Haughey 2002b) of the activities of African-led Pentecostal groups have similarly portrayed them as strategies that African immigrants have adopted to escape from or cope with the racism, alienation and ostracism they suffer in the Irish society.

According to Christiano et al (2002), Marx's description of religion as 'the opium of the people' was more revealing of the social conditions of English life in the mid-nineteenth century than it was of religion itself: "When Marx says that religion is the opium of the people, he means that the masses are not wealthy enough to afford the real opium that the rich in mid-nineteenth century England bought to make life's pains go away. When Marx's content is read in context, what he is saying is that religion is the only way the masses can solace themselves from the pains, both physical and psychological, that life brings them, because they can't afford drugs". Marx further contends that religion is a part of the ideology of oppression or as Christiano et al (2002: 127) put it, "a powerful conservative force that serves to perpetuate the domination of one social class at the expense of others". Religion, as an answer to and an explanation of man's conditions, produces illusions and divert believers away from the true solution to their problems, that is, the dismantling of

157

social and political structures of domination or oppression. It distracts them from their real essence in the world and makes them acquiescence in their own exploitation and degradation.

Marx has been criticised (Hamilton 2001) for classifying religion as an ideological tool of the ruling class to preserve or maintain its interests. One way to interpret Marx's analysis is that the ruling class consciously promotes or supports particular forms of religion and that, given different socio-economic and political circumstances, adherents would probably not practise religion. These arguments are not validated by the practices of Pentecostal African immigrants in Ireland. The majority of them had been Pentecostals before they arrived in Ireland and their groups have no obvious connections to Ireland's ruling class. The description of the journey to Pentecostalism offered by the participants in my study indicates they have individually played active role in choosing their present religion and in jettisoning their former ones. Whereas there is no doubt that religion has sometimes been used as an ideological tool to keep the oppressed satisfied and docile, there have been instances where religion has served as a tool of revolt or resistance.

A further analysis of Marx's view would suggest that religion is mostly a possession of the oppressed and dispossessed. Many analyses (Warner, 1993:1046-1048) of memberships of religious groups in the twentieth and twenty-first centuries suggest that they are, in many instances, comprised of people from all social and economic strata. In the specific case of Pentecostal African immigrants in Ireland, membership cuts across different social and economic strata, ranging from the unemployed asylum seeker, the low-earning factory hand or security guard to the high earning and upwardly mobile lawyer, nurse, diplomat and medical doctor—as my description of the churches' demographic characteristics in chapter five illustrates. What is however common to all of them is their 'immigrant' status and the consequent exclusion or 'detachment' from the majority society that this status mostly implies in many Western European countries.

Many of the earlier investigations of Pentecostal Caribbean immigrants in the United Kingdom similarly considered immigrant status and non active membership of the dominant society as forms of deprivation (see Becher 1995; Hill 1971b, 1971c; McRobert 1989; Parry 1993; Ramdin 1987). Whereas only a proportion of African Pentecostals is subject to economic hardship and perhaps poverty, the majority suffer varying degrees of social exclusion, 'diminished' social status and racism (Ugba 2004, Amnesty International 2001). But still it would be incorrect to argue that these disadvantages are the main reasons they are attracted to Pentecostalism, as proponents of the 'Deprivation Theory' (Glock 1964; Glock and Stark 1965) have argued, particularly in relation to the phenomenal growth of Pentecostalism in South America, Africa, The Caribbean and among immigrants from these places in Western countries (Corten 1999, Johns 1993).

The majority of participants in my study had been Pentecostals for many years before they arrived in Ireland. Whereas the substance of Marx's argument in this respect cannot satisfactorily account for the practices of African Pentecostals, his views are useful in understanding the particular forms their beliefs/practices have taken in Ireland. But as Hamilton (2001:95) notes, Marx's theory does not explain religion, only its uses: "To say...that religion can be turned into an instrument of manipulation is no more to explain it than saying that, because art or drama can be utilised for ideological purposes, this explains art or drama." Marx's analysis, Hamilton contends, "tends to ignore many aspects of religion, to oversimplify a complex phenomenon, and to make sweeping generalisations" (2001:96). Hamilton also derides the 'opium of the people' thesis as simplistic, saying it fails to recognise that religion could be "a means of preserving a sense of meaning and dignity in the face of difficult circumstances rather than the "mere opiate-like and resignation-generating compensatory fantasy" suggested by Marx. There is no doubt that Pentecostalism has been "a means of preserving a sense of meaning and dignity" in a strange and difficult immigration environment for some Africans in Ireland.

Take Blessing, for example. She, her husband and three children were facing imminent deportation when I interviewed her. Though two of her children were born in Ireland the government had stopped to grant residence permit to immigrant parents of Irish citizens—see my discussion of immigration policies in chapter two. Reflecting on their ordeal and quest for a legal status, Blessing notes:

> Since I came into this country, it has been one problem or the other. Today, the government will say 'we're not giving you paper', tomorrow they'll say, 'we're giving you paper'. In times like these, when I get to the church there are some messages that I hear that help me to keep calm. These messages let me know that God is still there for me. In this country, nobody is there for you except God

Durkheimian functionalism

Emile Durkheim (1965:47) supplied a famous definition of religion based on his study of ethnographic reports on Australian Aborigines: "A religion is a unified system of beliefs and practices relative to sacred things, that is to say, things set apart and forbidden—beliefs and practices which unite into a single moral community called a church, all those who adhere to them."

Durkheim's definition places no emphasis on the content of religion or the spiritual dimension of religious practices. He concentrated mainly on its social character. He was more concerned with the outcomes or functions of religious rituals than with the reasons believers have for engaging in rituals in the first case. In his view, religion was not only normal but also socially healthy or desirable. Though Durkheim's definition clearly asserts the sociological nature of religion and remains a useful tool for analysing the relationship between social values and societal integration, Christiano et al notes that it "is not, in fact, an accurate portrayal of the nature of religion in our time," mostly because Durkheim failed to acknowledge the role of the participant actor. In their view, Durkheim's analysis has limited application because it concentrated on "only one aspect of a multifaceted social process" (2002:12). Hamilton, in his criticism of Durkheim and other functionalists, states: "to say that religion is essentially about maintaining social order is to take a very limited view of it. Clearly, most religious traditions have been concerned with order and harmony in human affairs and relations but it does not follow that this is all religion is about" (2001:132).

Most participants in my research consider it their Christian obligation to respect the laws of the land and the authorities. However, respect for state-imposed orders or laws are valid to the extent that they do not conflict with God's laws or rather their peculiar interpretations of those laws. Some interviewees admitted they entered into Ireland illegally using fake travel documents but only because they believed it was 'God's will'. Some who have sought political asylum believe God has used that particular channel to facilitate their entrance into and settlement in Ireland for the purpose of preaching repentance and what they say is the imminent eternal damnation of the unrepentant. As an official of the Redeemed Christian Church of God puts it:

> What is paramount in God's heart is the expansion of his kingdom. To do this God needs people who are his children and he sends them to go out and preach the gospel. He uses different circumstances to accomplish his purpose. As a matter of fact what you're seeing here is a grand design of God which he has known from the foundation of the earth. What he has planned is to find a means—call it political asylum, economic migrant or whatever—to send people to different parts of earth to preach about the end of this world.

Other theorists who have adopted Durkheim's functionalist approach to religion include Bronislaw Malinowski, Radcliff Brown, and Talcott Parsons. Malinowski (1974) argues that the origin of religion could not be found in society itself but rather in the desire for a stable society where people would be able to find answers to their psychological and emotional needs. Humans encounter psychological problems when their plans conflict with the realities. In such situations of crisis, religion offers them guidance on how to conduct their lives and how to cope. The origin of religion is therefore traceable to the personal experiences of individuals. Though he agreed that religion was to a great extent a communal, rather than an individual affair, he notes that the most intense religious moments are felt in solitude, when the adherent is detached from the world. Religious rituals performed in public have a social function since they help to strength or renew unity among members.

Radcliffe-Brown, however, disagrees with Malinowski's analysis, stating that though religion can offer guidance in moments of crisis, religion itself can often be a source of psychological anxieties (Radcliff-Brown, 1952: 149). Brian Morris also sees Malinowski's thesis on the psychological importance of religion as a justification of religion (Morris, 1987; Mella, 1994). However, Orlando Mella (1994) concurs with Malinoski's interpretation and her study of religious practices among Catholic Chileans in Sweden reveals that stressful events like immigration can engender a deeper sense of religiosity among immigrants. In her view, "when people perceive their environment as threatening, challenging, demanding, and frustrating, they often recur to religion which becomes an answer to the individual's emotional need aroused in such a milieu" (Mella, 1994:11).

Mella's argument, in my view, explains the form or adaptations of religious activism among these immigrants, rather than the reasons they became Catholics in the first place. Radcliff-Brown also interprets religion as one element of a complex system, and says its main function is the role it plays in establishing and maintaining a particular social order. According to his interpretation, the religious form will depend on the structure of the social order in which it exists and of which it is a part. To understand a particular religion we would have to look at the social life/relations of the specific community in which it exists. While agreeing with the substance of Radcliff-Brown's argument, I suggest, as I have done above, that examining the social life/relations of any particular community can only tell us about the nature or forms of religious practices and not the reasons they become believers.

Talcott Parsons (1968) adopts Durkheim's definition of religion and the organismic interpretation of society where all parts worked together to make the whole work. He contends that religion promotes value orientations within the "institutionalised normative culture" which, along with other social-cultural and political mechanisms, help to prevent societal disorder. According to this interpretation, human society is possible primarily because its members posses certain ultimate values and share some overriding goals. As Parsons argues, order in society is possible through the "internalisation of the normative culture in the personalities of its members and in the institutionalisation of that in the normative structure of society". His contention that "religious values underpin general value consensus" has increasingly been invalidated by the now frequent confrontations between religious minorities and dominant cultures or value-system. Also, his assumption that general value consensus in a society are underpinned by religious values does not fit recent and current theories on the decrease of religious values and the ascendance of post-modern and secular ideas (Glasner 1977; Martin 1978; Norman 2003). In the specific case of Pentecostal African immigrants in Ireland, the values they define as their own conflict with those they ascribe to the dominant society, as I highlight in my discussion of identity and difference. This suggests that Parsons's analysis is unsuited for examining the practices of this group of Christians.

Rational Choice Theory (RCT) and its critiques

The paradigm shift in the sociological study of religion announced by Stephen Warner (1993) has come to be identified strongly with the Rational Choice Theory (RCT) even though Warner made clear that his theory has a multi-dimensional application. Rooted in the ideas of Adam Smith and other classical economists in eighteenth century Scotland, RCT views the individual as a rational actor capable of making choices based on a calculation of the costs and benefits (Ammerman 1997; Bruce 1993, 1999; Chaves 1995; Wallis and Bruce 1984, 1986). As Christiano et al (2002:42) explain: "The core proposition of this theoretical orientation is that …the decision processes that people use in their religious or spiritual life are not different from the processes that they use to buy a car, contract marriage, take a vacation, or choose a college or a career. What this means sociologically is that religion is not inherently more or less serious than other spheres of human endeavour, except as it is perceived to be by participant actors" (2002:42-43). RCT recognises that collective actions are the result of individual actions, unlike the Durkheimian analysis. In other words, the individuals that are engaged in a collective action are not robots. But as Christiano et al (p.44) explains: "Because actors are almost always in multiple situations simultaneously, the choice-making process is never simple. There are likely to be both conflicts and circumstantial idiosyncrasies that must be unpacked with the greatest of care".

Critics of the Rational Choice Theory like Christopher Ellison and Darren Sherkat (1995) and Sherkat (1997) have suggested that RCT could be made more sociologically realistic by giving greater recognition to the embedded nature of institutional practices. As Christiano et al (p.46) note: "Cultural, socio-economic, gender and other sociological factors play especially significant role in focusing the lenses through which we perceive religious experience…In many locales, religion comes to permeate the cultural atmosphere…one no more chooses religion to play a role in one's life than one chooses to initiate each breath that one takes."

Christiano et al (2001:47) contend that RCT represents religion as an inferior ideology desired only because of the needs it meets for the individual: "…if rational choice theory is any kinder to religion than old-time functionalism, it is because the theory harbours a less lofty view of the human being's state in the world, not because it possesses any superior measure of respect for its subjects". Wallis and Bruce (1984:14) also critique the RCT for assuming that there is "something inherently faulty or unsatisfactory in religion, that it could never be desired except as compensation for something better." They conclude: "...to admit that religion may provide compensation for failure to secure [a] present tangible reward is not to advance a theory of religion, only a theory about what religion is or does for some people" (p18). Christiano et al (2002:47) equally state that religious faith does not amount to an 'inferior brand of ideology' simply because it is not easily comprehended by non-adherents. The element of choice is dominant—perhaps over-emphasised—when Pentecostal African immigrants discuss their beliefs. Pentecostalism is mostly posited as an ideology they have consciously and rationally imbibed with little or no outside influences. Their narration of their Pentecostal journey often attenuates or negates the role played by structures and institutions in the 're-birth' decision and process.

Weber's substantive interpretation

Although Max Weber did not offer a formal definition of religion, Swatos and Gustatson believe that his definition, had he offered one, would have read something like this: "A religion is a patterning of social relationships around a belief in supernatural powers, creating ethical considerations" (Swatos and Gustatson 1992). The two main aspects of Weber's theorisation of religion that are of interest to my research are:

1) The fashioning of social relationships based on the belief in a supra mundane power
2) The manifestation of this belief in ethical, social and moral conducts.

Whereas religious ethics refer to "decisions about right and wrong, and corresponding actions, based on some sense of being pleasing to or not offending the Powers, the sacred, the holy" (Christiano, 2002:15-17), moral prudence refers to what is best on the long run for one's own selfish interest. Soteriology is the first of Weber's two ethical considerations as regards religiously-motivated actions. It addresses the question of what constitutes salvation and how it can be achieved. It refers to the actions believers engage in or refrain from, guided by the conviction that by taking such actions they are keeping in a right relationship with the Supreme Being.

Weber enunciates these ideas most thoroughly in *The Protestant Ethic and the Spirit of Capitalism* (1930). He argues that modern capitalism developed in part because of the existence of specific religious ethic among certain protestant groups in the West. The Calvinist brand of Protestantism created in believers a unique attitude towards economic and social activities, wealth creation and enjoyment. According to Calvin's doctrine of predestination, before people were born an all-knowing and all-powerful God had decided whether they would enjoy eternal bliss in heaven or languish in hell for eternity. This teaching, as Christiano et al (2002: 132-33) explain, "created the socio-psychological condition of 'salvation anxiety', producing considerable inner turmoil for believers who wanted to know something about the state of their eternal souls." The adherents searched for signs that they were in a right relationship with God and they found it in material wealth. They viewed wealth or material success as a sign of God's approval and grace or, as Christiano et al (132-33) put it, "…the tension of Calvin's austere doctrine of predestination was resolved by a belief (based principally on the Old Testament book of Proverbs) that God would reward in this life those whom he had elected to eternal glory". Believing that material success indicated the state of their standing with God, the protestant believers worked hard, played less and saved more.

Weber compared the devotion and dedication to work displayed by protestant entrepreneurs and workers to those of monks to their religious duties. As Christiano et al (2002:132) put it: "Like a monk who gives up the pleasures of the world to devote himself to an otherworldly of prayer and contemplation, the capitalist is an ascetic. Unlike the monk, however, the capitalist remains in the world and amasses wealth." Weber used the term 'innerwordly' asceticism to describe the asceticism of the modern capitalist and to differentiate it from the world-rejecting 'otherworldly' asceticism of the monk. He linked the emergence of inner-wordly asceticism to the specific religious teachings of Martin Luther. While rejecting the notion that "the highest form of religious calling demanded a withdrawal from the world into the monastery," Luther proposed a revolutionary idea that clothed secular vocation with sacredness or spirituality. Secular work was invested with a religious cloak or significance. Weber's series of essays suggest that the Protestant Ethic was a consequence of Martin Luther's teachings on vocation and the salvation anxiety provoked by the predestination doctrines of John Calvin.

Theodicy, Weber's second ethical consideration, refers to the believer's desire and attempts to explain the existence of evil. Here, the believer seeks explanation of why good people suffer evil or, as Weber himself put it: "the problem of how the extraordinary power of...god may be reconciled with the imperfection of the world that he has created and rules over" (Weber 1978:159). Based on their analysis of Weber's essays, Christiano et al (2002) enumerated five forms in which the religions of the world have tried to explain this dilemma: "A messiah who initiates the end of the world as we know it, the transmigration of souls, a universal day of judgement, predestination, or dual divinities of good and evil".

Geertz (reported in Hamilton 2001:179) echoes Weber when he asserts: "the enigmatic unaccountability of gross iniquity raises the uncomfortable suspicion that perhaps the world and man's life in the world have no genuine order at all". Put differently, when people observe the suffering that befalls those they consider good or innocent, they begin to doubt the meaningfulness or orderliness of the world around them or the logic behind life's events. In situations like this, Hamilton suggests that religion offers a moral explanation: "It (religion) attempts to show that these things are only apparently the case and that if one takes a wider view, they do fit into a meaningful pattern." He further surmised: "...religion tackles the problems of bafflement, suffering and evil by recognising them and by denying that they are fundamentally characteristic of the world as a whole—relating them to a wider sphere of reality within which they become meaningful" (Hamilton 2001:180).

Weber (1965) makes a difference between theodicy of misfortune and that of good fortune, associating the former with lower-class people and the latter with upper-class people. The theodicy of misfortune considered wealth and other forms of materialism as products of a world alienated from God. The soteriological side of this is that those who refuse to pursue the evil ways of wealth or material riches will receive rewards in heaven or in the life after the present. On the other hand, the theodicy of fortune contends that material riches are a well-deserved privilege. The upper classes use this form of theodicy to justify their rights to the riches that they own in comparison to the little or no riches of the lower classes. In analysing the conditions of African Pentecostals in Ireland it is clear that they rely on some of Weber's ideas on theodicy to explain what would appear to an outsider as the conflicts or contradictions between the tenets of their faith and the behavioural and practical consequences.

Like Weber, Peter Berger (1973) and Clifford Geertz (1966) highlight the role of religion in helping believers not only to interpret situations and events but also to construct a general sense of order and meaning. Geertz defined religion as "a system of symbols which acts to establish powerful, persuasive, and long-lasting moods and motivations in men by formulating conceptions of a general order of existence and clothing these conceptions with such an aura of factuality that the moods and motivations seem uniquely realistic". He made a distinction between a people's ethos, by which he meant the tone, character and quality of their life, its moral and aesthetic style and mood and their world-view, which he defined as "the picture they have of the way things in sheer reality are, their most comprehensive ideas of order". The role of religion, he argues, is to synthesise these two distinct elements, create a world-view for the believer and relate this view to their ethos (Geertz, 1966, quoted in Hamilton, 2001: 177). As Hamilton explains: "Sacred symbols make the ethos intellectually reasonable by showing it to be a way of life ideally adapted to the state of affairs the world-view express". But the ethos also re-enforces the world-view because "it is constructed in such a way that it fits the actual way of life" (Hamilton, 2001:177-78).

Although Geertz's definition veers thinly into the functionalist interpretation of religion, his emphasis on 'sacred symbols' as the main elements of religion puts his analysis in the substantive camp. The notion of religion as a set of sacred symbols that both express and shape the world for the believer resonates with Weber's ideas in the Protestant Ethic. As Hamilton explains, the symbols shape the social world of believers by "inducing dispositions to behave in certain ways by inducing moods" (Hamilton, 2001:178). These moods vary depending on what specific symbols are at work at any particular place and period. Geertz has been criticised for failing to detail the processes by which symbols induce the moods and motivations he alleges they do (Hamilton, 2001:181) and for omitting the issues of power and authority in relations to religion.

People, Geertz argues, require a general order of existence because they yearn to have a meaningful interpretation of their lives. People are generally unable to live with the idea of a chaotic world where events occurs haphazardly and by chance. According to him, bafflement, suffering and evil constitute the types of experience that threaten the meaningful world order of the believer. Geertz sees religion as attempting to offer explanations that are meaningful when that world order is threatened. He sees the human need for explanation and understanding as 'emotional' and said that any failure of an explanatory apparatus can lead to "a deep disquiet" (Geertz, 1966 in Hamilton, 2001). Although Geertz concentrates on anomalous or odd events of life in his analysis, Hamilton (2001: 179) reminds us that religion can also be used by believers to "make life significant in a broader context in the face of the sheer routineness of existence". He asserts that "the very ordinariness of much of daily existence may threaten at times to appear without significance precisely because of its ordinariness and routine character". By providing adherents with an explanatory framework grounded in a belief in spiritual things religion becomes the means of negotiating everyday lived experiences and for finding meaningful explanations of situations, events, circumstances and the anomalous occurrences.

Analysing suffering as a type of experience capable of disrupting our sense of meaningful order, Geertz disputes the 'opium of the people' theory of Karl Marx (Christiano et al 2002; Hamilton 2001) and the psychological explanations of religion offered by Malinowski (1974). He states that although people do embrace religion as a result of suffering, evil or a baffling event, authority or tradition constitute the basis of any religious beliefs. Rather than serving as 'opium', Geertz contends that religion does not offer illusory solutions to the problems of suffering or hardship but rather it helps to make suffering sufferable. Commenting on Geertz's views, Hamilton (2001:179) notes, "most of the world's religious traditions affirm the proposition that life entails suffering and some even glory in it…in its intellectual aspects religion affirms the ultimate explicability of experience. In its affective aspects it affirms the ultimate suffering of existence. It does this by providing symbolic means for expressing emotion. It attempts to cope with suffering by placing it in a meaningful context, by providing modes of action through which it can be expressed and thus understood. To be able to understand it is to be able to accept it and endure it."

Religion as one among many perspectives on the world is unique because faith is central to it. Ritual serves as mechanism both for generating and strengthening faith and as a demonstration of it. By stating that the 'mood and motivations' created by religion are uniquely realistic to the believers, Geertz acknowledges the subjective experience of religion. Hamilton agrees: "religious perspectives are each unique ways of approaching the world—ones which seem uniquely realistic to those who espouse them and eminently practical and sensible". Hamilton further explains that the potency of religious perspectives on society, and I would like to argue for the believers themselves, rests to a great deal on the believers' unwavering conviction about the rightness or unassailability of their unique perspectives: "The fact that believers within each religious perspectives regard their own perspective as obviously and self-evidently the most sensible and realistic one gives such perspectives great potency" (Hamilton 2001: 180).

Peter Berger (1973:31) agrees with the order-seeking thesis of Geertz and argues that social actors are "congenitally compelled to impose a meaningful order upon reality" through a process of physical and mental activity. He uses the Greek term 'nomos' to describe the social world thus created and states that the nomos shapes the actors' interpretation of experience even though it exists as an independent and external reality from the actors themselves. Although the *nomos* is socially constructed, it is often taken to be natural or, as he puts it, "in the nature of things". Religious beliefs act to normalise the socially constructed world and as Berger states, the *nomos* through religion, is invested with a sacred character and transformed into a 'sacred cosmos'. In this connection Berger describes religion as: "the audacious attempt to conceive the entire universe as humanly significant" (Berger 1973:37). The *nomos* serves to protect the social actors or believers against anomie and the tragic results of a world that threatens to be disorderly and meaningless.

Berger goes on to assert that the human society, through religious interpretations, is located within a bigger cosmic reality and this enables adherents to legitimise and make sense of the social order. Legitimation of the social order can take a number of ways but "always the precarious and transitory constructions of human activity are given the semblance of ultimate security and permanence" (Hamilton 2001:182). In addition to its legitimising role, religion helps the adherents to make sense of experiences, which would otherwise disrupt their sense of order. Hamilton states: "It legitimates marginal situations and experiences—those which are at the limits of everyday ordinary experience." He includes sleep and dreams, death, catastrophes, war, social upheaval, the taking of life, suffering and evil. Echoing Max Weber, Berger describes religious explanations of such experiences as theodicies and stated that theodicy acts as a force against anomie (Berger 1973:94).

In Berger's view, religion can be a "world-maintaining" or a "world-shaking" force. It can also be a force which alienates and de-alienates. Its alienating power gives religion the basis to foster stability and a continuation of the tenuous social reality. Hamilton (2001:183) points to "a lingering functionalism" in Berger's analysis and critiques it for failing to recognise that "the need for meaning might be the product of a specific type of social situation or relationship to nature" in line with Marx's explanation. Put differently, do social actors search for meaning in all and every situation? I would answer yes but I would also quickly add that the type and kind of meaning actors search for vary from one context to another. Hamilton (2001), however, commends Berger's analysis as "an ingenious synthesis of Durkheimian, Weberian and Marxist insights".

The arguments of Clifford Geertz and those of Peter Berger reinforce Max Weber's propositions in the 'Protestant Ethic' and in his discussion of soteriology. Although Weber's aim was to identify the reasons modern capitalism rose and spread quickly in particular places in Europe, his analysis demonstrates clearly that 'a belief in spiritual being' can be a motivation for and a determinant of social action/orientation (Weber, 1978:528). In a similar way I argue in the case of my respondents that specific Pentecostal teachings/practices, which are primarily meant to signify and reaffirm a relationship with the Supreme God, have become the basis for a new orientation to self and to 'others'.

Weber's analysis also suggests that the actions of social actors should not be viewed only in terms of their stated motives and goals but also in relation to their unintended consequences. It is therefore sociologically important to assess my respondents' beliefs/practices not only in terms of their stated goals but also in terms of their 'unintended' consequences for social relations and the construction of sameness/difference and of boundaries. Weber's 'Protestant Ethic' thesis clearly demonstrates that when human beings initiate and maintain relationship with God or a spiritual being, it can have consequences for the way they see themselves and their place in society. Believing that their actions helped them to please God and to maintain a right relationship with Him, the protestant believers that Weber studied redefined their relationship to work and to the society.

This point is most useful for my analysis of the situation of African Pentecostals in Ireland. For them, the 'new beginning' does not only signify the beginning of a deeper (given that Pentecostalism is not the first stage of their spiritual journey) personal relationship with God but also a new and heightened consciousness of who they are and want to be. Who they are and want to be, according to their own construction, is remotely connected to who they were and to the many other facets of their lives. On her experience, the respondent quoted at the beginning of this chapter, states:

> This experience happened in 1988... I went to the altar and I gave my life to Christ... It is a deep and personal encounter...that day when I met Jesus I knew it. I knew that something specific and deep had taken place in my life. I became a new creature. When I gave my life to Christ it was a new beginning. The old life passed away.

The 'new beginning' replaces received identity markers like skin colours, 'blood and soil' with a relationship with God and Jesus Christ, which allows them to escape, as Paul Gilroy (2000:120) writes, "the body-coded order of identification and differentiation". In a similar way, the Pentecostal prism enables Pentecostal African immigrants in Ireland to redefine their position and role in the Irish society. They re-conceptualised themselves not as a racialised minority immigrant group perching precariously on the periphery of Irish society but as agents of social and religious change with a God-ordained mission to preach moral regeneration and spiritual revival in Ireland. Detailed discussion of this point supported with quotes from my informants is contained in chapter eight.

In his analysis of the transformation of the former slave, Olaudah Equiano, Paul Gilroy equally notes that he (Olaudah) shed "the superficial differences of gender and social status, race and caste, marked on the body by the trifling order of man" when he was immersed in "the welcoming, baptismal waters of his new Christian faith." Similarly Nicole Rodriguez Toulis (1997:210) notes concerning her research on Jamaican Pentecostals in England:

> Being a 'Christian' offers members an alternative basis for the construction of identity and difference. It is their identity as 'Christians' which serves as the basis for their interaction with others in British society. Rather than define themselves as 'Black' in White society, church members identified themselves as model 'Christian' in an imperfect Christian society.

On the experience of re-birth, which signals a 'new beginning', she notes that "one of the issues at play was the rejection of an identity inscribed on the skin for one inscribed on the heart."

PROBLEMATISING THE 'NEW' PERSONALITY

Although 're-birth' implies radical attenuation of identity markers connected to 'blood and soil' and my informants speak of their new self-ascribed identity as unifying and inclusive, Woodward (2004: 16) reminds us that "there is never one fixed, coherent identity but several in play." Stuart Hall (1996: 4) also states that, "identities are never unified and, in late modern times, increasingly fragmented and fractured; never singular but multiple constructed across different, often intersecting and antagonistic discourses, practices and positions." I therefore argue that the 'new personality', articulated and essentialised by Pentecostal African immigrants, co-exists in multiple ways and to various degrees with the 'old personality' and with other 'personalities'.

Considering Stuart Hall's (1996: 4) reminder that "identities are constructed through, not outside, difference", it is essential to consider the multiple and degrees of 'difference' and 'sameness' constructed by my respondents based on religiously-informed understandings of 'self', 'others' and social location.

To elucidate these themes further, I have adopted Roger Brubaker's conceptualisation of identity. He proposes three clusters of words to replace the 'catch-all' phrase identity in order to eliminate the conceptual confusion that have surrounded the term 'identity'. As Brubaker (2004:35) puts it, the term identity "bears a multivalent, even contradictory theoretical burden". Stuart Hall acknowledges this shorrtcoming when he describes identity as a concept "under erasure". According to him, identity is "an idea which cannot be thought in the old way, but without which certain key questions cannot be thought at all." (Hall 1996:2). Brubaker's new way of thinking about identity appeals to me because it achieves a conceptual and analytical clarity that I believe has been absent in many articulations of 'identity' by various theorists. The term has often been used to encapsulate multiple, divergent and even contradictory aims and to capture both 'hard' and 'soft' understandings of self and 'others'.

Brubaker's critical intervention provides a way around these problems. He makes clear that his aim in suggesting alternative to the concept of identity is not to "deprive anyone of 'identity' as a political tool or to undermine the legitimacy of making political appeals in identitarian terms" (Brubaker 2004: 61). Rather he aims to eliminate the conceptual confusion or fuzziness that has surrounded the use of identity. The three clusters of terms specified by Brubaker (2004:41) are:

1) Identification and categorization
2) Self-understanding and social location
3) Commonality, connectedness and groupness

I have neither adopted Brubaker's suggestions un-prob-lematically nor accept every idea he associates with the clus-ters of words. I also do not believe that his classifications cannot be further deconstructed or that additional clusters of words or themes cannot be derived from them. Brubaker himself acknowledges the limitations of his classifications, some of which I have highlighted below. However, the sub-stance of Brubaker's analysis does not diverge from or con-tradict the substantial understandings of identity proposed by theorists like Stuart Hall (1996), Zygmunt Bauman (2000, 2004), Kath Woodward (2002, 2004) and Pierre Bourdieu (1990). In fact, my analysis demonstrates that Brubaker's 'new' insight and welcomed intervention is rooted in old usage and understandings of the term. His main contribu-tion lies in terminology and classification, as I demonstrate in the rest of this chapter.

IDENTIFICATION AND CATEGORIZATION

Brubaker (2004:41) asserts that, "self- and other-identifi-cation are fundamentally situational and contextual". Unlike the 'strong' notions of identity, identification is intrinsic to social life and it takes place consciously and unconsciously. Brubaker makes a distinction between relational and cat-egorical modes of identification and between self-identifica-tion and the identification and categorization of oneself by others. Self identification, he states, "takes place in dialectical interplay with external identification, and the two need not converge." (p.42). Whereas relational identification makes a connection to the position of the subject in a relational web, categorical identification focuses on "membership in a class of persons sharing some categorical attribute such as race, ethnicity, nationality or religion". In presenting my data, I will endeavour to demonstrate the interplay between self identification and the identification of the 'other' in the nar-ratives of my informants. I will also highlight the distinction between 'identity' and 'identification' in line with Brubaker's exposition.

Both Brubaker (2004) and Stuart Hall (Hall 1996) stress the role of the agents in the identification process. Whereas both self-identification and the identification of self by the 'other' (or external identification) take place 'in the ordinary ebbs and flow of social life", there is a form of external identification that is not reproduced in self-identification. Brubaker describes it as "the formalised, codified, objectified systems of categorization developed by powerful, authoritative institutions." (2004:41-42) Modern nation-states are the foremost of these powerful institutions. Hall also discusses the form of external identification that is carried anonymously through discourses or public narratives. Although such anonymous identifications can and are usually instantiated in particular narrative utterances, Brubaker states that "their force may depend not on any particular instantiation but on their anonymous, unnoticed permeation of our ways of thinking and talking and making sense of the world." (2004: 43-44). This idea resonates with those of Woodward (2002) and Hall (1996).

SELF-UNDERSTANDING AND SOCIAL LOCATION

Brubaker uses self-understanding to explain "one's sense of who one is, of one's social location, and of how (given the first two) one is prepared to act". His analysis ties the actions of social actors to particularistic interpretations or understanding of self in much the same way Pierre Bourdieu (1990) has used the concept of practical sense or *sens pratique* to describe the actor's cognitive and emotional sense of himself or herself and his or her social world. This interpretation of the actions of social actors marks the limits of both the symbolic and instrumental interpretations as well as those explanations that see such action as structurally determined. Brubaker's explication of self-understanding resembles Peter Berger's (Berger 1974: 162) analysis of identity that focuses on a sense of who one is and Craig Calhoun's enunciation of 'self-conception' (Calhoun 1991:68).

Brubaker (2004:44-45) notes that "the social processes through which persons understand and locate themselves may in some instances involve the psychoanalyst's couch or in others participation in spirit possession cults." In other situations, self-understanding may take place in "a grid of intersecting categories" or "a web of connections of differential proximity and intensity". Self-understandings, according to him, "may be tacit; even when they are formed, as they ordinarily are, in and through prevailing discourses, they may exist and inform action, without themselves being discursively articulated" (p.45). Self-understanding designates one's own understanding, not the designation of oneself by the 'other'. Describing this as a limitation, Brubaker notes: "...external categorizations, identifications, and representations may be decisive in determining how one is regarded and treated by others, indeed in shaping one's own understanding of oneself. At the limit, self-understandings may be overridden by overwhelmingly coercive external categorizations." (Brubaker 2004:45). Two other limitations of the concept of 'self-understanding' are its emphasis on "cognitive awareness at the expense of affective processes" and the fact that it does not imply objectivity in the same way as 'strong' definitions of identity do.

COMMONALITY, CONNECTEDNESS, GROUPNESS

Brubaker says these refer to "the emotionally laden sense of belonging to a distinctive, bounded group, involving both a felt solidarity or oneness with fellow group members and a felt difference from or even antipathy to specified outsiders" (p. 46). According to his analysis, "'Commonality' denotes the sharing of some common attributes" while 'connectedness' describes the relational ties that link people. Neither commonality nor connectedness alone engenders groupness defined by Brubaker as "the sense of belonging to a distinctive, bounded, solidarity group". But commonality and connectedness together may result in groupness. (p. 47) In addition to connectedness and commonality, the feeling of groupness is deepened by "particular events, their encoding in compelling public narratives, prevailing discursive frames, and so on". Relational connectedness is not always necessary to achieve a strongly bounded sense of groupness. It may rest on "categorical commonality and an associated feeling of belonging together". Brubaker further makes a distinction between the "strongly groupist, exclusive, affectively charged self-understanding and much looser, more open self-understandings, involving some sense of affinity or affiliation, commonality or connectedness to particular others, but lacking a sense of overriding oneness vis-à-vis some constitutive 'other'". Although both the strongly groupist and the much looser version (and the transitions between them) are important, Brubaker notes that "they shape personal experience and condition social and political action in sharply different ways".

CONCLUSION

In connection with Pentecostal African immigrants in Ireland, I have endeavoured to imitate Brubaker's typology in structuring my analysis of self conception, conception of 'others' and the construction of sameness/difference. My aim is to demonstrate that self conception and the articulation of groupness and interrelatedness emerge in a number of different ways through a series of identifications. The empirical data I have presented contradict the efforts of some informants to claim a single, overwhelmingly dominant and unitary identity. Though Pentecostal African immigrants essentialise the 'new personality', my analysis shows that they posses and demonstrate other identities in many aspects of their everyday conduct. In choosing symbols, images and language to signal self-conception and groupness, my informants are guided by specific Pentecostal teachings but also by national/ethnic affiliations and the realities of their voluntary or involuntary exile in Ireland, especially their status as immigrants and a minority group that have been the subject of racism and racially-motivated discriminations.

What we are is constructed, not given. As subjects we are constantly creating and recreating what we are. Erving Goffman (1975) compares the way we present ourselves to others to the roles of actors or actresses in a drama. In the case of social actors, the lines are scripted by the society or situation although there is scope for the actors to improvise and offer unique interpretations. In Woodward's view, Goffman's analysis implies "there are links between the society in which we live and the limitations offered by the roles or parts we play in that society." In linking the personal with the social, Goffman's analysis suggests that the actions of individuals are performances aimed at influencing the opinion of the 'other'. They are meant to make statements about ourselves and to elicit particular responses.

But there are often tensions between the subject's self perception and the perception of the subject by the 'others'. Kath Woodward (2002, 2004) notes that the subject's self-perception is complemented by the perception of the subject from the 'outside' or by the 'other'. According to her, the realisation of a particular self-ascribed identity status can be hindered or obstructed by how the subject is perceived from the outside: "How I see myself and how others see me do not always fit…material, social and physical constraints prevent us from successfully presenting ourselves in some identity positions—constraints which include the perceptions of others" (Woodward, 2004:7). Applying this idea to my investigation, a 'fuller' or more 'complete' understanding of the identity of Pentecostal African immigrants can only be articulated by measuring their self-perception against their perception by the 'others' in Irish society. This point is ultimately relevant to questions about their social location and participation in the Irish society in the long term.

Pentecostal African immigrants in Ireland inhabit a society saturated by stereotypes and negative views of Africans in general (see chapter three where I have described the conditions of African immigrants in Ireland). These negative views translate directly into the way their religious practices are perceived and interpreted. Public and academic discourses suggest that the religious practices of these groups of Christians are largely interpreted by the majority society as uniquely African, exotic and an escape from the difficulties of their immigration conditions. It is also perceived as a means used by adherents to affirm and rehearse life in their home-countries. These conflicts between 'self-interpretation' and the interpretation of self by the 'others' are relevant to the central questions of this research, as I demonstrate in chapter nine—the conclusion.

CHAPTER EIGHT

IDENTITY AND DIFFERENCE

INTRODUCTION

Based on Richardson's (1990) notion of synecdoche and Walcott's (1995) advice to eliminate unnecessary and repetitive details in presenting qualitative data, this chapter discusses two of the 18 in-depth unstructured interviews that I conducted. My decision to focus on these 'key' narratives is based on intellectual and methodological considerations and it does not mean that the chosen narratives are ideal types or are more important than the others (Richardson 1990; Aberle 1951, reported in Langness and Frank 1981). My focus on key narratives does not also suggest that the other narratives have not informed this research; indeed they have formed the basis of the other empirical descriptions (see chapters five and six) and have also informed my historical analysis in chapter four. Moreover, I sometimes 'interrupt' the key narratives in this chapter with the views of the other interviewees where I believe such views can add complexity, interrogate or enrich the main narratives.

However, the two key narratives that I discuss below are comprehensive and nuanced and they contain the necessary ingredients for a theorisation of the relationships between Pentecostal African immigrants' beliefs and social action/ orientation. This is one reason why I have chosen to focus on them. Another reason is that the Pentecostal, immigration and family backgrounds of the two interviewees are diverse and complementary at the same time. Although both of them were 'pushed' out of their home countries, the specific reasons for and circumstances of departure (and arrival in Ireland) differ. Whereas the female interviewee appears to have anticipated and wanted a leadership role in Pentecostal activities in Ireland, all that the male interviewee wanted was to worship God in the same way he did in his home-country. Her narration places a lot of emphasis on the trans-formational qualities of spiritual rebirth (born-again) and the power to conquer evils and difficulties that come with this experience. His narrative dwells less on these themes but rather emphasises the unique qualities of his Pentecostal group and the great attraction it holds for African immi-grants. Moreover, one of the most profound differences in my informants' narration of self and beliefs relates to gender. To highlight these differences I have chosen one narrative by a male and another by a female. The Pentecostal group of the female interviewee is connected to its Nigerian headquarters and its 'sister' churches in Ireland and other parts of Europe. The group that the male informant belongs to was founded in Ireland by him and four other Africans.

NARRATIVE STRUCTURE

Rogers Brubaker's (2004) re-conceptualisation of iden-tity but specifically the clusters of words he suggested as replacement for the problematic and all-embracing 'iden-tity' have offered a meaningful structure for the interview data discussed in this chapter. As I argue in chapter seven, Brubaker's critical intervention provides a way around the conceptual confusion implicated in the use of identity. This is the other reason—apart from methodological consider-ations—why I have adopted Brubaker's (2004:41) alternative clusters of terms. The three clusters of words are:

1) Identification and categorization
2) Self-understanding and social location
3) Commonality, connectedness and groupness

Drawing on Brubaker's suggestions, I have chosen to analyse my chosen 'key narratives' as a series of multi-layered identity positions, locating the two narrators in relation to:

- Their previous non-Christian selves
- Other immigrant African non-believers
- Majority Irish society
- The Catholic Church in Ireland
- 'Sinners', both Irish and Africans
- Identity positions on the basis of race, religiosity, nationality, etc.

The two narratives begin with information on the interviewee's biographical, immigration and Pentecostal background. This is followed by a discussion of beliefs, experiences and the relationships between beliefs and social action/orientation. The chapter concludes with a brief summary of my analysis.

MRS TOKUNBO OLUWA

Pentecostal background and immigration circumstances

Mrs Oluwa is a lawyer in her mid-40s. She became a Pentecostal many years before she relocated to Ireland. At the time she became a born-again Christian she was already a successful lawyer and a happily married woman and mother. Before she experienced rebirth she was, to use her own expression, 'churchy', which means she attended church services regularly and gave the appearance of devotion and commitment. During her first visits to Pentecostal congregations, she was amazed at the numbers of highly-placed personalities she saw or met there. It disabused her mind of the notion that Pentecostalism or religion was for the poor. She attended a Pentecostal service the first time because her husband, a successful Architect who had become a 'born-again' Christian months earlier, had persistently invited and nagged her.

Mrs Oluwa is forthright when she discusses the reasons she came to Ireland and the circumstances of her voluntary exile. She was in her 40s and expecting an unplanned baby. She had had one miscarriage and she wasn't prepared to take a risk. On the advice and persuasion of her friends and because of her husband's persistent appeal, she decided to go to the United States to have the baby, a privilege reserved for the very well-to-do in Nigeria. When she was denied a visa to America she settled for Ireland after she heard that babies born in Ireland were entitled to Irish citizenship. She was attracted by the opportunity to obtain dual citizenship for her child but not by the prospect of residing in Ireland. She had no intention to live outside of Nigeria. She was upwardly mobile and was at that time being considered for appointment as a magistrate.

Mrs Oluwa arrived in Ireland, gave birth to the baby, obtained necessary birth registration documents and headed back to Nigeria as soon as the baby was strong enough to cope with long hours of flights. She did not seek political asylum, as she never intended to stay. Back in Nigeria for a while her husband began to plead with her to go back to Ireland to establish legal residency, which would pave the way for their children to come to Ireland and have access to a better and more sophisticated education. Bent on advancing her career, Mrs Oluwa would not budge and for a long time the tug-of-war went on between her and her husband until, as she puts it, God intervened in a dream. While she slept in the night a voice told her to go to Ireland or she could end up in death and not get her magistrate appointment. Tearfully, she agreed to return to Ireland.

Back in Ireland she had a tough time financially. She received no stipends from the State and had to depend on her husband in Nigeria for financial support. Added to that was the problem of accommodation, getting her four children over to Ireland, and her spiritual responsibilities. She returned to the Redeem church where she had fellowshipped during her brief stay in Ireland. When she relocated to a suburb of Dublin where there was no Redeem Church, she decided to work towards establishing one. She liaised with other Redeem ministers in Ireland but direct financial help came from her parish in Nigeria. The church now has over 160 regular worshippers, three services a week, many ministers and an in-house magazine. The first time I met Mrs Oluwa she was still "praying and believing God" for her husband to be reunited with her and their children. She told me of the struggle she went through to get her children re-united with her and how her prayers and reliance on God softened the hearts of recalcitrant state officials. Her husband has since joined her and he has assumed leadership of the church although Mrs Oluwa continues to play a prominent role as a minister and leader.

Identification and self-understanding

A warm handshake and an uncomplicated self-identification marked the beginning of my interviews with Mrs Oluwa: "I'm Tokunbo, how're you doing, sir?", she said.

This introduction and many similar expressions in her narration do not speak of Mrs Oluwa's self-understanding. They were necessary because they facilitated our interactions but they did not represent the notions of self that she meant for me to have of her. She immediately launches into a detailed narration of her pre-born-again experiences but only because they emphasised and essentialised the 'self-understanding' that resulted from the born-again experience:

> I gave my life to Christ because what matters most is not joining a church but having a personal relationship with God. When I was growing up I was 'churchy' and I felt that I was okay. When I got married, I was still going to church. In fact, I was going to a Pentecostal church. But I was not born-again; I had not given my life to Christ. Even though fellow church members were calling me 'sister', I was still living my life the normal way, like everybody else. I was not different… My husband gave his life to Christ (became born again) in Redeem… On another day, he invited me to a different branch of the same church…When I entered into the church I could see that everything that was taking place—from the praise worship to every other aspects

of the service—wasn't ordinary. Everything was different from what I had seen or what I had been used to. I
saw some very important people that I knew in society,
including major-generals. They were dancing as if their
positions did not matter to them. I was totally trans-
fixed. I think God used the situation to speak to me
because I had always had a sense of self-importance. I
had always felt I was okay even though I was nothing.
I think the Holy Spirit used what I saw there to speak
me, to ask me, 'what do you think you are? Can you see
these people?' These were people I would need to book
appointments if I wanted to see them in their office.
Seeing them praising God and dancing without a care
in the world was a big challenge to me. They all looked
so happy. I knew that those people had something that
I didn't have... The pastor of the church happened to
be a lawyer, like myself. I knew that he was a very successful lawyer. He had a very big practice. I knew him
very well. That too was an eye-opener for me. Whereas
I had thought that Christianity was meant only for
the down-trodden, the hope of the hopeless, I now felt
that it was for everybody.

The stage was set for Mrs Oluwa to experience her metamorphosis from someone who had been 'like everybody else'
to a distinctive someone and a member of a group whose
members 'looked so happy' and have 'something' other people
do not have. The distinctions and boundaries between the
group she was about to join and the one she was coming out
from are not only many but multidimensional as my analysis
of 'commonality, connectedness and groupness' demonstrates.
In order to emphasise the 'something' she would become, Mrs
Oluwa describes herself and her professional and material
successes as 'nothing'. Her narration also reveals an interplay
between the 'self-understanding' she wants to articulate and
convey and self-identification or categorisation. For example,
she categorises herself as married, a lawyer and a nominal
Christian. The first two identifications are repeated (not necessarily emphasised) throughout her narration but the third
ceases and gives way to a new self-understanding from the
moment she experiences her transformation:

> As the church programme continued the Holy Spirit was working on me... By the time the sermon was finished, I felt overwhelmed. Most of what the pastor said related to my situation. It was as if he had discerned my thoughts and worries. It was as if he saw through me. I knew that he knew of me but he knew nothing about my personal life. So it must have been the Holy Spirit that was talking through him. The Holy Spirit was using him to address me specifically... I was touched in my heart by the things I heard. In fact while the pastor was still speaking I was crying. This experience happened in 1988... When the 'altar call' was made...I cried all the way to the altar. I couldn't control my tears. The pastor was saying to me, 'sister, don't worry, Jesus paid the price, don't worry.' Maybe he thought that my sin was bigger than that of the others. But that wasn't the reason I was crying. I cried because I was reflecting on my life and the emptiness it had been. I was just thinking, 'what if I had died before that day, what would have been my portion'? That was what made me cry. So I went to the altar and I gave my life to Christ. I thank God that I did.

Again, Mrs Oluwa emphasises the 'emptiness' of the life she had been living in order to essentialise the 'new' life and the self-understanding that comes with it. Having already mentioned the 'important personalities' she saw in the church and the impression that this made on her, she describes the role of the pastor in the church and in her conversion. However, she makes clear that her conversion did not come from the pastor or 'important personalities' but from the 'Holy Spirit', which she says 'was working on me' and talking specifically to her through the pastor.

In Mrs Oluwa's narration of her 'new life' and her sojourn in Ireland there is more evidence of the interplay between identification and self-understanding. There is also evidence of the interplay between self-identification (internal identification) and identification of self by the 'other' (external identification). Her narration problematises self-understanding and demonstrates the connections between 'self-understanding' and social action. She begins her narration of the 'new' life by reflecting on the 'old':

Where would I be without Jesus? If I had died before that day *(the day she got born-again)*, I would have gone to hell. Although I was attending a Pentecostal church and they were calling me 'sister', I wasn't a Christian, I knew that I wasn't born again. When you meet Jesus you'll know. Your life will experience a profound change. You'll become a new creature. It is a deep and personal encounter, different from going to a church, different from any thing else. So that day when I met Jesus I knew it. I knew that something specific and deep had taken place in my life. I became a new creature. When I gave my life to Christ it was a new beginning. The old life passed away. If fact, there was this joy that came into my life. Before then, I had personal problems. Even with my education and all that I had, I had no feeling of contentment and no inner joy. My happiness depended on circumstances and it was very erratic. It was just the deceit of the devil, the devil made me feel contented. The devil made me feel I was somebody when in reality I was nobody. But the day I met Jesus there was a change in my life...I became so excited about my Jesus that wherever I went I was not ashamed to say that 'Jesus is Lord'. I would take the bus from Ikeja to CMS in Lagos Island and I would preach. I would enter another bus back to Ikeja and I would preach. Any spare time I had, I would board a commercial bus so I could preach.

In the narration above, Mrs Oluwa problematises the term 'Christian', saying it is not synonymous with membership of a church or attending church services. She only became a 'Christian' when she became 'born-again' although she had been an active member of a church. There is a clear distinction between the 'self-understanding' associated with the 'old' life and that of the new. The new self-understanding speaks of someone who has suddenly realised the lordship of Jesus Christ and is not deterred by physical difficulties or timidity from proclaiming it publicly. The 'old' understanding of self is associated with discontentment, lack of inner joy, unhappiness, problems, and the devil. The new understanding of self portrays a believer who is able to cope with problems because Christ goes through the problems with her:

It's not that there have not been problems…I've gone through problems. I've gone through difficult situations. I've gone through trials. In every thing, I've come out victorious. Most of the time when I'm going through tribulations, the way I would have felt as an unbeliever I don't feel that way anymore. As an unbeliever, I used to be depressed. Any little thing would weigh me down. But now each time I go through situations, I see Christ going through it with me and because of that I'm not afraid, I don't get moved.

In this narration, Mrs Oluwa goes so far as to use the term 'unbeliever' to describe herself and her pre born-again 'Christian' commitments or activities. It becomes increasingly clear as her narration progresses that the born-again experience is considered by her (and most interviewees) as the 'true' mark of Christianity and that any belief or practice that contradicts or falls outside of it is inferior. Next, Mrs Oluwa narrates her experience of illness and 'miraculous' recovery to demonstrate her new self-understanding of the empowered individual who is neither deterred nor defeated by problems of any sort:

After I gave my life to Christ, there was a time I was seriously sick. It was not the kind of sickness where I would be in pain or bed-ridden but I knew that I was not okay. My health was deteriorating seriously and I wasn't mentally alert…I was going round the hospitals. They couldn't diagnose what was wrong with me…I realised that I had left undone what I should have done. It occurred to me that I was letting the devil dictate to me what I should do. I took action immediately. I registered in a prayer school…We had fasting, long-term fasting…The essence of fasting is to kill the flesh and lift up your spirit-man so you can receive from God…I attended the prayer school for one year. It was an evening course. During the prayer school, there was a seven-day programme in the camp. Through that programme I was thoroughly blessed because there were different kinds of spectacular miracles…God healed me too. In my dream, God spoke to me on the first night of the programme. I saw an angel of God taking my blood sample to the laboratory. It was like a laboratory scene. He said, 'see, you're not sick, it is well with you'. And the next day I just discovered that I was okay. I was absolutely okay.

The other major instance, according to her, where God intervened in a dream to instruct and guide her relates to her return to Ireland to set up a home. As I have stated in the introduction to her narration, she returned to Nigeria after giving birth to her baby in Ireland and having completed the necessary documentations. In Nigeria her husband suggested she return to Ireland to set up a home so their children would have better education and more opportunities for advancement. Mrs Oluwa resisted both because she was on the verge of being appointed a magistrate and she did not want to go through the pains of uprooting and permanent migration at her age:

> When my husband saw that I was adamant, that I wasn't going to do it, he said, 'okay, don't worry'. That night I went to sleep. In my sleep God spoke to me. He said, 'you want to take appointment on the Bench, what if you take the appointment and die? I own your life.' That was what I heard. When I woke up from that sleep, I didn't have peace again. At first I could not bring myself to tell my husband about the dream. I was still thinking I could maybe plead with God to have mercy and to let me stay because I was at the pinnacle of my career. I felt that giving up my career at that time would be too costly for me. I could not disobey God's instruction to me. His words were very clear when I heard them in my dream. I had my plans and desires but His plan and desire for me prevailed. As a born-again Christian and a child of God, the first thing you learn is to listen to God and to obey. That is what the new relationship with him means. After I gave my life to God, I surrendered everything—my future, plans and freedom—to him. The decision to return to Ireland to stay was a big test of my loyalty to God. I'm happy I listened to him…Looking back now I believe God had a different plan for me. He needed me here. Eventually I made up my mind to return to Ireland and I went and told my husband my decision. I told him with tears in my eyes. My husband

> was surprised by my sudden change of mind...I told
> him it was because God asked me to.

Again, Mrs Oluwa's understanding of self as one who is unquestionably loyal to God comes through in the narration above. Submission to God comes before self-interest and what she would not readily do for her husband and her children she would easily do for God. This understanding of self essentialises the relationship to the Supreme Being and it dominates Mrs Oluwa's narrative and those of the other Pentecostals. It forms a basis of social action, even those actions that go against societal norms or specific state policies. It is also a basis for erecting and collapsing boundaries or for constructing commonality and groupness, as I now discuss.

Commonality, connectedness, groupness

Mrs Oluwa's experience of re-birth did not only mark the transformation from the 'old' self understanding to the 'new', it also laid a 'new' basis of commonality, connectedness and groupness. Whereas the Pentecostal group in its different manifestations in Nigeria and Ireland is portrayed as the 'new' basis of commonality, connectedness and groupness, the former basis is variously interpreted as that which is 'ordinary', to which every person who is not a Pentecostal belongs, the African communities in Ireland and the larger Irish society. However, her narration reveals differing degrees of commonality with, connectedness to and groupness with the 'others'. In other words, although the various boundaries have been set up because the 'others' do not have the same orientation towards God as Mrs Oluwa's 'new' group, they are enforced in different ways and to different degrees:

> To me, people who don't know Jesus are like children
> walking towards fire. To a child, the fire is glowing
> and beautiful but he or she doesn't know it can be
> dangerous. When you have Christ, that's the way you
> feel towards those who don't have Christ. You want to
> warn as many people as possible so their blood will not
> be on you. When I gave my life to Christ, I just wanted

everybody to know that hell is real and heaven is true. A life without Christ is like a chicken in a cage. In Nigeria, at the beginning of the year, they buy chicken, they call it 'agric' chicken and they keep them in the cage. They give them the best of feeds and the best attention. Why do they do this? They are preparing them for the day of slaughter. That's the Christmas day. They bring the chickens out during Christmas and sell them and they are slaughtered. The lives of these chickens are like the lives of people who do not know Christ...So that is the way I feel about it and that is why I just want to share the goodness of God with them.

In the above narration, Mrs Oluwa establishes a boundary between 'people who don't know Jesus' and those who have Christ (the born-agains). It is a boundary that polarises and homogenises. It does not recognise degrees of 'knowing' or 'not knowing' Jesus and it also obliterates social differences within the two groups and any form of interrelationships between the two groups, except that one is a pre-condition for the other.

Later in Mrs Oluwa's narration it is discernable that the broad category of 'those who know Jesus' refers to both the wider born-again family or all those who have "received Christ into their lives" and the members of her distinct Pentecostal group, the Redeemed Christian Church of God (Redeem). Her attachment to the latter could be explained by what Brubaker describes as "the strongly groupist, exclusive, affectively charged self-understanding" while her relationship with the former is a "much looser, more open self-understanding, involving some sense of affinity or affiliation, commonality or connectedness...but lacking a sense of over-riding oneness" (Brubaker 2004: 46). Below is her articulation of her early encounters in Ireland with her Pentecostal group:

When I came back to Ireland I was so busy...I was busy in His work. I was serving God in the church. I had already been ordained as a minister. I was ordained about four or five years ago in Redeem, in Nigeria...I got a place in Drogheda. Financially, it was very tough because I wasn't working. I had to pay the rent. I just rented a room and I was paying 250 pounds (about €350) per month. It was very tough. It was very traumatic. I didn't apply for social welfare allowance because if I did my children would not be able to join me. The reason I returned to Ireland was to bring my children over. That purpose would have been defeated had I applied for social welfare allowance. It was a big sacrifice...But the first thing I did was to go to church. I asked where Redeem was. The nearest Redeem was in Mosney.[1] So I went there. The first Sunday I fellow-shipped with them, they welcomed all first-time visitors and put down our names. The Area Pastor visited me and they discovered that I'm an ordained minister. He encouraged me. There was a house fellowship that had just started in Drogheda where I live. I was leading the house fellowship.

Redeem offered Mrs Oluwa a welcoming environment and provided some respite from the hardships and trauma she was encountering in the larger Irish society. The pastor paid her a personal visit and provided some encouragement. More importantly she was given the responsibilities of organising the nascent group in Drogheda, signalling her full admission into a family of believers but also providing her with a platform to cultivate and nurture relationships. Given her background as a lawyer who had been very active in her home-country, her new role provided an outlet for her energy and creativity. The 'small group' of believers she spear-headed in Drogheda grew into a church of about 160 members but it remained a close-knit group where she continued to provide and also receive help, encouragement, friendship and acceptance:

> Within a short time the group became so big...we needed a bigger accommodation and possibly transform into a full church... The church was inaugurated on August 21, 2001 but we had been holding meetings since June of that year. When we started we had 45 people. We are over 160 now...The church has been a pillar of strength to members. In the area of immigration, I've been useful to members. I advise them

on how to go about their applications. And I help to hire barristers for some, work with solicitors to hire barristers. In fact the whole of Redeem calls me when they have immigration problems—all the branches. They'll call me and I'll advise them. At least three of those that I helped got their papers *(resident status)*. And those that received rejection we advised them on how to go about the appeals, the procedure to follow and all those things…I've done that—and most of the time free of charge. It's only for members that I know cannot pay…It is the church platform that has brought us together. We are co-workers for God. When they are distressed or depressed, we hold their hands, pray together, show them love, show them care. You know many people here don't have their husbands, they don't have their parents, and when things happen, the church would always be there to fill the vacuum. And we've always been there. I've always been there. That is why I said sometimes I don't get home till 2a.m. or 3a.m. Sometimes they're in the hospital, they call me. I've to be there. I'm the relative they have here. They call me in the middle of the night and I go. My children would get up and lock the door.

In this narration, Mrs Oluwa paints a vivid picture of commonality, interconnectedness and groupness. The things that connect them are their common orientation towards God and the problems they face—immigration, loneliness, depression and lack of close family ties. The search for solution involves a common reliance on God and on the support of fellow church members. She describes the physical act of holding hands together to pray, thus highlighting the sense of groupness and connectedness. She also compares her role of visiting sick ones and supporting members to that of a relative. Mrs Oluwa says that she offers free legal advice only to members of Redeem, including members in other branches. In this instance the larger born-again family is grouped among the 'other' that is not entitled to free legal advice despite the commonality.

The boundaries Mrs Oluwa draws between her group and the 'constitutive other' are many and multidimensional as the following narration relating to the impact of Pentecostalism on her family demonstrates:

> My husband is not here yet. I'm the head. Well Jesus is the head and we're the under-shepherds...As the minister in charge and a mother with five children, there is a lot of pressure on me. I'm a lawyer. I'm having to retake my professional exams because my earlier qualifications are from Nigeria... I've just passed the professional exam and I'm now qualified to be a solicitor... It has been very tough. So I won't say it doesn't affect my family...The reason it's easier for me to cope is because our children were raised in the Lord. They have been taught Bible principles, at home and in the church. They were brought up with Christian principles and ideals. If they were not raised up in the Lord, they would probably not understand why we live the way we do and why we do things the way we do. My first child is 16, the second is 13, the third is 11, the baby is three years old. I also have a 15-year-old child that I raised. He's my nephew... Chances are I would have had problems with these children when we came here, especially as some of them are in their teenage years. You know, the Irish society is different from where we come from. There is so much permissiveness and immorality here. It is not an easy place to bring up children. At 16, children are supposed to be free to do what they like. But the Christian values that I've taught my children since infancy have made them amenable to my advice and instructions. If not for these Christian principles, things would have been a lot harder. I know of many Africans that have lost their children; their children are with the Social Welfare authorities, they are living in hostels because they revolted against their parents. They formulate all sorts of stories and tell all sorts of lies to the Social Welfare authorities...So it takes the grace of God to bring up children in this society. I'm happy that my children see things differently because of the different values that result from studying the Bible. A classmate of my son was asking him, 'why is it that you don't smoke?' He is being made to feel anti-social because he does not smoke and do the other immoral things that the Bible condemns...They want to teach my 16-year-old to go to the pub, to the cinema and to go out

with guys. But the grace of God and the education the Bible offers have made it easier for my children to resist these pressures. Even though I'm very busy with the things of God, they too are busy. They're in youth fellowship, my daughter that's going to be 16 soon is in the choir in the church, my boys are drumming for the church. My 11-year-old is in the children's section. We're all involved in the work of God. It makes things easier. It doesn't affect their education or cut them off from the larger society. They go to school and they are active socially. They have outings. We've youth fellowship, where the youths go to places as a group. They go to the beach.

In the above narration, Mrs Oluwa acknowledges contacts and conflicts among the three groups—her group, the majority society and the larger African communities. She portrays her group and her family as distinct from and parallel to the larger Irish society. They rely on Bible principles for guidance and direction but the larger society is permissive and it grants self-destructive freedom to its young ones to engage in immorality, smoking and visit pubs. Here we find an example of what Brubaker calls "a felt difference from or even antipathy to specified outsiders." (Brubaker 2004: 46). This polarisation is achieved through a homogenisation that refuses to recognise differences within the groups. The larger African community is also identified as belonging to this group of 'specified outsiders'. Their children are rebellious and have taken on the characteristics of the larger Irish society. Pentecostalism and specific Bible principles on morality are constructed as the boundaries that divide and protect. However, the narration reveals some interconnections between Mrs Oluwa's group and the larger society. This, among other things, suggests that boundaries are not physical but social, religious, ideological and perhaps psychological. She is working to restart her career and has just passed her law exams. Her children attend the same school as the children from the majority society but there is a clash of values and the children of her group resolutely resist the invitations and pressures to join the way of life of the majority society, thus perpetuating boundaries and contributing to a homogenised identity formation.

Reversed identification

Mrs Oluwa's narration of the relationship of her group with 'Christian' Ireland is complicated. She compares Ireland of the past where Christianity and missionary activities flourished to Ireland of the present where religiosity has decreased and the younger generations are far-removed from God and the ways of their fore-fathers. She portrays the image of an African immigrant Pentecostal group whose main motivation in Ireland is to restore the country's past glories and 'true' Christianity. Her portrayal imbues the presence of African immigrants in Ireland with a higher and far nobler objective than the popular association with political asylum and economic motives. In this narration, Mrs Oluwa reverses the popular image of African immigrants as a racialised minority group on the periphery of Irish society. She constructs an alternative basis of identification and self-understanding that is not only dignifying and empowering, but rejects the identification and conceptualisation of African immigrants by the 'other'. She constructs early Ireland as based on Pentecostal principles, thus bridging differences and reversing the dialectic position of Africans versus Irish people. In Mrs Oluwa's narration, African Pentecostal immigrants are ascribed a superior position:

> The foundation of this nation (Ireland) was built on Christ. When St Patrick (Ireland's Patron Saint) came, he came as a Pentecostal minister...He made Christians and ministers out of many Irish people. As a result, many Irish people were in a position to go to the nooks and corners of the world, to preach the good news...They took the gospel to the other parts of the world but now they are sleeping. You see young Irish children, they are not interested in things of God, they are not. They don't follow their parents to church. The Irish are sleeping. Children are not following the examples set by their parents. The link is broken. The present Ireland is unconnected with the Ireland of the past where Christianity and Christian values thrived.

Parents are not handing over the spiritual heritage
that they had received from their parents and, grand-
parents and great grand-parents. As I said, the link is
broken and we are here to try and restore it. It may be
the youths are not interested because the church has
disappointed them, especially with all the paedophile
scandals involving priests. So our main mission is to
restore Christianity in this country. In fact, we meet
together and pray for this nation all the time. We pray
for Ireland, we pray for spiritual revival in this country.
Our presence in this country is divinely ordained
although that may not be manifest at the moment. As
time goes on, it will become clear. In the years and
decades to come people will look back and understand
that we had been brought to Ireland by God for a specific reason. That reason is the spiritual health of the
nation.

In the above narration, African immigrants are recon-
structed as the empowered givers, contrary to the image of
the helpless (and devious) receivers that is often propagated
in popular and media discourses. They are on a divinely
ordained mission to shine a spiritual light on a nation that
has regressed into unbelief and moral disintegration. It is an
image of African immigrants that encourages them to hold
their heads high up and re-conceptualise their self-understanding.

MR JAMES OLU ESAN

Pentecostal background and immigration circumstances

Mr Esan is the pastor and leader of Gospel Faith Mission
(GFM), which he co-founded with four other Nigerians in
2000. My first and subsequent meetings with him took place
in his office in the church premises, a derelict one-storey terraced house near Parnell Square in Dublin city centre.[2] I had
phoned many times to arrange for an appointment but for
various reasons connected with his busy pastoral duties we
could not meet. When I arrived in his office he was in a
prayer and counselling session with a female church member.
I waited in the reception. The sound of his voice rose and fell

as he prayed and spoke in tongues. I was ushered in just after the lady departed. There is an air of contentment around Mr Esan as he narrated the triumphs and travails of GFM as well as his own spiritual journey.

His encounter with Pentecostalism began in Lagos in 1994 when he became a born-again Christian. His decision to be born-again marked a milestone for someone born in a family that 'worshipped idols' and who had attended a Pentecostal church for about ten years without a clear or definite idea of his relationship with God. Once he became born-again, Mr Esan served in various capacities within the church. He also maintained his business activities, buying and exporting cocoa pods. On arrival in Ireland in 1998, he joined Graces Church, an Irish-led Pentecostal church but he soon left the group and formed the GFM. He came to Ireland to seek asylum but he and his wife have acquired residence permits by virtue of their citizen children. Mr Esan says his primary goal is to win "more souls for the kingdom every day."

Identification and Self-Understanding

There are similarities between Mr Esan's journey to Pentecostalism and that of Mrs Oluwa. Both had been nominal Christians who had attended church services regularly but without a clear idea of their relationship with God. The experience of re-birth marked a new self-understanding built around their connection to God. It also marked the beginning of an active Pentecostal life:

> I had been attending a church for over ten years before I became a born-again Christian. I was going to a Pentecostal church for over ten years before I became a born-again Christian. But I got born again in 1994—I know that was the year I gave my life to Christ. We had been idol worshippers. My family worshipped idols. No one attended church in my family. By the grace of God, my father, my mother and everyone now go to church. Our house in Nigeria is being used as a place of worship now. When I became born-again I started praying for the salvation of my parents. One

day another group…went and counselled them and
they gave their lives to Jesus; they became born-again.

In the narration above, born-again Christianity is constructed as the genuine Christianity and the re-birth experience marked the beginning of Mr Esan's personal concern
about the spiritual welfare of others—his parents. The narration also reveals a new and empowered individual who is
able to force changes in the circumstances of other people
through prayer. His parents got born-again as a result of
his prayers on their behalf. There are clearly echoes of Mrs
Oluwa's experiences in this account. Whereas the rebirth
experience kindled in both Mrs Oluwa and Mr Esan a
concern for the spiritual welfare of other people, the impact
was slightly different in the case of Mr Odukoya (another
interviewee) whose parents were born-again Christians. He
was raised in a born-again family and he attended his father's
Pentecostal church before he got born-again:

> But at a point in my Christian life I discovered that
> apart from being born in a Christian family, there is
> a time you personally must make up your mind that
> you want to live for God. I came to the realisation that
> serving God is a personal thing, it's not a collective
> thing, it's not a tribal thing, it's not a family thing.
> It's a one-to-one thing with God…giving your life to
> Christ must cost you something. There must be some
> things you used to do that you can't do again. That is
> the meaning of the word born-again…old habits and
> relationships that do not meet the Bible's standards
> must be discarded. Bible standards become the yard-
> stick for judging and measuring everything…I had to
> give up my girlfriend in order to live for God. I stopped
> going to parties. I loved music so much, I loved music.
> I had huge collections…I had to give them up. That
> was very painful; that was the really painful one, not
> the girlfriend. I didn't think I could survive without
> my music…At first I didn't see what the big deal was
> about listening to worldly music like Marvin Gaye's
> 'Sexual Healing' but then I started seeing things in the
> scriptures that do not really support listening to such
> music in the sense that my heart now belongs to God…
> The more I listen to negative things, the more I watch

> the wrong films, the more I read pornographic books, the more they affect my soul, my spirit and I will not be able to live a holy life. The negative thoughts will keep coming into my mind…Now I spend more time listening to godly music and reading the scriptures.

Mr Odukoya's account of his re-birth makes a distinction between the 'mundane' and the 'spiritual'. Girlfriends, parties, pornography, 'wrong films' and 'worldly music' are, in this instance, markers of the boundary that separates the old world from the 'new'. The other markers of this boundary in the narrations of the other participants are alcohol, drugs, pre and extra-marital sex, dishonesty and all forms of criminal activities. Mr Odukoya's construction of his new relationship with God differs slightly from that of Mrs Oluwa and Mr Esan as he emphasises the desire to separate from the world and to acquire holiness.

The concern for the spiritual welfare of others has remained the major motivation for Mr Esan's Pentecostal activities in Ireland, as he explains below:

> My primary goal is to make sure that more souls are won for the kingdom every day. I just want to see spiritual revival in Ireland. To be honest with you, I am after the souls, all sorts of souls—Africans, Irish—the colour doesn't matter. Souls have no colour; they are colourless. What matters most is that more souls are won for the kingdom of God. Every other thing could be added but my primary goal is to see that more souls come to the Lord through our ministry. That includes every people, not just Africans.

In the above narration, Mr Esan is no longer the helpless asylum seeker who is after the mundane goal of amassing money and capital with the eventual aim of returning to exportation of cocoa pods. Rather, he is the non-racial or 'colour-blind' Christian who is after 'colourless' souls in his country of exile. Although this re-articulation of his presence and purpose in Ireland contradicts the understanding of him by the 'other', it creates in Mr Esan a sense of self-satisfaction and fulfilment:

I know that the original reason I came to Ireland was not for this purpose but the fact is; God has said, 'My thoughts are not your thoughts'. I had my plans but the thoughts and plans of God prevailed. I have fulfilment in this country. Honestly speaking, I'm fulfilled. Some of my colleagues that studied Mutual Funds with me are working in the banks now. I tell them one thing, 'I'm fulfilled here'. I tell my friends, 'I thank God for your lives but I'm fulfilled'. I have never had peace in any other thing than preaching the gospel. I've been in business, I have actually, by the grace of God, been successful in business but I had no peace; no fulfilment. This is the first time in my life that I have peace. I'm doing what God has called me to do—preaching the gospel.

Commonality, connectedness and groupness

Like Mrs Oluwa, Pentecostalism became the basis for constructing commonality, connectedness and groupness. However, 'race' and 'colour' also feature in Mr Esan's construction of difference and sameness. The first evidence of this is in his articulation of the beginning of the Gospel Faith Mission, which he co-founded with four other Nigerians:

> Gospel Faith Mission started nearly four years ago at No 8, Castle Ryder Drive. That is where I was living then. We started with five people. We started as a prayer group. We didn't start as a church. We started as a prayer group in my living room. We met together to pray. We decided to form the group because the way they worshipped in the Irish Pentecostal church we were attending was quite different from the way we pray in Africa. That was why we decided to have a prayer group. Our little group of five persons grew into a church and today we have a branch in London and three churches in Ireland.

This narration casts doubts on the universalism of Pentecostalism and introduces 'racial' or 'cultural' qualifiers. One Pentecostal group is described as 'Irish' and the other as 'African'. But more importantly, the 'Africans' that found their way to the 'Irish' Pentecostal could not cope with the way of worship. This view of Pentecostalism as racialised and divided along colour lines re-echoes in the views of some other participants. It also features prominently in its history and development as I have demonstrated in chapter five. Mr Esan's encounter with 'Irish' Pentecostals has been at least as important for self-definition and entrenchment of boundaries as the encounter with non-Pentecostal 'others'.

As their little group expanded, Mr Esan and his co-founders struggled to find a bigger venue. In narrating the efforts they made and the groups they had contacts with, Mr Esan discusses conflicts and differences that highlight the peripheral location of their Pentecostal group in the cultural and religious landscape of Ireland:

> ...we started with five people in my sitting room. After two months the sitting room could not accommodate us because people *(African immigrants)* from far and near had started to come to the prayer meetings. So we moved to what we call CB shop on Dorset Street.[3] We rented a basement but it was a terrible time because the other users of the hall would organise overnight parties, mess up the place and we would have to clean it for our Sunday service...We thought we had a big accommodation in CB shop but after six months the place was overfilled with members and visitors. We relocated to a church in Aungier Street. But after some time the priest of the church, the Irish church, complained that members of his congregation were getting attracted to what we were doing, they were taking positive interest in our worship. Because of that the priest gave us a quit notice. He said we could in time draw away members of his congregation if we continued to use his church auditorium *(a long hilarious laughter followed)*. It was a Catholic church on Aungier Street. As a result we relocated to the YMCA building. From YMCA building we moved to the present place.

In this narrative, the constitutive 'other' is, in the first instance, portrayed as alcohol-loving and uncaring party animals (most certainly members of the larger Irish society, given the location of CB shop in the North inner city) that contributed only misery to the efforts of Mr Esan's group to maintain the routine of meetings and worship. In the second instance, the 'other' is portrayed as an edgy, envious and hostile Catholic priest bent on disrupting the efforts of Mr Esan's group to worship their God. But the antipathy towards Catholicism, Ireland's dominant religious group, is also doctrinal as another participant explains:

> The fact is there are lots of things that they practise in the Catholic Church that do not conform with what the Bible teaches. One example is the use of the crucifix. The Muslims also use it. Christ, by the grace of God, is no longer on the cross. He has been resurrected. He has ascended into heaven. Why should we use the crucifix, ask Mary to pray for us, ask dead saints to pray for us? In the book of Corinthians the Bible makes clear that you are a saint of God the moment you are born again. As a saint of God, you cannot begin to ask dead saints to pray for you... Thank God Mary is the one that brought forth Christ but Mary is not the road, she is not the way, at all. Jesus said, ask anything in my name, not in the name of Mary. These are some of the areas where we disagree with the Catholics. I'm not just criticising them for criticism's sake and I'm not saying that Catholics will not make heaven, no, no, no. I believe equally that there are some Catholics that will make heaven...As a born-again Christian, my life should be based on the Bible. When people see me they should know that I live by the Bible. This is not often the case with Catholics. Catholics simply go through catechism and the Simple Prayer book.

However, the 'constitutive other' in Mr Esan's narration is not only the Catholic Church. Sometimes it is all Christian groups where 'human philosophies' rather than 'the truth' or 'the gospel of our lord Jesus Christ' is preached. Mr Esan, who describes his church as the fastest-growing African-led Pentecostal church in Ireland, explains the reasons for the rapid growth:

> We are not getting new members because of my own ability. One thing I have discovered is that people are fed up with lies. They are actually hungry for the truth. The truth is that if you preach the gospel, if you preach

the gospel of our lord Jesus Christ, there will be an increase. But if you preach human philosophies it may affect the growth of the church…by the grace of God, in this church, we *(including all the ministers and church leaders)* are determined to preach the truth. Three Sundays ago we preached on the benefits of salvation and 31 people gave their lives to Jesus. Thirty-one people were born-again in the course of one service! We sincerely believe we are not preaching human doctrines here…We are preaching the gospel of our lord Jesus Christ and I sincerely believe that that is actually what people are looking for today. That is why they are coming to us. They are fed up with lies.

Implied in this discourse is the notion that the other groups, including other African-led Pentecostal groups, are not sites for reproducing the authentic gospel or the 'truth'. Rather, they teach human philosophies and lies. Despite some commonality and inter-connectedness (for example, membership of 'Joy in the Nation', the umbrella body of African-led Pentecostal groups), one cannot use the concept of groupness to describe these churches because denominational differences and competition for converts and societal recognition are deep-rooted. Another participant articulated these differences and antipathy much more emphatically:

I will never support any form of criminal activities among the membership of the church. If they catch any person from my church involved in credit card fraud or stealing, let them lock him or her up. I won't visit anybody in jail. If you know how to steal, you should know how to go to jail. These are harsh words but I don't believe in saying, 'God bless you, God loves you' while you continue to trade in cocaine, commit credit card fraud and bring the money to the church…Such money is bloody money and God will never bless it. It has negative effects on our faith and on our lives…I know that there are a few genuine churches that the many Africans have set up in Ireland in recent years but I cannot deny the fact that there are impostors. I cannot deny the fact that some people are working to fill their own pockets…There are some that are preying on people, they prey on people's problems…

> They're killing them. It's wickedness. Like I said, I'm
> not a judge but I know currently there are bits of dis-
> agreement…I will not allow anyone to manoeuvre me
> and make the church a business. I'll not do that, no
> matter how close I am to you. We cannot be involved
> in ungodly practices. Some things may look good but
> they are not godly. If they are good but not godly and
> you try to invest in them, they will bring problems.

In the above narration, the constitutive 'other' are other
African-led Pentecostal churches whose members are
involved in various forms of criminal activities. Still there
is some recognition of commonality or interconnectedness
between the two groups as they have all been set up by
'Africans'. But this commonality does not lead to groupness
as the narrator constructs definite boundaries between his
group and the other groups. These boundaries are marked by
the dubiousness of the leaders of the other groups and the
nefarious activities of their members.

In Mr Esan's narration, the larger Irish society is constituted as the 'other' and the site of many practices that God
abhors. Within his group, 'wholesome' alternatives are fashioned to stop its members from crossing the boundaries but
also to attract members of the dominant society. The social
habits named in his narrative constitute boundary markers:

> We consider polygamy, extra-marital affairs and sex
> before marriage as abominations…Members of this
> church do not drink alcohol. We preach against taking
> alcohol because the Bible says you should be filled with
> the holy spirit rather than wine…members know that
> it is against Bible principles to drink alcohol. Going
> to the pubs…it depends on what you're going to do in
> the pub. We don't support members visiting pubs to
> drink or socialise and to engage in conducts the Bible
> does not approve…But whatever they are enjoying in
> the pubs we have in the church. They are dancing in
> the pub, we dance here. They get drunk in the pub,
> we have God's holy spirit. Whatever it is that takes
> them to the pubs, we want to create a better alternative
> in the church. You see, we are planning to move to
> another place of worship *(in Ballyfermot)*. It is located

in the midst of addicts, drug addicts. We are working out ways to win their souls...we're going to take the drugs from them and give them something different and better...There is greatness in them and we want to bring out that greatness in the addicts. God can use any human being irrespective of their colour, position or social class.

In this narration, the 'we' is Mr Esan's group which is out to perform spiritual and social transformation in the lives of the constitutive 'other', defined in this instance as drink-loving, pub-crawling and drug addicted members of the majority society. Drugs, pre and extra-marital sex and alcohol-fuelled revelries in pubs symbolise the boundaries that divide the two distinct groups. Mr Esan's group is constructed as occupying a superior moral and spiritual position. Its members are on a mission to help the helpless. This is contrary to the way they are conceptualised by the 'other'. As Mr Esan explains below, his group and other African-led Pentecostal groups are perceived by the dominant society in racial and 'colour' term. The perception and attitude of the dominant society constitute an impediment to the mission of African Pentecostals:

The Irish society has been finding it difficult to accept what God has decided to do. With all humility I appreciate the Irish and I love them. And I can say without reservation, they are a wonderful people to live with but they are still finding it difficult to accept what God is doing. They are still asking themselves, 'is God actually using these Africans?' But God can use any people irrespective of their colour. The problem is that they (Irish) have not accepted that God is using us Africans to bring the message of salvation to them in these end times. We'll not give up. The fact is that God has brought us Africans here to bring spiritual revival to Ireland. It will happen if they accept. Their blood will not be upon us if they don't accept...Oh, how I wish the Irish would just grab this vision so that they will enjoy God in the twenty-first century! They should forget about our colour. Colour has nothing to do with what God wants to do in Ireland now...I know of many great men of God that came to Ireland in the month of August. We're expecting more next year. They are coming from Africa…the truth is, if God is determined to do anything, he will do it whether you accept it or not. The Irish people should accept now that God is using us Africans.

In the above narration, commonality and groupness are constructed in religious and racial terms. The 'we' on a mission to bring spiritual revival to Ireland are 'Africans' while the 'other' or beneficiary is the 'Irish people'. This narration does not recognise differences among the 'we'. It also homogenises the 'other'. The 'we' is constructed as agents of religious and social change but also as foreigners of a different skin colour who are considered inferior by the 'other'. The experience of racism also features in the narration of other participants. For example, Mr Odukoya says the experience of racism and racially-motivated attacks have made it difficult for African Pentecostals to preach or interact with members of the dominant society:

> Unfortunately we don't at the moment have an environment that is conducive for the work we've been called to do, where we can really get our message across to the Irish people. Our people…because of some challenges they face in this society—verbal abuse, racial abuse and everything—they are really hiding in their shells, they are afraid, they are withdrawn from society and people even without realising it sometimes. Will they pick on me? What will happen when I go down the street with my baby in pram? What if they spit on me or on the baby? How would I feel? I mean…it is difficult for any one who has experienced that to go out and start saying, 'God loves you'. So these challenges make it difficult for many of us to cross the boundaries, the lines that separate us from them. By the nature of the work we are here to do, by the nature of our calling we should cross the boundaries. We should reach out to every one—black, white, Irish, Africans, in fact everyone and anyone. And that is what we're trying to do but the circumstances are difficult. The climate is not conducive but we'll keep trying. We'll not abandon our calling. But like I said, it is difficult to go telling people 'Jesus loves you' when you believe you're not loved by

the same people. You really have to have a large heart to try to reach out after you've been treated this way. When you have been treated like that, abused, spat on, you are scarred and withdrawn. That is the truth. I've been able to do the little I've done because I know that if they knew better they wouldn't behave that way. I know that a lot of these things is caused by ignorance. But how will they get rid of their ignorance unless we tell them, if we don't mix with them?

In this narration 'our people' are the racialised African Pentecostals while the constitutive 'other' are the ignorant but racist 'Irish people'. Differences are constructed in racial and religious terms. The larger society is constructed as a hostile place where African immigrants experience racially-motivated attacks. Implied in this narration is the denotation of African-led Pentecostal groups as places that these victims of racism withdraw into, the place of respite from these attacks.

CONCLUSION

For Ireland's Pentecostal African immigrants, the experience of rebirth lays the basis both for articulating a new conceptualisation of self which has direct implications for social actions and motives and for constructing commonality, connectedness and groupness. Their re-articulation of self focuses mostly on their Pentecostal beliefs, activities and morality which contradict the dominant understanding of them in the media and popular discourse. In this instance, Pentecostalism provides a basis for an alternative, subversive and empowering articulation of self. In their self analysis, African Pentecostals are not the racialised minority immigrant group sitting precariously on the periphery of Irish society but empowered agents of social and religious change in an increasingly secular Ireland whose younger generations have swapped the spirituality of their forefathers for drugs, alcohol and revelries in pubs.

Commonality and groupness involve the dual but paradoxical tasks of establishing and tearing down boundaries or of building bridges and erecting boundaries at the same time. Boundaries are generally erected to set the narrators apart from non-Pentecostals while the bridges are mostly aimed at connecting one Pentecostal group to another. My analysis reveals that the boundaries set up by Ireland's African Pentecostals are multidimensional and based mostly on their unique interpretation of the Bible. But in some cases, the boundaries are also marked by moral and racial/ethnic symbolisms. Such boundaries homogenise in order to essentialise sameness within distinct groups or the larger born-again family.

My analysis also demonstrates that the degree to which these boundaries are enforced depends on who the constitutive 'other' is. For example, the boundaries that separate the narrators from non-Pentecostals generally, from the dominant society or from the Catholic establishment are strongly articulated and rigidly enforced, while those that set distinct African Pentecostal groups apart can sometimes be blurred and weak. The boundaries between them and the larger society permit some connections and interrelationships which some Pentecostals argue would facilitate their eventual integration into the larger Irish society. I take this analysis forward in the next chapter—the conclusion—where I examine, among other things, the implications of my findings for the place and future of these groups in twenty-first century Ireland.

Notes

1. The little town of Mosney is located about 50 kilometres north of Dublin. It has housed one of the government-designated accommodation centres for asylum seekers after the introduction in 2000 of the policy of 'dispersing' asylum seekers all over Ireland. The centre in Mosney became the largest in the country. Of the 6,127 asylum seekers in 63 accommodation centres at the beginning of 2005, Mosney housed 761 (Sanctuary 2005, 2006, Tróicare/ICJP 2002).

2. The church has since relocated to a refurbished warehouse which it purchased in 2004 in the Greater Dublin Area.

3. Dorset Street is located in north central Dublin and it is still largely populated by native Irish. It is part of what is known as 'Dublin Inner City' which has a disproportionate high rate of unemployment and social problems.

Chapter nine

Identity and Social Location

This research on Pentecostal African immigrants in twenty-first century Ireland has revealed clear and definite influences of beliefs on self-conception and the social construction of 'others', differences and boundaries. It has shown that Pentecostalism is perceived as different from 'ethnic' or ancestral religions (Gans 1994; Herberg 1960; Winter 1996) by portraying it mostly as a social category which adherents consciously and actively acquire, nurture and showcase. The study also demonstrates a clear articulation of the specific material, social and emotional uses of Pentecostalism in precarious immigration circumstances. In the case of some informants, the conception of self as a willing and amenable tool in the hands of God had a direct influence on their decision to relocate specifically to Ireland, as illustrated both in Mrs Oluwa's narration in chapter eight and Danielle's experiences documented in chapter four. According to their accounts, they heard clear instructions from God and 'saw' his fingers pointing them in the direction of Ireland. It is therefore not surprising that these informants understand and interpret their presence and experiences in Ireland through the Pentecostal prism. The findings of this study suggest that the multiple and complex relationships African immigrants maintain with Pentecostalism cannot be explained by relying on a single theoretical framework. A triangulation of functionalism, critical and substantive theories of religion is needed to explain these relationships.

The outcome of this research, therefore, contributes to and derives from the sociology of religion and the social constructionist view of identity. It interprets identity and boundary markers not as 'natural' or 'essential' characteristics connected with 'blood and soil' (Gilroy 2000) but the result of social performances and interactions (Berger and Luckmann 1979; Hall 2002; Woodward 2002). This concluding chapter, building on the major findings of the study, expands on the implications for the sociology of religion and the social constructionist view of identity. It also assesses the implications of identity and boundary construction for the place and participation of Pentecostal African immigrants in twenty-first century Ireland. It concludes by briefly articulating the relevance and usefulness of my methodology and the relevance of this study to future research on this theme.

BETWEEN ETHNICITY AND POLITICS

The core of this study centres on the relationship between beliefs and the construction of social realities. However, it has also identified some material, social and emotional uses of Pentecostalism in difficult and precarious immigration circumstances, in line with Emile Durkheim's (1965) functionalist theorisation of religion, and as other researchers of immigrants' religious practices (e.g. Glazer and Moynihan 1963; Ter Haar 1998a, 1998b; Kalilombe 1998; Mella 1994) have documented. In connection with politics and immigration, membership of Pentecostal groups and specific Pentecostal teachings on the willingness and ability of God to intervene in mundane affairs in the interest of the faithful have constituted the core of Pentecostal African immigrants' responses to dramatic changes in Ireland's residency and citizenship policies that threatened to truncate their residence or continued stay in Ireland—see detailed discussion in chapters two and three. Here we find an example of the application of specific Pentecostal doctrines in a diasporic context. Details of these changes and their impact have been discussed in chapter two. Pentecostal African immigrants caught in the immigration quagmire expressed a belief that

God would intervene in Ireland's domestic politics and cause the Minister for Justice and other decision makers to change the state's immigration policies. When the government soft-pedalled and introduced less strident policies, they interpreted it as a victory of and for their God, believing that campaigners and pressure groups may have merely served as God's agents of change.

Turning to the celestials for solutions to tangible earthly problems brings to mind Karl Marx's notion of religion as an illusory solution (Hamilton 2001; Birnbaum 1973), although it must be added that these Pentecostal groups also served as sources of practical help. As I have noted in chapter eight, church members with legal expertise and experience gave advice, in some cases for no fees, to fellow worshippers on how to lodge and process applications for residence permit. At the same time, fellow worshippers commiserated with or consoled those in difficulties with words of hope. They held their hands and prayed with and for them. In songs, sermons and prayers, the afflicted expressed their desire to be freed of these problems.

The policies and politics of that era also promoted racism and racially-motivated attacks, many of them directed at sub-Saharan Africans, as I have explained in chapter three. Whereas most of these churches did not join in marches meant to protest against such attacks (though individual members may have participated), they provided a physical space where members could withdraw into for relative safety and support. Specific Pentecostal teachings also formed the basis of intellectual response to these attacks, enabling members to come to terms with them. Pentecostal teachings on forgiveness, loving the 'enemy' and the oneness of the human family helped members to be less bitter about their experiences and, where possible, seek means of reconciliation. They blamed 'ignorance' and the devil for the racially-based hostilities that they suffered and said the solution lay in the conversion of the perpetrators to Pentecostalism. As one participant told me, "we have only one enemy—the Devil. Our fight is against the devil and his demons. They are responsible for all the wrong that people commit". In this sense Pentecostal teachings helped the members (of these churches) to assume a morally superior position by refusing to engage in retribution or openly expressing hatred towards the perpetrators.

Racial bias and discrimination often result in social isolation and the loss of societal recognition and prestige (Essed 1991). As I have illustrated in several chapters, but especially in chapters five and six, many Pentecostal African immigrants are successful professionals who had enjoyed respect and recognition in their home-countries. A survey I conducted in 2003 with African immigrants in the Greater Dublin Area revealed that many were worried about the diminished social status imposed on them by their condition of voluntary or involuntary exile (Ugba 2004). African-led Pentecostal churches have transpired into spaces where members could counter social isolation and also reclaim a measure of the respect and recognition they once enjoyed in their home-countries, as Mella (1994) argues in relation to Chilean Catholic immigrants in Sweden. These churches are perhaps the only institutions in Irish society where Africans experience a sense of ownership and full belonging, according to my interviewees. This sense of ownership and belonging engenders trust and a sense of security and freedom that African immigrants do not generally experience in Irish society. It is therefore not surprising that they exhibit a more confident and positive disposition within these settings than they do outside of them. As one respondent puts it: "If you want to know the true African, go and observe him or her in the church".

The other connection between these Pentecostal groups and politics, according to some participants, is that the churches are providing training and electoral bases for future civic and political leaders. The leaders of African-led Pentecostal groups in Ireland do not advocate the separation of religion from politics or the non-participation of members in politics. Rather they consider Pentecostal teachings on honesty and morality as qualities political leaders should possess. They also predict that increased and expanded memberships and inter-church cooperation will in future work for the benefit of members who aspire to political office. The participants who make this prediction buttress their opinion by pointing to the increased participation of Pentecostals in politics in some countries in Africa, South and North America and among Black Americans. However, available evidence suggests little or no direct involvement in political mobilisation among African-led Pentecostal groups in the United Kingdom and continental Europe (Hunt 2002a; Ter Haar 1998a, 1998b; Mella 1994). Moreover, recent political developments in Ireland, including the election in 2004 of the first two local councillors of African origin, do not suggest that African Pentecostal groups have played a significant and overt role in political mobilisation.

This study has also revealed a gender dimension in the uses of Pentecostalism among African immigrants (see Ekué 1998 for a gender analysis of African Christians in Germany). There are more women than men in the four churches covered in this study, according to church officials and interviewees. In the days when Ireland still granted citizenship rights to children of immigrants, pregnant women came to Ireland ahead of their spouses as part of a strategy to gain residence rights. They would later apply for their spouses to join them. In reality, the application and re-unification process was slow, bureaucratic and emotionally burdensome. These difficulties were aggravated after the government abolished the rights of immigrant parents to residence permit and about 11,500 parents whose applications had not been decided were caught in a quagmire, until the government re-opened the application process in January 2005, as discussed in chapter two. Pentecostal African immigrants caught in this debacle, including single mothers and wives whose spouses had not joined them in Ireland, found acceptance, companionship and support in these churches. Many participants link the active involvement of women in these churches to the social and domestic problems they face.

Ethnicity

Chong (1998), Galush (1977), Lewins (1978), Lucas (1955) and Williams (1988), among others, have interpreted the relationship between religion and ethnicity in two principal ways: Religion as the essence of ethnic identity and religion as support for ethnic identity and cohesion. For example, Galush (1977), who studied early Polish immigrants in the United States, contends that their national identity was inseparable from Roman Catholicism, while Lucas (1955) postulates that religion, rather than nationality or ethnicity, was the glue that held early Dutch Calvinist groups in America together. Kurien (1998) makes a connection between Hindus in America and the maintenance of ethnic identity. In the case of Asian Indians, Williams (1988) notes that they used religion to support or maintain other forms of group identities, including ethnically-based ones. In her analysis of the role of religion in the maintenance of group identities in Northern Ireland, Clare Mitchell (2005:17) asserts that "masses, priests and sacraments continue to be involved in the transmission of communal identity". Chong (1998:265) similarly notes the "highly significant role" played by religion "as a source of and support for emergent ethnic identity and group cohesion" among second generation Koreans in America.

While Pentecostalism cannot be described as an 'ethnic' or 'ancestral' religion despite the many influences specific African cultures and traditions have had on it (see MacRobert 1988; Raboteau 1978, 2001; Wilmore 1983), African-initiated Pentecostal churches in Ireland have been forums for re-enacting or perpetuating particularistic ethnic and cultural signifiers. For example, the Christ Apostolic Church, one of the four churches covered by this study, had services in English and in Yoruba, a language spoken in the southwest of Nigeria where many of its members in Ireland come from. Although English is the official language in the four churches, there are songs in native languages and dialects on some occasions. Also, interpersonal interactions before and after church services are conducted mostly in native languages. Language, Ngugi wa Thiong'o (1993) contends, does not only facilitate communication and interaction but it is a repository and a transmitter of a people's culture. By offering African immigrants unique opportunities in a situation of exile to maintain regular and frequent contacts with their native languages, African-led Pentecostal churches have translated into institutions that enable these immigrants to retain, revive and rehearse aspects of their native cultures and ways of life.

The churches also provide other opportunities for the re-enactment of cultural or 'ethnic' signifiers and for the inter-generational transmission of cultural practices. Dress is one form of signifying culture or ethnicity. Most adults as well as children dress in native attires to church services, the only such opportunity in Irish society, apart from when they attend parties organised by fellow Africans or attend formal award ceremonies, to showcase this aspect of their cultural heritage. Fredrick Barth (1969:14) names 'dress' among the "overt signals" or "diacritical features" used by groups to showcase identity. Lori Peek (2005:219) similarly includes "religious dress" among the "important identity markers that help promote individual self-awareness and preserve group cohesion". By means of dress, "ethnic and national heritage is displayed and thus maintained". Like dress, food is also used by church members to delineate groupness and inter-relatedness. Children are served biscuits and beverages on Sundays and on special occasions. However, in the Christ Apostolic Church, a lady member sells 'jollof' rice and *moin moin*, baked beans prepared in the traditional African way, after the church service. Her food is bought by parents and their children, providing unique opportunities for re-enforcing particularistic eating or consumption choices and thus re-signifying group members' ethnicity.

The churches covered by this study frequently receive ministers from Africa. Although the main aim of these visits is evangelistic and pastoral, they often have the unintended consequences of re-enforcing ties with the native lands. In many cases, the sermons delivered by visiting ministers are suffused with examples or illustrations from the homelands, thereby re-focusing the attention of church members on these places. In other cases, visiting ministers make direct appeal to national or ethnic sentiments or loyalty. They tell church members that they are on a journey and that the expected and successful conclusion of the journey is a return to their lands of birth. Members are reminded that only 'foolish' sons and daughters forget their parents or land of birth.

Lastly, another major connection between the practices of these churches and the promotion of ethnic identity can be explained through what Chong (1998:265), in imitation of Max Weber (1965), has described as the 'sacralization' of ethnic/cultural values or clothing particular ethnic traits, values and practices with the aura of spirituality. In the case of Koreans in America, she notes that certain cultural traits and traditional values were legitimated as Christian values. Pentecostal African immigrants in Ireland have a similar tendency to equate what they call African moral values and the traditional respect for parents and the elderly with Christian values. Thus what is good and African is also Christian. This sort of sacralization or legitimation of cultural or traditional values and practices strengthens the attachment of African immigrants to them, as Kelly Chong also concludes in the case of Korean Americans. I now turn to discussing the connections between the substance of Pentecostalism and the social construction of reality.

FOR GOD AND IN HIS NAME

This section summarises and interprets Pentecostal African immigrants' specific understandings of self and 'others' and the complex and multiple ways they construct boundaries and differences. I want to argue that the experience of spiritual rebirth (born-again) is central to the analysis of the connections between Pentecostal beliefs and the construction of social realities by African immigrants. The subjective experience of spiritual rebirth marks both the beginning of a new and heightened consciousness of their relationship with God and the believer's admission into the core of the Pentecostal fold (see chapters four, seven and eight). The instantaneous (sometimes dramatic) experience of rebirth is articulated and sustained through individual devotion and social performances (prayers, songs, conducts, speech, general orientation etc) achieved through association with fellow Pentecostals mostly in group settings. Barth (1969:15) refers to these types of social performances as "continual expression and validation". As Weber (1978, 1965, 1930) argues in the case of the Calvinists in seventeenth century Europe, the heightened awareness of the believer's relationship with God translates into a new understanding of self, of 'others' and of society and social relations.

Other scholars (Bellah 1976; Berger 1973; Geertz 1966; Gilroy 2000; Peek 2005) have similarly acknowledged the transformative capacity of religious ideas or beliefs and their role in the social construction of reality. For example, Peek (2005: 219) concludes that "...religion remains an important organizing factor in the hierarchy of identities that compose the self". For Pentecostal African immigrants in Ireland, religious beliefs rooted in the experience of re-birth constitute the main basis for articulating a new self understanding, which has direct implications for a broad range of social actions, including the construction of difference, commonality, connectedness and groupness, as argued in chapter eight. The rest of this section will summarise participants' self-understanding, their understanding of 'others' and types/dimensions of the difference/boundaries they construct.

ALTERNATIVE/SUBVERSIVE CONCEPTION OF SELF

Pentecostalism provides African immigrants a basis for an empowering understanding of self that contrasts with and subverts their identification and conception by the 'others' in Irish society. The 'other' is used in this instance to refer to the larger Irish society. The self-understanding and self-articulation of African Pentecostals attenuates racial/national identity markers while emphasising their Pentecostal credentials, beliefs, activities and mission. In direct opposition to how they are perceived perception in media and popular discourses as economic sojourners and a minority group on the fringe of Irish society (see chapter three), Pentecostal African immigrants construct themselves as agents of religious and social change who have arrived in Ireland to preach the 'true' Christianity, restore Ireland's past religious glories and rescue the younger generations of Irish men and women who, according to their interpretation, have swapped the spirituality of their forefathers for a life of sexual immorality, drugs, alcohol and night-long revelries in pubs.

Similar to this finding, Paul Gilroy notes that Christianity, particularly the baptismal experience, gave the former slave, Olaudah Equiano, an alternative basis for re-imagining himself and his place in society. In the case of Pentecostal Jamaican groups in the United Kingdom, Nicole Rodriguez Toulis notes that beliefs offered members an alternative basis for articulating self: "Rather than define themselves as 'Black' in White society, church members identified themselves as model 'Christian' in an imperfect Christian society" (Toulis 1997:210).

COMMONALITY, CONNECTEDNESS AND GROUPNESS

According to Eisenstadt (1998), the major codes used in constructing collective identity include primordiality, civility, and transcendentalism or sacredness. Describing these codes as ideal types, Eisenstadt notes that real live application usually combines elements of the three. The relative importance of each code is situational. His notion is useful for understanding the ways Pentecostal African immigrants construct commonality, groupness and difference. As with self-conception, they rely less on national/ethnic and phenotypical markers and more on specific Pentecostal teachings on salvation/redemption and moral uprightness when articulating commonality, connectedness and groupness. They construct categorical distinctions or boundaries between the 'saved' and the 'unsaved' (the defining criteria being spiritual re-birth and active membership of a Pentecostal group) and construct commonality and connectedness on this basis. Michael Piore (1995) notes that narrowly-focused "communities of meaning" formed on the basis of distinctions are "incapable of cross-boundary exchange", while Michele Lamont's (1992) research on upper-middle class men in France and the United States concludes that the importance of boundary types varies across space and time. Her research also demonstrates that boundaries grounded in widely-held beliefs are stronger in generating hierarchies and in affirming collective identities. These notions are relevant to my analysis of the 'place' of African Pentecostal immigrants in Ireland and their participation in the larger society.

Whereas the concept of groupness always seems to apply to members' particular Pentecostal group and biological family, commonality and connectedness are constructed in multiple and complex ways. For example, the connections to mainline churches in Ireland does not always translate into closer spiritual or even social association despite the fact that some African-led Pentecostal groups have used the meeting halls of these churches for little or no fee. Although Pentecostal African immigrants construct the larger non-Pentecostal African communities as the 'others', they unintentionally but sometimes strategically articulate some connections and commonalities, especially when they discuss the larger social and political conditions of their voluntary or involuntary presence in Ireland. While portraying Pentecostalism as the major, or sometimes, the only definer of social reality, they occasionally appropriate racial and ethnic symbolisms to either articulate commonality/difference or to explain the discrimination and social isolation they encounter in the dominant society.

Generally, the multiple and complex boundaries they construct homogenise in order to essentialise sameness within distinct Pentecostal groups or the larger 'born-again' family. But boundaries are not enforced with equal severity. The degree to which a particular boundary is enforced depends on who the constitutive 'other' is. The boundaries that separate them from the larger African communities admit some connections, while differences are sometimes, even if unintentionally, weakly articulated. The differences and boundaries between them and the larger non born-again Irish society are constructed as binary opposites and they are strongly articulated and rigidly enforced, while those that set distinct African-led Pentecostal groups apart can sometimes be blurred and weak. The commonality and sameness they sometimes portray between themselves and Irish-led Pentecostal groups is tainted with ethnic and cultural bias. Their encounter with 'Irish' Pentecostal 'others' is as important for self-definition and entrenchment of boundaries as the encounter with non-Pentecostals generally.

The boundaries between Pentecostal African immigrants and the larger society allow for some connections and inter-relationships which, some Pentecostals argue, would facilitate their eventual integration into and more active participation in the larger Irish society. Before I assess this prospect based on specific theories of immigrant enclaves and ghettos, I want to conclude this section by reiterating the contribution of the findings of this research to ongoing sociological debates on primordialist and social constructionist views of identity. Earlier analyses of individual self-conception and group identity formation emphasised primordial or bio-logical traits over religious, social or political traits. While emphasising the central role played by language, customs, traditions and nationality in group identity and cohesion, analysts (e.g. Barth 1969; Geertz 1963; Isaacs 1975) tend to construct these features as 'natural' and static and the sources of irreconcilable differences between groups. In such analyses, group members are said to internalise group qualities and construct their sense of self on this basis.

However, recent studies (e.g. Gilroy 2000; Hall 2000; Woodward 2002) question essentialist interpretations of individual and collective identity, promoting instead post-modern interpretations of social constructionism, emphasising social agency and the interactional influences on self-conception and group identity. In their attempts to make up for what they consider the shortcomings of social constructionism, post-modern critiques emphasise variations within social categories, the role of power in the classification process and a recognition of the limits of discourse as a means of interpreting or articulating social realities (see Calhoun 1995; Connell 1987; Gilman 1985). For example, Stuart Hall (2002) rejects the notion of identities based on essentialist definitions of cultural and ethnic collectives in favour of cultural fluidity, hybridity and diaspora.

According to Paul Gilroy (2000: 111), the very idea of diaspora, "disrupts the fundamental power of territory to determine identity" and constitutes alternative ways of articulating an identity that does not essentialise primordial ties and roots. The web or networks resulting from diasporic formations, he argues, have made possible "new understandings of self, sameness, and solidarity". I contend, as have Gilroy (2000) and Toulis (1997), that Pentecostalism has offered African immigrants a new/additional basis for constructing understandings of self, sameness, solidarity and difference. The new basis emphasises Pentecostal credentials while de-emphasising race, nationality and immigrant status. The new understanding of self contradicts and subverts the dominant interpretation of African Pentecostals (and African immigrants in general), which emphasises race, nationality, immigrant status and social marginality.

ENCLAVES OF SOLIDARITY OR GHETTOS OF EXCLUSION?

The findings of this research indicate that African-led Pentecostal churches are socially and culturally on the fringes of Irish society despite the complex and multiple ways the members of these churches articulate their role and position. Dominant Irish society does not see these groups as belonging to it. Rather, they are conceived as the 'other', mainly in racial terms (for analyses of the modern Irish state as racial, see Lentin and Lentin 2006; Lentin and McVeigh 2006). In addition to the way they are perceived, the ideals, doctrines and practices of these churches locate them outside the dominant society, not in a physical sense but culturally and socially.

Moreover, the churches are populated mostly by sub-Saharan Africans whose routes to and reasons for membership include the desire for a 'deeper' relationship with God, the search for safety and succour in a difficult immigration environment and the quest for the companionship of co-ethnics. Given the high concentration of sub-Saharan Africans in these churches and the various functions (including the opportunities to re-live particularistic cultural traits and affirm loyalty to motherlands and co-ethnics) they fill in the lives of their members, I want to argue that these churches are comparable to economic enclaves and other institutions set up by immigrant groups in the United States at the beginning of the twentieth century. Sociological analyses (e.g. Thomas and Znaniecki 1974; Marcus 1997; Portes 1995; Portes and Bach 1985; Cutler and Glaeser 1997) acknowledge that immigrant institutions meet important needs and provide important services for new arrivals despite the controversy (see Schelling 1971; Kundnani 2002; Wirth 1938; Wellman 1979; Logan et al. 1996) over their long-term contribution to the immigrants' efforts to integrate into the larger society and to the maintenance of social unity and cohesion.

At the beginning of the nineteenth century, social scientists of the Chicago School used terms such as The Ghetto, Little Sicily, Greektown, and Chinatown (Burgess 1925: 47-62) to describe immigrant institutions and neighbourhoods that had become common in many cities in the United States. Conceptually, there have been attempts to differentiate immigrant enclaves from ghettos. From the emphasis on the immigrant business sector in the early stages of migration and of this debate, the term immigrant enclave is now used to designate all places where immigrants from a particular geographical region and who define themselves as members of one ethnic or religious group congregate with the aim of maximizing their economic, socio-cultural and political advantages (Marcuse, 1997: 242). Massey (1985) theorises immigrant enclaves as an aberration, a useful and practical way-station for the immigrants in their journey to become part of the larger American society. Massey's thesis, supported by Portes and Jensen (1987), states that a measure of segregation was natural as immigrant groups entered the United States, but that segregation is eventually overcome by the processes of individual socio-economic mobility and acculturation.

Ghetto is the other side of the immigrant neighbourhood. Whereas in contemporary usage the enclave connotes a positive meaning, denoting voluntary segregation, socio-economic mobility and acculturation, the term Ghetto connotes involuntary segregation, lack of socio-economic mobility and acculturation. Peter Marcuse's analysis depicts Ghetto as the result of the involuntary spatial segregation of a group or groups that are also in a subordinate relationship—politically and socially—with the dominant groups in a particular society (Marcuse 1997: 228). His views reflect those of Clark (1965) on black neighbourhoods in the United States, which he studied in the 1950s and 60s: "The dark ghettos are social, political, educational, and—above all—economic" (Clark, quoted in Marcuse, 1997: 235).

However, Richard Sennett (1992, also reported in Marcuse 1997) conferred some positive elements on the term Ghetto when he said it (the ghetto) could at once be a space of repression and a space of identification. Sennentt's view finds resonance in Clark's argument (1965) about the great "psychological safety" the ghetto provides against racism and discrimination by the majority society. Other studies (e.g. Bonacich 1973; Horton 1995; Zhou 1992; Zhou and Logan. 1991) reveal that immigrant groups can sometimes choose 'self-segregation' in order to symbolise and sustain a particular group identity. These debates inevitably lead to concerns about the future of African-led Pentecostal churches in twenty-first century Ireland: Are they foci of enclaves or of ghettos? Will they help or hinder the integration or participation of Africans in Irish dominant society?

In the case of second-generation Koreans in the United States, Chong (1998) contends that Korean Protestant churches could cease to be useful or relevant when "Korean

Americans are successful in achieving a sense of full assimilation". Similarly some participants in my research indicate that the 'mainstreaming' of African-led Pentecostal groups will happen when they are dominated and led by the second and subsequent generations. While acknowledging that this is an issue for future researchers, this view appears to be overly optimistic as it does not take into consideration Pentecostal ideologies of salvation, moral uprightness and spiritual re-birth.

Having already acknowledged that African members of these churches have constructed a socio-cultural and moral universe that is parallel to the one inhabited by Irish society, it is worth pointing out, as some participants note, that there are tangible interconnections between the two universes. Pentecostal African immigrants interact with the social, educational, economic and financial institutions of the dominant society. They live in neighbourhoods and some of them maintain social contacts with people from other social, racial and cultural groups. Some participants have argued that such interconnections will facilitate their fuller integration into Irish society. However, I contend that such integration into the mainstream society will be difficult to achieve unless the walls of boundaries and differences erected on both sides are dismantled. In the main body of this book I have identified various boundaries and identity markers constructed both by these churches and by Irish society. At the beginning of the twenty-first century it is difficult to be optimistic about the transformation of these boundaries, and of African-led Pentecostal groups becoming more fully involved in Irish society in the foreseeable future.

CONCLUSION

Employing a variety of investigative and analytical techniques, this pioneering research on Pentecostal African immigrants in twenty-first century Ireland has produced a nuanced analysis of the interconnections between beliefs and social action/orientation. It challenges the over-reliance on functionalism in interpreting immigrants' religious participation and demonstrates that a cogent and comprehensive explanation of such a complex and multifaceted phenomenon can be achieved only through a triangulation of theories and investigative techniques. My research complexifies concepts of belonging, boundaries and sameness/difference and furthers the debates on social construction of commonality and groupness. Concluding by discussing theories of immigrant enclaves/ghettos, this research has also highlighted the complexities of integration and the participation of Pentecostal African immigrants in Ireland.

POSTSCRIPT

BOUNDARIES, BELONGING AND ACCESS: REFLECTION ON THE RESEARCH PROCESS

This book is the outcome of a research process that lasted from 2001 to 2005. The bulk of the empirical investigation took place in the Greater Dublin Area. The process of establishing the research focus was long, challenging and, not unexpectedly, marked with a few false starts. Initially I had intended to compare and contrast the role of immigrant institutions in the settlement and integration of recent African immigrants in Ireland and Germany. I had chosen Germany because, like Ireland, the large-scale presence of African immigrants in that country is a relatively recent phenomenon. I had also lived in Germany for many years and I believed my knowledge of African communities in both countries would make access less problematic and enrich the research process. This initial idea and various versions of it were eventually abandoned, but not before exploratory investigations that included a week-long ethnographic work among African immigrants in Cologne, Germany. However, I became acutely aware of the pivotal role that religion plays in the lives of individual African immigrants and in inter-community relations following my visit to Germany and because of my experiential knowledge of African communities in Ireland, gained through formal and informal contacts with groups and individuals in the Greater Dublin Area since 1998. My interest and enthusiasm was, to a large extent, tinged with curiosity and worries about the implications of memberships of these churches for boundary construction and for the participation of African immigrants in Irish society.

I had arrived in Ireland from Germany in April 1998 (having emigrated from Nigeria in 1992) and enrolled for post-graduate studies in journalism later that year. While studying I published articles in *The Irish Times* and *The Irish Independent* on themes relating to Africa and African immigrants in Ireland. These articles marked the beginning of my involvement with individuals and groups in the African communities in Ireland. My interaction with the communities deepened and widened when I became the founding editor and one of the publishers of *Metro Eireann* (www.metroeireann.com), Ireland's multicultural newspaper. Eventually, I became a member of or served on the boards of several 'African' community groups, including the Africa Centre and the theatre company *Arambe*. Involvement in these projects further broadened and deepened my contacts in these communities.

After initial ethnographic observation of places of worship in the Greater Dublin Area and some informal discussions with African friends and acquaintances, I decided to focus on African-led Pentecostal churches, not only because they provide prominent evidence of African immigrants' religious participation, but also because they constitute a new and innovative intervention in Ireland's social and religious landscape. Another reason why I was attracted to this theme was my interest in the sociology of religion and my personal religious experiences as a member of a minority religious group. The decision to examine specific themes relating to identity and the construction of boundaries/difference emerged inductively, following repeated contacts with members of these groups and the analyses of preliminary semi-structured interviews and a focus group meeting. The focus group, which consisted only of church members who had taken part in the semi-structured interviews, provided new insights as it gave the participants the opportunity to articulate their beliefs and practices. During the meetings, the participants exchanged views and occasionally contradicted or challenged one another's interpretations. The meetings also brought me closer to the leadership of the various churches and helped to establish a working relationship between us.

Once I had established the focus of my research it quickly became clear that I would have to triangulate my investigative techniques in order to elicit the data I needed to answer the main questions, because "each practice makes the world visible in a different way" (Denzin and Lincoln 2003: 5). Thus I have triangulated four investigative techniques in order to elicit valid data that enabled me to both produce relevant background information about these churches and also explore issues of identity and difference. These techniques are ethnographic observation, unstructured in-depth interviews, analysis of print and audio materials and a quantitative survey. In addition, I also spent many informal hours of interactions, and conversation with those informants who had become my acquaintances and would visit me and my family at home with their family members. At other times, I (sometimes with my children) visited them in their homes and spent hours of 'informal chats' while my children played with theirs. We also had delicious and elaborate dinners prepared in that uniquely 'African' way at my home and at theirs.

After such visits or interactions, I would use the next convenient opportunity (usually immediately after the visit) to recall and document essential and relevant details or comments. No doubt some important details were lost as a result of the time lapse and the limitations of the human memory, but the real benefits of those informal interactions were not limited to what was said or remembered. Rather, it was the unspoken and the unique opportunities to observe my informants in as natural environment as could be, to have them converse and interact with me and with one another without any consciousness that they were being observed or documented. For example, I learnt much about Pentecostal teaching on fasting during one of these social interactions when on one of these visits to my house, Blessing politely declined a meal of Pounded Yam and Egusi that I had prepared, but her husband and two children tucked into it. I insisted on knowing the reasons for her refusal to eat. For a long time she said nothing except that she could not and would not eat. After I reminded her that it was discourteous and un-African to reject hospitality, she was compelled to say she could not eat for religious or spiritual reason. "Are you fasting", I asked pointedly. "Well, you are not supposed to tell people you're fasting," she responded, adding: "You know what the Bible says about the left hand not knowing what the right hand is doing." Thereafter, we entered into a long conversation on fasting and related issues. Discussions like these were the main features of our informal social meetings and they provided deeper and robust insights into the beliefs, experiences and perceptions of my informants and they have indeed enriched my accounts.

In the rest of this chapter I describe the research process and highlight the challenges involved in gaining access to participants and ethnographic sites. I also discuss my inter-action and relationship with the informants and my 'outsider within' status as an African investigating other Africans and a member of a 'minority' religion investigating another minority religion.

ACCESS TO PARTICIPANTS AND ETHNOGRAPHIC SITES

The CAC was the first group that I contacted because I had established connections with an official of the church before I began this research. In selecting the other churches I was guided both by the ease of access and my intention to concentrate on the largest, fastest-growing, most active and influential groups and, to a large extent, the four churches I have selected meet these criteria. My contacts with the Christ Apostolic Church started as far back as 2000 when I was still the editor of *Metro Eireann*. The church had, through one of its officials, placed advertisements in *Metro Eireann*, inform-ing the public about the venue, days and times of its weekly services. The official became my acquaintance and, later, one of my key informants. I had many preliminary discussions with him and the other church officials I met through him in the initial stages of fashioning this research project. In 2001, soon after I registered for a PhD, I conducted semi-structured interviews with him and five other members of his church, including the pastor. I also convened a focus group meeting of all the interviewees to discuss the results of the individual interviews. The outcomes of these preliminary interviews and the focus group were instrumental in defining the course and central questions of this research.

While I had conceived of these churches, in line with media and public discourses, solely as platforms where African immigrants seek to meet specific socio-cultural, practical and emotional needs, my initial interviews and interaction with CAC members revealed that deeper and more complex issues were involved. It became clear that Pentecostalism is not simply 'what they do' but, more fundamentally, 'what they are'. As a result of these initial discoveries, I decided to focus as much on what Pentecostalism makes members do as what it does for them. My preliminary findings made me realise, for the first time, that the beliefs/practices of these groups could be investigated using non-functionalist theoretical frameworks.

The majority of CAC members who participated both in the interviews and in the survey were recruited with the assistance of my key informant in the church. It thus became clear to me that I needed to cultivate a key informant in each of the four groups. My key informants were mostly officials or influential members who attended church services regularly and have a good insight into both beliefs and practices. Although the relationships we formed varied from one informant to the other, their role in my research was very similar. In the case of my key informant in the CAC, his role was sometimes limited to introducing me to fellow church members but at other times he arranged meetings between the interviewees and me. On one occasion, an after-service announcement about me and my mission was made to the entire congregation after my key informant interceded with his fellow officials. Thereafter, I experienced greater cooperation from church members in completing the questionnaires

I had prepared. My informant also played the role of a 'cultural interpreter', supplying detailed background information of specific church events and ceremonies (Richardson 1990, 1995; Van Mannen 1995; Walcott 1995). The insight I gained in the initial encounters with my key informant and other CAC members played a significant role in my decision to include more churches in my investigations.

It quickly became clear during our meetings and discussions that their life stories and the history of the CAC were connected in sociologically interesting ways to, at least, three other African-led Pentecostal churches in Ireland. Some of the connections were individual but others were institutional. For example, one of the informants had been a member of Redeem before he relocated to CAC, while another had worked in the same firm as the founder/pastor of the Gospel Faith Mission. I also discovered that the founders of two other African-led churches had been members of CAC before they seceded. These and other interconnections kindled my interest in the other churches and in the interrelationships among the churches. After I indicated that I would like to include Redeem in my study, my CAC key informant volunteered to link me directly with a senior Redeem pastor and he put a call through to the pastor while we were still conversing. I was able to talk to the pastor on my informant's mobile phone and we arranged a meeting. My key informant also provided information on how I could contact some members of the other churches.

'THE OUTSIDER WITHIN'

However, despite the generous assistance and guidance of my key informants and many other participants, access to individual interviewees was sometimes problematic for a number of reasons. My racial background, my membership of the 'African community' and phenotypical features did not always guarantee access to individual interviewees although it made access to ethnographic sites and observation/documentation less problematic. For example, I did not stand out in the midst of church members as would a researcher of a different colour or racial background. Consequently, my presence aroused little suspicion and caused minimum or no disruption of normal interaction among church members. Apart from our common racial background, many participants felt a sense of oneness with me because of our common immigration experiences. They interpreted my research but especially the expected outcome—'Doctor of Philosophy'— as both a personal benefit to me and a source of prestige for the entire community. As one female key informant in Redeem said to me: "You're my brother. Your progress is my progress. And our progress is the progress of all Africans in Ireland". However, there were limits to this affinity or commonality. At other times in the ethnographic process my 'outsider' status, defined mainly but not solely by my non-Pentecostal status, proved problematic. I will return to this point shortly.

During observation and documentation, my writing material and audio equipment did not constitute a distraction because church members often bring their own writing and recording equipment. Many church members take notes during meetings or sermons. It is also not uncommon for others to take photographs or use audio and video recording machines. My presence and documentation activities did not therefore strike church members as unusual. As far as the majority of church members were concerned I was no more than a worshipper bent on jotting down every word from the pastor's mouth. Although Denzin and Lincoln (2003: 49) argue that "the effect of the observer's presence can never be erased," I believe that my presence in ethnographic sites in the course this research caused little or no disruption for the reasons I have mentioned. I therefore do not believe that the majority of participants "assumed situational identities that may not be socially and culturally normative," as Denzin and Lincoln (2003:31) argue.

On the other hand, my privileged access and insight into the activities of these groups made me the 'outsider within' which, according to Patricia Hill Collins (1991), possesses "a special standpoint" that enables him or her to produce "distinctive analyses". Collins notes that the distinctive stand-point of the 'outsider within' derives from the encounter with the "paradigmatic thought of a more powerful insider community". She argues that African-American women intellectuals developed distinctive analyses of race, culture and feminism because their unique platform provided them "with the benefits of white male insiderism" while repudiating its "taken-for-granted assumptions" (Collins 1991: 53). Her notion of the 'outsider within' and Du Bois's (1996) idea of 'double consciousness' resonate with Georg Simmel's (1921) conceptualisation of 'the stranger'. In describing the peculiar composition of the stranger as simultaneously near and remote, concerned and indifferent, Simmel states that the 'stranger' has the ability to see patterns that may be more difficult for those immersed in the situation or completely removed from it to see. Du Bois and bell hook (hook 1984, quoted in Collins 1991) focus on the double worlds of the African-American, which they both argue, have imparted on them a keener insight into issues of race and belonging. Du Bois (1996:5) refers to the distinctive and keener insight of the African-American as 'second-sight' while bell hook calls it looking "both from the outside in and from the inside out" (hooks 1984, in Collins 1991:36).

Applying the concepts of marginality and double vision to sociological inquiries, Collins (1991: 36) notes that, "'marginality' has been an excitement to creativity". She further states: "As outsider within, black feminist scholars may be one of many distinct groups of marginal intellectuals whose standpoints promise to enrich contemporary sociological discourse. Bringing this group—as well as others who share an outsider within status vis-à-vis sociology—into the centre of analysis may reveal aspects of reality obscured by more orthodox approaches" (p.36). In a similar way I believe the unique relationship I have cultivated with Pentecostal African immigrants and the privileged access this has afforded me have enabled me to produced a distinctive analysis of the interrelationship between their beliefs/practices and social action. However, my 'outsider within' status was counter-balanced by my 'outsider' status at some stages in the ethnographic process, as I now explain.

'THE OUTSIDER'

Many encounters or interactions with individual informants highlighted the complexities of belonging and emphasised my problematic 'outsider' status. The main criterion that defined my outsider status was my non born-again and non-Pentecostal status as this pre-interview discussion between a male informant (and MFM member) and me illustrates:

Abel: *As I explained on the phone, I'm researching Pentecostal African immigrants in Ireland. I suppose we can begin the interview by hearing about your religious background, how you became a born-again Christian and a Pentecostal*

Informant: *Are you born-again yourself?*

Abel: *If you don't mind I would rather keep my personal religious convictions out of this at this stage. I'm quite happy to talk about it when we've finished with the interview...*

Informant: (cuts in) *No, no, no, you've come to introduce your research to me; I want to introduce my Christ to you. So, are you born-again?*

Abel: *I really don't want this meeting to be overshadowed by my personal religious history...I never shy away from discussing my own conviction; it's just that I'm here as a researcher and I would rather discuss my research first and my faith...*

Informant: (cuts in again) *Look, Christ died for you and for me. I'm under obligation to proclaim this message and warn of the consequences of lack of faith. This is my opportunity to proclaim it to you. Have you received Christ into your life? Are you born again?*

Abel: (I realised that I wasn't going to win) *I'm a Christian. Born again? It depends on what you mean by it.*

Informant: *Born-again is a biblical term. It doesn't have two meanings. It is clearly stated—to be born-again is to be washed in the blood of Jesus, to repent of your sin, to give your life completely to God, be filled with the Holy Spirit and...*

After he ended his explanation I told him about my religious convictions and briefly explained the reasons for them. He acknowledged them but he made clear that I was in need of salvation and spiritual light and that spiritual re-birth was the only answer. Thereafter we proceeded to the interview. For the most part he cooperated and we had an exhaustive discussion of his own spiritual journeys, Pentecostalism and Pentecostal African immigrants in Ireland. However, there was no doubt that our initial exchanges affected and reversed the power relations and the dynamics of our conversation. I had arrived at his office as an 'important' researcher from a respected Irish university, but our initial exchanges punctured this image by exposing my 'lamentable' spiritual state, according to his definition of spirituality. The interview was no longer just about explaining his background and beliefs but also about educating and convincing me, given the passion and conviction with which he spoke.

Another informant, a female pastor (and a lawyer) in Redeem, waited till after our interview to pose similar questions:

> Informant: *Are you born-again?*
> Abel: *I'm a Christian.*
> Informant: *That's what I thought when I saw your name. But are you born-again, spirit-filled and heaven-bound?*
> Abel: *I think a lot depends on what you mean by born-again?*
> Informant: *I've just explained it. Have you repented of your sins and given your life to Christ? You see, it's not enough to be a Christian. The Bible says, 'you must be saved'. That is what the Bible says, not me. Are you convinced in your heart that you're saved? Which church do you go to?*
> (I told her about my religious affiliations)
> Informant: *Hallelujah! Thank God for that but church membership will not save you. You remember what I said, before I became born-again I was very churchy, I attended church services regularly and they even called me 'sister'. But church does not save. Christ saves. You must receive him into your heart, he died for you...*

Again, the roles and power relations were reversed in the exchanges above. My informant did most of the questioning and I struggled to supply answers. Buoyed by her passion and convictions (but also by the presence of two subordinates), she imparted knowledge about spirituality and salvation and she consistently sought to expose my 'hollow' spiritual state, according to her own definition of spirituality. We remained acquaintances since this encounter and she became one of my key informants and distributed questionnaires on my behalf.

Most encounters with individual interviewees had similar elements to the two I have reproduced above. Although they re-emphasised and reminded me of my 'outsider' status, they contributed to robust discussions and outcomes. Most interviewees felt a need to proselytise or defend their faith the moment they interpreted our encounter not just as a meeting between a researcher and a respondent but also a clash between divergent religious views. They tended to be more prolific and nuanced in their analysis when they were impassioned and they almost always were when they felt a need to proselytise or defend their faith.

The other markers of my outsider status included my relatively settled immigration status and my membership of an elite Irish university. A few participants addressed me as 'Dr' or 'Prof' although they knew I was still to complete my doctoral programme. This could be interpreted as a sign of respect but it could also have been their way of indicating that this was their heart's desire for me. I had not only been living in Ireland longer than many of them but I had also been post-nuptially naturalised. Many of the participants had precarious immigration status as asylum seekers or parents of Irish children still waiting for valid residence permits. I was sometimes compelled to discuss my own residence or immigration status in response to direct enquiries by some participants. On one occasion, after I told a male informant (in response to his questions) that I did not need a visa to enter the United Kingdom because I travel with an Irish passport, he responded: "Ah, I thought we were the same. You've no problems. You're an Irishman". Remarks like this re-articulated boundaries and differences that I had wrongly believed were not there, and they complexified concepts of sameness and belonging.

DATA COLLECTION

In-depth interviews

Most of my interviews took place in multiple sessions and they lasted for at least two hours on each occasion. They were tape-recorded. In these encounters with the informants, I was primarily interested in *what* they believe and *what* they do and *their* interpretations of the connections between beliefs and social action/self conception. However, I did not initiate the conversations by asking these specific questions but rather by asking about their Christian or Pentecostal background. My commonest opening sentence was: When and how did you become a Pentecostal? Most informants responded by narrating theirs as well as their family's religious background and activities. Although they inevitably touch on the *why* in the process of tackling the *how*, I used probes which sometimes included long silences, inquiring stares or vigorous and rapid nods to elicit detailed and specific explanations relating to self conception and the construction of identity and difference.

As Denzin and Lincoln (2003: 64) note: "Each interview context is one of interaction and relation; the result is as much a product of this social dynamic as it is a product of accurate accounts and replies." While careful not to present the impression of challenging their accounts or their interpretation of the Bible, I was determined to elicit complete, coherent and relevant accounts that touch on the central questions of my investigation. This was particularly the case where the informant knew about my own religious conviction. I did not want them to interpret our meetings as a clash of competing religious views. That would have easily led to a breakdown of communication, interaction, trust and rapport. I was not necessarily interested in why the informant had accepted a particular interpretation of the scriptures but rather in the implications of that interpretation for self conception and social action. The enterprise of ascertaining the validity or otherwise of beliefs, in my view, falls outside the remit of sociology. Where I suspected that my probe or request for detailed explanation could be interpreted as casting doubts on their narration, I would rephrase the question using different terms. But in the majority of cases, I would simply note down the issue in my field notebook, let the interchange continue uninterrupted, and then revisit it after about half an hour or so. For the majority of respondents, including those who became Pentecostal much later in their lives, the story of their Pentecostal journey equates to the story of their entire life. Their Pentecostal journeys make sense mostly in relation to their pre-rebirth non-Pentecostal experiences.

According to Denzin and Lincoln (2003: 48), the interview is not a neutral tool but "a negotiated text" and a site "where power, gender, race, and class intersect". Because two or more people are involved in a specific interview situation, they argue that "the interview produces situated understandings grounded in specific interactional episodes", and that the outcome is influenced by "the personal characteristics of the interviewer, including race, class, ethnicity, and gender." Racial or ethnic factors did not pose major challenges in my interactions with the informants. As I have explained earlier, they made interaction easier while serving as markers of my 'outsider within' status. Although my membership of an Irish elite university became a definer of my 'outsider' status, it did not appear to have mattered much in the interactional interview moments because the themes of the interviews were those that informants felt very comfortable with and they often assumed the superior 'expert' position, as my earlier illustrations demonstrate.

Fontana and Frey (2003) suggest that a feminist interviewing ethic transforms the relationship between the informant and the researcher into a relationship between co-equals and the exchanges are carried on in a conversational manner. I tried to achieve this aim mostly by allowing the informants to control the pace, but not necessarily the direction of the interview. I also endeavoured to show that I was interested in their well-being and their struggles to survive in a new immigration environment. I made an effort to give the impression that I would still be interested in them even if they were not participants in my research. Sometimes, this could mean hours of listening to 'personal' troubles, and at other times, it meant offering advice in connection with specific immigration problems or writing a job reference or a letter of support to the Department of Justice.

Some church members who had agreed to do inter-views with me failed to live up to their promises. They were either preoccupied with other commitments or were simply not motivated enough. Appointments with some pastors or church leaders were rescheduled many times as many of them appeared to spend the bulk of their time attending to 'emergencies' or 'urgent matters'. Church members who were directly affected by the changes and uncertainties of Ireland's immigration and citizenship laws were too upset and unset-tled to honour interview commitments. A few informants repeatedly made and cancelled appointments with me. It also became obvious that some members could either not appre-ciate the intellectual rationale for this research or did not agree with it. In a few cases, apathy bordering on disrespect marked the reaction of some church members to my invita-tions or entreaties. I was often asked the reasons or purpose for my investigations. I was sometimes asked to name the beneficiaries. Some of those who demanded such explana-tions did so out of suspicion and mistrust. Others simply did not want to spend time on a project that they believed had no direct or immediate benefit to their groups or that could even damage their reputation.

However, patience and caution on my part yielded good results in such circumstances. I was always prepared to painstakingly explain the purpose of my research and why I believe it would help, rather than harm them. I often told informants that their groups were among the foremost socio-cultural African-led institutions in Ireland and that my aim was to highlight this development and to document the role of their groups' beliefs/membership and the way members negotiated identity and difference. This sort of explanation was often followed by the question: 'How does it benefit us?' In some cases I explained the likely political and social capital that could accrue to them when the State and the public recognise their pivotal position in the African communities. At other times I told them that my research would inscribe and document the important role their institutions have played in the formation of African communities in Ireland for future generations.

Interpretation of interviews

Once I had transcribed the interviews I realised almost immediately that I had too much material for the size of the project that I envisaged. The vast majority of my participants were passionate and articulate narrators who were willing not only to share their stories but to do so extensively. Even though I had originally set out to hear narrations of their Pentecostal beliefs and journeys and to measure them against theories of identity, what I got in many cases were rich narratives of life stories, articulately constructed and reflecting on self and 'other'. Most narratives demonstrate the connections between ideals or beliefs and the individual orientation to social action. They also highlight particularistic interpretations and application of beliefs. The quantity and the quality of data were swelled because these multiple themes were woven into many of the narratives and, in some cases, they constituted the essence of the narratives. I had to make a selection from the 18 narratives in order to achieve the depth of analysis necessary to address my research themes and also to make my data manageable. I selected two narratives based on methodological and intellectual considerations and because they are robust and rich enough to form a solid basis for theorising identity and belonging in relation to Pentecostal African immigrants. As Walcott (1995:86) notes, "the rationale for capturing and reporting details in ethnographic presentation is not to recount events as such, but to render a theory of cultural behaviour."

Having read the interview transcripts many times over, it also became clear that despite their diversity, the narratives were connected by similar interpretations of Pentecostalism that mostly emphasised its transformative capacity and role which often manifested in social action and conduct. Although each narration is anchored in the unique position of the narrator as parent, church leader, successful professional, asylum seeker or single mother, there were striking similarities in their interpretations of the relationships between Pentecostalism and social action and between religious beliefs and self-conception. Concerning the female informants in her study, Laurel Richardson (1990: 30) similarly notes: "...because the individual stories of the single women were similarly contoured, I began to think of these women as a social category...the particulars of the stories were different, and there were different subplots, but the main thematic was the same."

Although I agree with Richardson's view, as demonstrated by my reliance on two main narratives in the analysis of identity and difference in chapter eight, I do not believe that the narrations I have chosen as key stories typify the experiences of the other informants. For this reason I have used the views of the other respondents to interrupt, contest, disrupt and problematise the two key narratives. Using the key narratives to represent the experiences of all informants would contradict my proposition that identity and group experiences are not only heterogeneous but also internally contested and complex. As Finlay (2004 : 232) equally notes, "culture can no longer be understood simply as the way of life of a group or a people; rather it is better understood as symbolic practice, a contested process through which we attach meaning to our lives and our world"—also see Clifford and Marcus (1986).

In *Sun Chief*, published in 1942, Simmons (reported in Langness and Frank 1995: 64) suggests that individuals are creatures and carriers of the mores of their groups. Therefore, life narratives provide "a level of continuity in behaviour that is more fundamental than either biological, environmental, societal, or cultural determinants, being in fact a synthesis of all four". David Aberle (1951, reported in Langness and Frank 1995: 64-65) who later undertook a psychological analysis of *Sun Chief*, concludes that life history offered a suitable means of investigating "the complex relationship of motivations and actions to norms and beliefs". The subject of Aberle's life history was Don Talayesva, a member of the Hopi society. He felt that by examining Talayesva's interpretation of and reaction to the problems he faced, an insight into the lives of all Hopi and the Hopi society could be gained without suggesting that Talayesva was a typical Hopi or that his life course was typical. Aberle's summation suggests that although the life course of individual members of a cultural or religious group is not the same, it is possible to gain insight into group norms, orientation and motivations by examining the lives of key members. This notion harmonises with the concept of synecdoche enunciated by Laurel Richardson (1990). Describing synecdoche as "a rhetorical device through which a part comes to stand for the whole, such as an individual for a class", Richardson (1990: 17-18) argues that "social science reasoning, generally—indeed science reasoning—is based on synecdoche, because we are usually studying parts, examples, experiments, or samples which we intend to represent a whole."

I have chosen one narrative by a male and another by a female to reflect gender differences in the informants' narratives. The other reasons I have chosen the two narratives are their richness, the differences and similarities in the migration history and status of the narrators and the differences in the histories of their Pentecostal groups. Whereas my male informant came to Ireland to seek political asylum, my female informant did not. The Pentecostal group of the female informant has its headquarters in Nigeria and it has 'sister' churches in Ireland and other parts of Europe. The group that the male informant belongs to was founded by him and four other Africans in Ireland and it was still at the early stages of establishing contacts with African-led Pentecostal groups in the United Kingdom and in Africa.

Structuring the narratives

Denzin and Lincoln (2003: 37) note that the presentation and interpretation of data "is both artistic and political" while Richardson (1990: 9) states that writers can use literal and rhetorical structures to create "a particular view of reality." I have therefore approached the presentation of my interview data fully aware that I am engaged in a theoretical, moral, political and methodological exercise or challenge. Roth (1989, quoted in Richardson 1995:215) is pessimistic about the prospects of surmounting this challenge: "there is no principled resolution, no alternative, to the problem of speaking for others." Richardson (1990: 12) similarly notes: "No textual staging is ever innocent...It is unavoidable. When we write social science, we are using our authority and privileges to tell about the people we study. No matter how we stage the text, we—as authors—are doing the staging." The conventions of the social sciences can be additional obstacles for, as Richardson (1990: 12) notes, they "hold tremendous material and symbolic power over social scientists." With these criticisms at the back of my mind, I have endeavoured to highlight the narrative structure and tone of the informants by making their voices prominent, strong, true and respected.

The narrative tone, according to Richardson (1990: 39), offers writers a unique opportunity to reduce "their authority over writing for others" and consequently amplify their own "credibility as writers of interpretive social science." The tone of a narrative is measured, among other things, by the "organization of material, how a quotation or a person's experience is framed and treated by the narrator, what and how much the narrator lets who say..." I have endeavoured to make my informants' voices prominent and strong but I have neither obliterated my presence nor abdicated my position/authority as author/writer. As Wolf (1992: 130) notes, "the ethnographer should be decentred in terms of the authority of voice, but at the same time should be front and centre in the text so that the reader is constantly aware of how biased, incomplete and selective the materials being presented are".

To erase my presence would also suggest an attachment to "ethnographic realism" and create the false notion that nothing is standing between my informants and the reader (Kirshenblatt-Gimblett 1989; Marcus and Cushman 1982), when I have, in fact, played a pivotal role in originating, structuring and interpreting the research. The structure of my data also speaks to and critiques the view that personal narrative accounts are transparent and objective or that they "speak for themselves" (Behar 1990). As Minh-ha (1991: 13) reminds us, "…the story and its telling are always adaptive. A narration is never a passive reflection of a reality." Silverman (2003) states that interview texts are produced and used in social contexts. To simply content-analyse interview texts is to disregard the interpretive process involved in its production. According to Behar (1990: 225), narratives should be structured in a way that reveals "the subjective mapping of experience, the working out of a culture and a social system that is often obscured in a typified account."

I have endeavoured to achieve this by using 'lead-ins' and 'lead-outs' to frame the actual words or quotations of my informants. The reader is therefore both able to 'hear' for themselves the voices of my informants and read my interpretation, contestation or 'reminders'. While the participants' voices bring the reader back to the informants' actual experiences and interpretations of those experiences, my 'lead-ins' and 'lead-outs' supply the wider contexts both for interpreting those experiences and for making them sociologically relevant and interesting. Through this dialogic exchange I have successfully de-centred my voice and compromised my own authority as the final arbiter while increasing the presence and power of my informants. Although Atkinson and Silverman (1997) debunk the idea of "polyphonic voices", saying that collaborations between the interviewer and the informant produce a monologic view of reality, I am convinced that my dialogic approach has enhanced my credibility as an interpretive analyst. Framing or, as Richardson (1990: 40) calls it, 'embedding' the narratives has served a second major purpose of preparing the reader for changes in themes or in the direction of the narratives. I have used long quotations and extensive biographical details both to enhance the presence and power of my informants but such framing also enhances the understanding of the complex sociological issues that are at the centre of the narratives.

Survey

I conducted the survey in order to elicit pre-determined (De Vaus 1991) basic socio-demographic information on the membership of the churches because I could not obtain such information from reliable secondary sources, including the churches themselves. The absence of a sampling frame meant that I could not adopt the random sampling technique to select the participants (De Vaus 1991). Participation was therefore mostly voluntary, although I aimed to have most social categories (gender, age, officials, non-officials, married, single etc) represented. I made many trips to places of worship to administer the questionnaires. My key informants solicited the cooperation of fellow church members and participated in handing out and recovering the questionnaires. Some pastors or church officials made announcements to the entire congregation, requesting members to complete the question-naires. A few church leaders completed the questionnaire in the presence of the congregation both to encourage members to complete them and to disabuse their minds of any suspi-cion. Out of a total of 300 questionnaires I distributed, 144 (or 48%) were completed and returned.

Visits to ethnographic sites

My visits to ethnographic sites began in 2001 and lasted till 2004 with month long breaks in between. My aim was to observe every kind of public meeting and also attend group or committee meetings, where permission was given. While my presence at large public gatherings was hardly notice-able, it was definitely intrusive in small group situations. As Denzin and Lincoln (2003: 49) note, "interactive observers are by definition intrusive." They also argue that objective observers and observations do not really exist because "any gaze is always filtered through the lenses of language, gender, social class, race, and ethnicity." They therefore conclude that all observations are "socially situated in the worlds of—and between—the observer and the observed" (2003: 31). I have no doubt that I was able to overcome many of these limitations because of the common background contexts that I share with my informants.

Lofland (1995) makes a connection between ethnographic observations and interviews, saying that the data gathered in the field often come through or are enhanced by informal interviews. This observation reflects my own experiences. However, I want to suggest a dialectical flow of influences rather than the cause and effect structure suggested by Lofland. While ethnographic data were enhanced by on-site interviews, the interview themes were most times based on the feedback from ethnographic observations in my case.

Note-taking was a major feature of my ethnographic activities. The nature and volume of notes depended on circumstances and themes. There were some occasions, as I have already explained, when I could not take notes during the events but had to engage in a post-event recollection and documentation. I often had to re-write and structure my hurriedly scribbled notes at the first opportunity after I had left the ethnographic site. Sometimes, I recorded events in a chronological order, especially if I was observing a service or group meeting for the first time. At other times, it was a real challenge to document the various activities that were taking place simultaneously. Normally, I would arrive at the venue of a meeting or church service well ahead of the official starting time. In that case, I had enough time to describe and document the setting, including the seating arrangements, furniture and pre-meeting activities. It also afforded me the opportunity to talk to the early arrivals about their expectations and nature of involvement in the programme. My notes usually included details about members' dress code, the dominant medium of conversation, the themes of pre-meeting interactions, the order of meetings, the names and ranks of participants and the degree of the pastor's involvement. Data from ethnographic observations have enriched every part of this book but especially my analyses of the histories and activities of the groups, their membership, administration and identity/difference.

Secondary documents

Sources of secondary data include church pamphlets, in-house magazines, church programmes, invitation leaflets, posters that advertise special programmes and audio tapes of pastors' sermons. These materials were collected over a period of three years, beginning 2002. On a few occasions they formed the basis of formal and informal interaction with the informants. In analysing invitation leaflets and posters, I paid particular attention to the circumstances of their production, the use of pictures and the concept of self which was projected through them. For example, some churches take particular care to include people of different racial backgrounds in posters/leaflets meant to advertise their presence and activities in order to signify a universal or inclusive attitude. They also use 'universal' images like the opened pages of the Bible or the image of a dove which, they say, implies peace. At other times, the faces of prominent African Pentecostal leaders are splashed across these posters/leaflets but only if such leaders are participating in the programmes being advertised. The faces on posters often reflect contentment, happiness and joy. Some posters specifically invite people to come and receive the solutions to their problems, including all sorts of illness. It was interesting to compare the self portrayal of these churches as indicated in their own media and their portrayal in the secular national Irish mass media. The data I gathered from printed material, including Redeem's in-house magazine, has enhanced my analyses of the history, activities, membership and administration of these churches. I also transcribed some sermons, read the transcribed texts many times and extracted themes relevant to my analysis of identity and difference.

CONCLUSION

Laurel Richardson (1995:198) names informants' oral accounts, in-depth interviews, case studies and ethnographic observations as some of the techniques of qualitative research. In this chapter I have demonstrated how and why I have applied these and other techniques. Despite their limitations, including well-founded concerns about their neutrality, I believe that these techniques succeeded in providing unique insights into church members' interpretations of beliefs and social experiences. My research has progressed inductively, fashioned and re-fashioned by my experiences with informants and my encounters in ethnographic sites. It can therefore be concluded that my informants have unwittingly taught me how to research them without limiting my inquisitiveness and experimentations.

This book focuses on a particular socio-cultural group in a defined geographic area and under specific socio-political and historical circumstances. I have approached the data gathering both as an 'outsider' and an 'outsider within'. I therefore have no intention of denying the implications of my circumstances and location for objectivity and partiality. However, Richardson (1990: 28) reminds us that partiality and subjectivity "are not the research and writing disadvantages that positivist empiricism proposes." She further argues that there is no objectivity in social analyses because all perspectives are situated. As she puts it: "There is no view from 'nowhere', the authorless text. There is no view from 'everywhere,' except God. There is only a view from 'somewhere,' an embodied, historically and culturally situated speaker." This is a situated analysis rendered from a particular viewpoint.

BIBLIOGRAPHY

Aberle, David, F. 1951. The Psychosocial Analysis of a Hopi Life-History. *Comparative Psychology Monograph*, Vol. 21, No. 1.

Achebe, Chinua.1983. *The Trouble with Nigeria*, London: Heinemann.

Olukushi, Adebayo. 1993 (ed.) *The Politics of Structural Adjustment in Nigeria*. Portsmouth, N.H.: Heinemann.

Adedeji, Adebayo, Teriba, Owodunni and Bugembe, Patrick. 1991. *The Challenge of African Economic Recovery and Development*. London: Cass.

Adogame, Afe. 2000. The Quest for Space in the Global Spiritual Marketplace: African Religions in Europe. *International Review of Mission*, Vol. LXXXIX; No. 354; pp. 400 – 409.

_____.2003. Betwixt Identity and Security: African New Religious Movement and the Politics of Religious Networking in Europe. *Nova Religio:* Vol 7, Issue 2; 24-41.

African Refugee Network. 1999. *African Refugees Needs Analysis*. Dublin: ARN.

Ake, Claude. 1996. *Democracy and Development in Africa*. Washington, D.C.: Brookings Institution.

Ammerman, Nancy. 1997. Rational Choice Theory and Religious Vitality. In L. Young (ed.) *Rational Choice Theory and Religion: Summary and Assessment.* New York: Routledge; 119-132.

Amnesty International. 2001. *Racism in Ireland: The Views of Black and Ethnic Minorities.* A Report by FAQs Research for Amnesty International. Dublin: Amnesty International.

Anderson, Allan. 1999. Introduction: World Pentecostalism at a Crossroads. In Anderson and Hollenweger (eds.) *Pentecostals after a Century: Global Perspectives on a Movement in Transition.* Sheffield: Sheffield Academic Press.

_____.2000. *Evangelicalism and the Growth of Pentecostalism in Africa.* (http://artsweb.bham.ac.uk/aanderson/Publications - accessed Dec.)

Anderson, Allan H and Hollenweger, Walter J. 1999. (eds.) *Pentecostals after a Century: Global Perspectives on a Movement in Transition.* Sheffield: Sheffield Academic.

Atkinson, Paul and Silverman, David. 1997. Kundera's Immorality: The Interview Society and the Invention of Self. *Qualitative Inquiry*, 3: 304-325.

Bade Klaus, J. 2003. *Migration in European History.* Malden, MA: Oxford: Blackwell Publishing.

Barret, David, Kurian George and Johnson Todd. 1982. *World Christian Encyclopaedia.* Nairobi, Oxford: Oxford University Press.

Barrett, David B and Johnson, Todd M. 1999. Annual Statistical Table on Global Mission. *International Bulletin of Missionary Research* 23 (January): 24-25.

Barron, B. 1987. *The Health and Wealth Gospel.* Downers Grove, Ill.: InterVarsity Press.

Barth, Frederick. 1969. (ed.) *Ethnic Groups and Boundaries: The Social Organisation of Culture Difference.* London: George Allen & Unwin.

Baumann, Martin. 1998. Sustaining "Little Indias": Hindu Diasporas in Europe. In Gerrie ter Haar (ed.) *Strangers and Sojourners: Religious Communities in the Diaspora.* Leuven: Peeters; pp. 95-132.

_____.1995. Conceptualizing Diaspora: The Preservation of Religious Identity in Foreign Parts, exemplified by Hindu Communities outside India. *Temenos* 31: 19-35.

Bauman, Zygmunt. 2000. *Liquid Modernity.* Cambridge: Polity Press.

_____.2004. *Identity: Conversations with Benedetto Vecchi.* Cambridge Polity Press.

Becher, Virginia. 1995. *Black Christians. Black Church Traditions in Britain*: A resource pack produced jointly by the Centre for Black and White Christian Partnership and Westhill RE Centre, Birmingham: Sellyoak Colleges.

Bellah, Robert N. 1976. *Beyond Belief: Essays on Religion in a Post-traditional World.* New York & London: Harper and Row.

Behar, Ruth. 1990. Rage and Redemption: Reading the Life Story of a Mexican Marketing Woman. *Feminist Studies*, Vol. 16; pp. 223-258.

Berger, Peter L. 1967. *The Sacred Canopy.* Garden City, New York: Doubleday.

_____.1973. *The Social Reality of Religion.* Harmondsworth: Penguin.

_____.1974. 'Modern Identity: Crisis and Continuity'. In Wilton S. Dillion (ed.) *The Cultural Drama: Modern Identities and Social Ferment.* Washington: D.C.: Smithsonian Institute Press; pp. 159-81.

Berger, Peter L and Luckmann Thomas. 1967. *The Social Construction of Reality: A Treatise in the Sociology of Knowledge*. London: Allen Lane.

Bhardwaj, Surinder M and Madhusudana Rao. 1990. Asian Indians in the United States: A Geographic Appraisal. In C. Clarke, C. Peach and S. Vertovec (eds.) *South Asians Overseas: Migration and Ethnicity*. Cambridge: Cambridge University Press; pp. 197-217.

Birnbaum, Norman. 1973. Beyond Marx in the Sociology of Religion? In Charles Y. Glock and Phillip E. Hammond (eds.) *Beyond the Classics? Essays in the Scientific Study of Religion*. New York; London: Harper and Row; pp. 3-70.

Blasi, Peter J. 1998. Functionalism. In *Encyclopaedia of Religion and Society*, William H Swatos Jr. (ed.) Walnut Creek, California: Alta Mira. pp. 193-97.

Bodnar, John. 1985. *The Transplanted: History of Immigrants in Urban America*. Bloomington: Indiana University Press.

Bonacich, Edna. 1973. A Theory of Middleman Minorities. *American Sociological Review* 38:583 - 594.

Bourdieu, Pierre. 1990. *The Logic of Practice*. Stanford: Stanford University Press.

Brouwer, Steve, Gifford Paul and Rose, Susan D. 1996. *Exporting the American Gospel: Global Christian Fundamentalism*. New York; London: Routledge.

Brubaker, Rogers. 2004. *Ethnicity Without Groups*. London & Cambridge, Mass.: Harvard University Press.

Bruce, Steve. 1993. Religion and Rational Choice: A Critique of Economic Explanations of Religious Behaviour. *Sociology of Religion* 54: 193 – 205.

_____.1999. *Choice and Religion: A Critique of Rational Choice Theory*. New York: Oxford University Press.

Burgess, Ernest W. 1925. The Growth of the City: An Introduction to a Research Project. In Robert E. Park, Ernest W. Burgess, and R. D. McKenzie (eds.) *The City: Suggestions for Investigation of Human Behaviour in the Urban Environment*. Chicago: University of Chicago Press; pp. 47 – 62.

Burgess, Stanley and McGee, Gary (eds.) 1988. *Dictionary of Pentecostal and Charismatic Movements*. Grand Rapids, MI: Zonderman.

Calhoun, Craig. 1991. The Problem of Identity in Collective Action. In Joan Huber (ed.) *Macro-Micro Linkages in Sociology*. Newbury Park, California: Sage Publications; pp. 51-75.

_____.1995. *Critical Social Theory: Culture, History, and the Challenge of Difference*. Oxford, UK: Blackwell.

Calley, Malcolm J. 1965. *God's People: West Indian Pentecostal Sects in England.* Oxford: Oxford University Press. (Issued under the auspices of the Institute of Race Relations).

Carling, Jørgen. 2005. *Trafficking in Women from Nigeria to Europe.* (www.migrationinformation.org/Feature).

Central Statistics Office. 2003. *Population and Migration Estimates* April 2003. Dublin: CSO.

Chaves, Mark. 1995. On Rational Choice Approach to Religion. *Journal for the Scientific Study of Religion,* Vol. 36; pp. 574 – 83.

Chong, Kelly H. 1998. What It Means to Be Christian: The Role of Religion in the Construction of Ethnic Identity and Boundary among Second-Generation Korean Americans. *Sociology of Religion,* Vol. 59; 259 – 286.

Christian History. 1998. *The Rise of Pentecostalism.* Issue 58, Vol. XVII No. 2.

Christiano J. Kevin, Swatos, William H Jr. and Kivisto, Peter. 2002. *Sociology of Religion: Contemporary Developments.* Walnut Creek, Lanham, New York and Oxford: Altamira Press.

Clarke, K. 1965. *Dark Ghetto: Dilemmas of Social Power.* New York: Harper & Row.

Clarke, Colin, Ceri Peach and Steven Vertovec .1990. Introduction: themes in the study of the South Asian diaspora. In C. Clarke, C. Peach and S. Vertovec (eds.) *South Asians Overseas: Migration and Ethnicity.* Cambridge: Cambridge University Press; pp. 1-29.

Clifford, John and Marcus, George. 1986. *Writing Culture: The Poetics and Politics of Ethnography.* Berkeley; London: University of California Press.

Coleman, Simon. 2004. The Charismatic Gift. *Journal of the Royal Anthropological Institute,* Vol. 10, Issue 2; pp. 421 – 442.

Collins, Patricia Hill. 1991. Learning from the Outside Within: The Sociological Significance of Black Feminist Thought. In Mary Margaret Fonow and Judith A. Cook (eds.) *Beyond Methodology: Feminist Scholarship as Lived Research.* Bloomington and Indianapolis: Indiana University Press; pp. 35 -59

Collinson, Sarah. 1993. *Europe and International Migration.* London: Pinter for Royal Institute of International Affairs.

Connell Robert W. 1987. *Gender and Power: Society, the Person, and Gender Politics.* Cambridge: Polity Press.

Corten, André. 1999. *Pentecostalism in Brazil: Emotion of the Poor and Theological Romanticism.* Basingstoke: Macmillan.

Corten, André and Marshall-Fratani, Ruth. 2001 (eds.) *Between Babel and Pentecost: Transnational Pentecostalism in Africa and Latin America.* London: Hurst and Company.

Bibliography

Cox, Harvey. 1996. *Fire from Heaven: The Rise of Pentecostal Spirituality and the Reshaping of Religion in the Twenty-first Century.* London: Cassell.

Cox, James L. 2003. The African Christianity Project and the Emergence of a Self-Reflexive Institutional Identity. In Gerrie ter Haar and John Cox (eds.) *Uniquely African? African Christian Identity from Cultural and Historical Perspectives.* Trenton, NJ: Africa World Press. pp. 215-40.

CSO. 2002. *Census Results*: www.cso.ie/census.

_____.2006. *Census Results*. www.cso.ie/census.

Cullen, Paul. 2000. *Refugees and Asylum Seekers in Ireland.* Cork: University Press.

Cutler, David M and Glaeser, Edward L. 1997. Are Ghettos Good or Bad? *Quarterly Journal of Economics* 112 (3), 827–872.

Dahya, Badr. 1974. The Nature of Pakistani Ethnicity in Industrial Cities in Britain. In A. Cohen (ed.) *Urban Ethnicity.* London: Tavistock; pp. 77-118.

Dempster, Murray W, Klaus, Byron D and Petersen, Douglas. 1999. (eds.) *The Globalization of Pentecostalism: A Religion Made to Travel.* Oxford: Regnum.

Denzin, Norman K and Lincoln, Yvonna S. 2003. Introduction. In Norman K Denzin and Yvonna S. Lincoln (eds.) *Collecting and Interpreting Qualitative Materials.* London; New Delhi: Sage Publications.

DTEE. 2003. Tánaiste Announces Changes to the Work Permit Scheme. *Press Release,* Dec. 04.

_____.2006. Work Permits Statistics by Nationality. www.entemp.ie (visited website in May).

De Vaus, David A. 1991. *Surveys in Social Research.* London: UCL Press.

DFID 2001. *The Causes of Conflict in Sub-Saharan Africa: Framework Document/Department for International Development.* London: DFID.

Dublisch, J. and. Michalowski, R.1987. Blessed Are the Rich: The New Gospel of Wealth in Contemporary Evangelism. In M. Fishwick and R. Browne (eds.) *The God Pumpers: Religion in the Electronic Age.* Bowling Green, OH: Bowling Green State University Popular Press: pp. 33-45.

DuBois, William Edward. B. 1996. *The Souls of Black Folk.* New York; London: Penguin Book.

Durkheim, Emile. 1965 [1912] *The Elementary Form of Religious Life.* New York: Free Press.

Ebaugh, Helen. R, Jennifer O'Brien and Janet Saltzman Chafetz. 2000. The Social Ecology of Residential Pattern and Memberships in

Immigrant Churches. *Journal for the Scientific Study of Religion* 39(1): 107-116.

Ekué, Amele Admavi-Aho. 1998. How Can I Sing the Lord's Song in a Strange Land? In Gerrie ter Haar (ed.) *Strangers and Sojourners: Religious Communities in the Diaspora*. Leuven: Peeters; 221 -234.

Eisenstadt, Shmuel N. 1998. Modernity and the Construction of Collective Identities. *International Journal of Comparative Sociology*, Vol. 39, no.1, 138-158.

Ellison, Christopher G and Sherkat, Darren E. 1995. The 'Semi-Involuntary Institution' Revisited: Regional Variations in Church Participation among Black Americans. *Social Forces* 73: 1415-37.

Essed, Philomena. 1991. *Understanding Everyday Racism: An Interdisciplinary Study*. London: Sage Publications.

Faist, Thomas. 2000. *The Volume and Dynamics of International Migration and Transnational Social Spaces*. Oxford: Oxford University Press.

Fanning, Brian, Mutwarasibo, Fidéle and Chedamoyo, Nelta. 2003. *Positive Politics: Participation of Immigrants and Ethnic Minorities in the Electoral Process*. Dublin: Africa Solidarity Centre.

_____.2004. *Negative Politics, Positive Vision: Participation of Immigrants and Ethnic Minorities in the 2004 Local Elections*. Dublin: African Solidarity Centre.

Findley, Sally E. 2001. Compelled to Move: The Rise of Forced Migration in Sub-Saharan Africa. In Saddique M.A.B (ed.) *International Migration into the Twenty-first Century*. Cheltenham, Edward Elgar Publishing Limited. pp. 50 – 73.

Finlay, Andrew (ed.) 2004. *Nationalism and Multiculturalism Irish Identity, Citizenship and the Peace Process*. Muster: LIT verlag.

Finnegan, Ruth. 1992. *Oral Traditions and the Verbal Arts*. London: Routledge.

FLAC, 2003. *Direct Discrimination? An Analysis of the Scheme of Direct Provision in Ireland*. Dublin: Free Legal Advice Centres.

Fontana, Andrea and Frey, John H. 2003. The Interview: From Structured Questions to Negotiated Text. In Norman K Denzin and Yvonna S. Lincoln (eds.) *Collecting and Interpreting Qualitative Materials*. London & New Delhi: Sage Publications.

Frazier, Edward F. 1964. *The Negro Church in America*. New York: Schocken Books.

Freston, Paul. 1997. Charismatic Evangelicals in Latin America: Mission and Politics on the Frontiers of Protestant Growth. In Stephen Hunt, Malcolm Hamilton and Tony Walter (eds.) *Charismatic Christianity: Sociological Perspectives*. London: Macmillan Press.

Galush, William. J. 1977. Faith and Fatherland: Dimensions of Polish-American Ethno-religion. In R. Miller and T. D. Marzik (eds.)

Immigrants and Religion in Urban America. Philadelphia, PA: Temple University Press.

Gans, Herbert J. 1994. Symbolic Ethnicity and Symbolic Religiosity: Towards a Comparison of Ethnic and Religious Acculturation. *Ethnic and Racial Studies 17:*577-592.

Geertz, Clifford. 1963. The Integrative Revolution: Primordial Sentiments and Civil Politics in New States. In Clifford Geertz (ed.) *Old Societies and New States: The Quest for Modernity in Asia and Africa.* New York: Free Press of Glencoe: 105-157.

_____.1966. Religion as a Cultural System. In M. Banton (ed.) *Anthropological Approaches to the Study of Religion.* ASA Monographs No 3. London: Tavistock.

Gerlach, Luther and Hine Virginia. 1968. Five Factors Crucial to the Growth and Spread of a Modern Religious Movement. *Journal for the Scientific Study of Religion; pp.* 7:23-40.

_____.1970. *People, Power and Change: Movements of Social Transformation.* Indianapolis, IND: Bobbs-Merrill.

Gerloff, Roswith. 1992. *A Plea for British Black Theologies: The Black Church Movement in Britain in its Transatlantic Cultural and Theological Interaction.* (2 vols.) Frankfurt a.M: Peter Lang.

_____.1999. Pentecostals in the African Diaspora. In Allan Anderson and Walter Hollenweger (eds.) *Pentecostals after a Century: Global Perspectives on a Movement in Transition.* Sheffield: Sheffield Academic Press.

Gifford, Paul. 2004. *Ghana's New Christianity: Pentecostalism in a Globalising African Economy.* London: Hurst & Co.

_____.1992. (ed.) *Dimensions in African Christianity.* Nairobi: All Africa Conference of Churches; pp. 236-44.

Gilman Sander L. 1985. *Difference and Pathology: Stereotypes of Sexuality, Race, and Madness.* Ithaca, NY: Cornell Univ. Press.

Gilroy, Paul. 2000. *Between Camps.* London: Penguin Books.

Glasner, Peter E. 1977. *The Sociology of Secularisation: A Critique of a Concept.* London: Routledge and Kegan Paul.

Glazer, Nathan and Moynihan Daniel P. 1963. *Beyond the Melting Pot: The Negroes, Puerto Ricans, Jews, Italians and Irish of New York City.* Harvard, Ma: M.I.T. Press.

Glock, Charles Y. 1964. The Role of Deprivation in the Origin and Evolution of Religious Groups. In Robert Lee and Martin E. Marty (eds.) *Religion and Social Conflict.* New York: Oxford University Press.

Glock, Charles Y and Stark, Rodney. 1965. *Religion and Society in Tension.* Chicago: Rand-McNally.

Goffman, Erving. 1975. *The Presentation of Self in Everyday Life.* Harmondsworth: Penguin.

Goldstone, Katrina. 2002. Christianity, Conversion and the Tricky Business of Names: Images of Jews and Blacks in the Nationalist Irish Catholic Discourse. In Ronit Lentin and Robbie McVeigh (eds.) *Racism and Anti-Racism in Ireland*. Belfast: BTP Publications Ltd.

Gordon, Milton M. 1964. *Assimilation in American Life: The Role of Race, Religion and National Origins*. New York: Oxford University Press.

Guerin, Patrick. 2002. Racism and the Media in Ireland: Setting the Anti-immigration Agenda. In Ronit Lentin and Robbie McVeigh (eds.) *Racism and Anti-racism in Ireland*. Belfast: Beyond the Pale Publications ltd. pp. 91 – 101.

Hackett, Rosalind. 1987. *New Religious Movements in Nigeria*. Lewiston: The Edwin Mullen Press.

Hall, Stuart. 1996. Who Needs Identity? In Stuart Hall and Paul du Gay (eds.) *Questions of Cultural Identity*. London: Sage Publications.

Hamilton, Malcom. 2001. *The Sociology of Religion: Theoretical and Comparative Perspectives*. London: Routledge.

Handlin, Oscar. 1951. *The Uprooted: The Epic Story of the Great Migrations that Made the American People*. Boston: Little Brown.

Hannon, Michele, 2003. *Enterprise Supports, Training and Start-up Assistance for Ethnic Minority Entrepreneurs*. Dublin: Terenure Enterprise Centre.

Harrison, Graham. 2002. *Issues in the Contemporary Politics of Sub-Saharan Africa: The Dynamics of Struggle and Resistance*. Basingstoke: Palgrave Macmillan.

Herberg, Will. 1955. *Protestant-Catholic-Jew: An Essay in American Religious Sociology*. Garden City, NY: Doubleday.

Hill, Clifford. 1971a. *Black Churches: West Indian and African Sects in Britain*. London: British Council of Churches, Community and Race Relations Unit.

_____.1971b. From Church to Sect: West Indian Sect Development in Britain. *Journal for the Scientific Study of Religion*, 10, pp. 114-23.

_____.1971c. Pentecostal Growth - Result of Racialism? *Race Today*, 3 (3), pp. 187-90.

Hollenwenger, Walter J. 1976. *The Pentecostals*. London: SCM Press.

_____.1973. *New Wine in Old Wineskins: Protestant and Catholic Neo-Pentecostalism*. Gloucester: Fellowship Press.

_____.1999. The Black Roots of Pentecostalism. In Allan Anderson and Walter Hollenweger (eds.) *Pentecostals after a Century: Global Perspectives on a Movement in Transition*. Sheffield: Sheffield Academic Press.

Hollinger, D. 1989. Enjoying God Forever: An Historical Profile of the Health and Wealth Gospel in the USA. In P. Gee & J. Fulton (eds.) *Religion and Power: Decline and Growth*. BSA, Sociology of Religion Study Group: London, pp.147-63.

hooks, bell. 1984. *From Margin to Centre*. Boston: South End Press.

Horton, John. 1995. *The Politics of Diversity: Immigration, Resistance, and Change in Monterey Park, California*. Philadelphia: Temple University Press.

Hunt, Stephen. 2002a. Neither Here nor There: The Construction of Identities and Boundary Maintenance of West African Pentecostals. *Sociology*: Vol. 36 (1); pp. 147-169.

_____.2002b. Deprivation and Western Pentecostalism Revisited: The Case of 'Classical' Pentecostalism. *PentecoStudies*, vol. 1, nr. 1.

_____.2002c. Deprivation and Western Pentecostalism Revisited: Neo-Pentecostalism. *PentecoStudies*, vol. 1, nr. 2.

Hunt, Stephen, Hamilton, Malcolm and Walter, Tony. 1997a. Introduction: Tongues, Toronto and the Millennium. In Stephen Hunt, Malcolm Hamilton and Tony Walter (eds.) *Charismatic Christianity: Sociological Perspectives*. London: Macmillan Press Ltd. pp. 1 – 16.

_____.1997b (eds.) *Charismatic Christianity: Sociological Perspectives*. London: Macmillan Press Ltd. pp. 1 – 16.

Hunt, Stephen and Lightly, Nicola. 2001. The British black Pentecostal 'revival': Identity and belief in the new Nigerian churches. *Ethnic and Racial Studies*. Vol. 24 No. 1; pp. 104–124.

ICC, 2003. *Research Project into Aspects of the Religious Life of Refugees, Asylum Seekers and Immigrants in the Republic of Ireland* (part of Churches Together in England project). Belfast: Irish Council of Churches.

Ifekwunigwe, Jayne O. 1999. *Scattered Belongings: Cultural Paradoxes of Race, Nation and Gender*. London: Routledge.

Inglis, Tom. 1998. *Moral Monopoly: The Rise and Fall of the Catholic Church in Modern Ireland*. Dublin: University College Dublin Press.

Ingoldsby, Brian. 2002. *Regular Migration to Ireland*, a paper delivered at the Incorporated Law Society Seminar: Rights to Reside in Ireland on 14 May 2002 at Blackhall Place, Dublin.

Integrating Ireland. 2005. *International Students and Professionals in Ireland: An Analysis of Access to Higher Education and Recognition of Professional Qualifications*. Dublin: Integrating Ireland.

Isaacs, Harold Robert. 1975. Basic Group Identity: The Idols of the Tribe. In Nathan. Glazer and Daniel Moynihan (eds.) *Ethnicity*. Cambridge, MA: Harvard University Press; pp. 29-52

Johns, Jackie David. 1999. Yielding to the Spirit: The Dynamics of a Pentecostal Model of Praxis. In M.W. Dempster, B.D. Klaus, and D. Petersen (eds.) *The Globalization of Pentecostalism*. Carlisle, CA: Regnum Books (with Paternoster Publishing).

Johns, Cheryl Bridges. 1993. *Pentecostal Formation: A Pedagogy among the Oppressed*. Sheffield: Sheffield Academic Press.

Jumare, Ibrahim. 1997. The Displacement of the Nigerian Academic Community. *The Journal of Asian and African Studies*, 32, pp. 110-19.

Kabbaj, Omar. 2003. *The Challenge of African Development*. Oxford and New York: Oxford University Press.

Kalilombe, Patrick. 1997. Black Christianity in Britain. *Ethnic and Racial Studies* 20 (2), pp. 308 – 15.

_____.1998. Black Christianity in Britain. In Gerrie ter Haar (ed.) *Strangers and Sojourners: Religious Communities in the Diaspora*. Leuven: Peeters; pp. 173-193

Kalu, Ogbu U. 1998. The Third Response: Pentecostalism and the Recon- struction of Christian Experience in Africa, 1970-1995. *Journal of African Christian Thought*, 1:2, 3.

_____.2003. Globecalisation and Religion: The Pentecostal Model in Contemporary Africa. In Gerrie ter Haar and John Cox (eds.) *Uniquely African? African Christian Identity from Cultural and His- torical Perspectives*. Trenton, NJ: Africa World Press. pp. 215-40.

Keogh, Dermot. 1998. *Jews in Twentieth-Century Ireland: Refugees, Anti- Semitism and the Holocaust*. Cork: Cork University Press.

Kirby, Peadar, Gibbons, Luke and Cronin, Michael. 2002 (eds.) *Rein- venting Ireland: Culture and the Celtic Tiger*. London: Pluto.

Kirshenblatt-Gimblett, Barbara. 1989. Authoring Lives. *Journal of Folk- lore Research*, Vol. 26: 123 -149.

Kolm, Richard. 1971. Ethnicity in Society and Community. In Otto Feinstein (ed.) *Ethnic Groups in the City*. Massachusetts, London and Toronto: Heath Lexington Books.

Koser, Khalid. 2003. New African Diasporas: An Introduction. In Khalid Koser (ed.) *New African Diasporas*. London and New York: Rout- ledge.

Kundnani, Arun. 2002. *Asians do Mix, say researchers*. Institute of Race Relations: www.irr.org.uk/2002/december/ak000008.html (visited Dec. 2003).

Kurien, Prema. 1998. Becoming American by Becoming Hindu: Indian Americans take their place at the Multicultural Table. In R.S. Warner and J.G. Wittner (eds.) *Gatherings in Diaspora: Religious Communities and the New Immigration*. Philadelphia: Temple Uni- versity Press; pp. 37-70.

Lamont, Michele. 1992. *Money, Morals, and Manners: The Culture of the French and American Upper-middle Class*. Chicago, IL: University of Chicago Press.

Langness, Lewis. L and Frank, Gelya. 1981. *Lives: An Anthropological approach to Biography*. Novato, California: Chandler and Sharp.

Bibliography

Larbi, Kingsley. E. 2001. *The Eddies of Ghanaian Christianity.* Accra: Centre for Pentecostal and Charismatic Studies (CPCS).

Lentin, Ronit. 2001. Responding to the Racialisation of Irishness: Disavowed Multiculturalism and its Discontents. *Sociological Research Online,* 5/4, http://www.socresonline.org.uk/5/4/lentin.html.

Lentin, Ronit and Lentin, Alana. 2006. (eds.) *Race and State.* Newcastle: Cambridge Scholars Press.

Lentin, Ronit and McVeigh, Robbie. 2006. *After Optimism? Ireland, Racism and Globalisation.* Dublin: Metro Eireann Publications.

Lewins, Frank William. 1978. Australia: Religion and Ethnic Identity. In H. Mol (ed.) *Identity and Religion.* Beverly Hills, CA: Sage Publications, pp. 19-38.

Lofland, John. 1995. *Analyzing Social Settings: A Guide to Qualitative Observation and Analysis.* Belmont, Calif. & London: Wadsworth.

Logan, C. 1975. Controversial Aspects of the Movement. In: Malcolm Hamilton (ed.) *The Charismatic Movement,* Grand Rapids, MG: Eeerdmans. pp. 102-45.

Logan, John R., Richard D. Alba, and Shu-Yin Leung. 1996. Minority Access to White Suburbs: A Multi-Region Comparison. *Social Forces* 74: 851-82.

Logan, John R, Richard D. Alba, Michael Dill and Min Zhou. 2000. Ethnic Segmentation in the American Metropolis: Increasing Divergence in Economic Incorporation, 1980-1990. *International Migration Review* 34:98-132.

Logan, Penny. 1988. *Practising Hinduism: The experience of Gujarati Adults and Children in Britain.* Unpublished report, Thomas Coram Research Unit, University of London Institute of Education.

Lucas, Henry. S. 1955. *Netherlanders in America: Dutch Immigration to the United States and Canada, 1789-1950.* Ann Arbor: University of Michigan Press.

Luckman, Thomas. 1967. *The Invisible Religion: The Problem of Religion in Modern Society.* New York: Macmillian.

Mac Éinrí, Piaras. 2001. Immigration Policy in Ireland. In Farrell and Watt (eds.) *Responding to Racism in Ireland.* Dublin: Veritas Publications; pp. 46-87

_____.2000. *Immigration into Ireland: Trends, Policy Responses, Outlook.* Cork: ICMS: www.migration.ucc.ie/irelandfirstreport.htm.

MacRobert Iain, 1988. *The Black Roots and White Racism of Early Pentecostalism in the USA.* Basingstoke: Macmillan.

McRobert, L.1989. The New Black-Led Pentecostal Church in Britain. In P. Badman (ed.), *Religion, State and Society in Modern Britain,* Lampeter: Edwin Mellen.

Malinowski, Bronislaw. 1974. *Magic, Science and Religion, and other Essays.* London: Souvenir Press.

Marcus, George E and Dick Cushman. 1982. Ethnographies as Texts. *Annual Review of Anthropology*, 11:25-69.

Marcuse, Peter. 1997. The Enclave, the Citadel, and the Ghetto: What Has Changed in the Post-Fordist U.S. City? *Urban Affairs Review.* Vol. 33, No 2 :228-64.

Marren, Patrick, 2001. Causes of International Migration. In Whelan, Thomas R. 2001 (ed.) *The Strangers in our Midst: Refugees in Ireland: Causes, Experiences, Responses.* Dublin. Kimmage Mission Institute of Theology and Cultures.

Marshall, Gordon. 1982. *In Search of the Spirit of Capitalism: An Essay on Max Weber's Protestant Ethic Thesis.* London: Hutchinson.

Marshall, Ruth. 1993. 'Power in the Name of Jesus': Transformation and Pentecostalism in Western Nigeria 'Revisited'. In Terence Ranger and Olufemi Vaughan (eds.) *Legitimacy and the State in Twentieth-Century Africa: Essays in Honour of A.H.M. Kirk-Greene.* Basingstoke: Macmillan in association with St. Antony's College, Oxford.

Marshall-Fratani, Ruth. 1998. Mediating the Global and Local in Nigerian Pentecostalism. *The Journal of Religion in Africa* XXVIII 3.

Martin, David. 2002. *Pentecostalism: The World their Parish.* Oxford: Blackwell.

_____.1978. *A General Theory of Secularization.* Oxford: Blackwell.

Martin, Susan F. 2001. *Global Migration Trends and Asylum.* Journal of Humanitarian Assistance: http://www.jha.ac/articles/u041.htm.

Massey, Douglas. 1985. Ethnic Residential Segregation: A Theoretical Synthesis and Empirical Review. *Sociology and Social Research* 69: 315-50.

_____.1994. Economic Development and International Migration in Comparative Perspective. *Population and Development Review.* 14: 383 – 413.

McCarthy, Patricia and Rafferty, Michael. 2002. Ethnicity, Class and Culture in Dublin. *Studies.* Vol. 94, Number 364: 338 – 364.

McKeon, Barbara. 1997. Africans in Ireland in the Eighteenth Century. *African Expression,* No. 4 Autumn.

McVeigh, Robbie. 2002. Is there an Irish Anti-racism? Building an Anti-racist Ireland. In Ronit Lentin and Robbie McVeigh (eds.) *Racism and Anti-Racism in Ireland.* Belfast: BTP Publications; pp. 211-225.

_____.1992. The Specificity of Irish Racism, *Race and Class,* 33/4.

Mead, George. 1934. *Mind, Self and Society from the Standpoint of a Social Behaviorist.* Chicago: The University of Chicago Press.

Mella, Orlando. 1994. *Religion in the Life of Refugees and Immigrants.* Stockholm: Centre for Research in International Migration and Ethnicity (CEIFO).

Metcalf, Barbara. 1996. Introduction: Sacred Words, Sanctioned Practice, New Communities. In B. Metcalf (ed.), *Making Muslim Space in North America and Europe*. Berkeley: University of California Press; pp. 1-27

Minh-ha, Trinh T. 1989. *Women, Native, Other: Writing Postcoloniality and Feminism*. Bloomington, Indiana: Indiana University Press.

Mitchell, Clare. 2005. Behind the Ethnic Marker: Religion and Social Identification in Northern Ireland. *Sociology of Religion*, Vol. 66; No. 1; pp. 3-21

Morris, Brian. 1987. *Anthropological Studies of Religion: An Introductory Text*. Cambridge: Cambridge University Press.

Mutwarasibo, Fidéle. 2002. African Communities in Ireland. *Studies:* An Irish Quarterly Review; Vol. 91, No. 364, pp. 348 – 358.

Norman, Edward R. 2003. *Secularisation*. London: Continuum.

Nwajiuba, Chinedum. 2005. International Migration and Livelihoods in South-eastern Nigeria. *Global Migration Perspectives*, No. 50; published by Global Commission on International Migration; Geneva, Switzerland.

Ojo, Matthew. 1998a. The Contextual Significance of the Charismatic Movements in Independent Nigeria. *Africa*. Vol. 58 (2), pp. 23-27.

_____.1988b. Deeper Life Christian Ministry: A Case Study of the Charismatic Movement in Western Nigeria. *Journal of Religion in Africa*, 18 (2), pp. 17-28.

Olupona, Jacob K. 1991 (ed.) *African Religions in Contemporary Society*. New York: Paragon Press.

ORAC, 2006. Monthly Asylum Statistics, published by the Office of the Refugees Application Commissioner. www.orac.ie/Pages/Statistics. htm (May).

Parry, Tony. 1993. *Black-Led Churches in West Yorkshire*, Leeds: CANA.

Parsons, Talcott. 1968. *The Structure of Social Action: A Study in Social Theory with Special Reference to a Group of Recent European Writers*. New York: Free Press; London: Collier-Macmillan.

Peek, Lori. 2005. Becoming Muslim: The Development of a Religious Identity. *Sociology*, Vol. 66, No. 3 pp. 215 – 242.

Piore Michael J. 1995. *Beyond Individualism*. Cambridge, MA: Harvard Univ. Press.

Poloma, Margaret. 1982. *The Charismatic Movement: Is There a New Pentecost?* Boston, Mass: Twayne Publishers.

_____.2000. *The Spirit Bade Me Go: Pentecostalism and Global Religion*. Paper prepared for presentation at the Association for the Sociology of Religion Annual Meetings, August 11-13, Washington DC.

_____.2001. The Pentecostal Movement. In Stephen Hunt (ed.) *Christian Millenarianism: From the Early Church to Waco*. London: Hurst.

Portes, Alejandro. 1995. *The Economic Sociology of Immigration: Essays on Networks, Ethnicity and Entrepreneurship*. New York: Russell Sage Foundation.

Portes, Alejandro and Bach, Robert, L. 1985. *Latin Journey: Cuban and Mexican Immigrants in the United States*. Berkeley & London: University of California Press.

Portes, Alejandro and Leif Jensen. 1987. What's an Ethnic Enclave? The Case for Conceptual Clarity. *American Sociological Review* 52:768-771.

Pryce, Ken. 1979. *Endless Pressure: A Study of West Indian Life-Styles in Bristol*. Harmondsworth: Penguin.

Raboteau, Albert J. 2001. *Canaan land: A Religious History of African Americans*. Oxford: Oxford University Press.

_____.1978. *Slave Religion: The 'Invisible Institution' in the Antebellum South*. New York: Oxford University Press.

Radcliffe-Brown, Alfred R. 1952. *Structure and Function in Primitive Society: Essays and Addresses*. London: Cohen & West.

Ramdin, Ron. 1987. *The Making of the Black Working Class in Britain*. London: Gower.

Rasmussen, Hans Korno. 1996. *No Entry: Immigration policy in Europe*. Copenhagen: Copenhagen Business School Press.

Riccio, Bruno. 2003. More than a Trade Diaspora: Senegalese Transnational Experiences in Emilia-Romagna (Italy). In Khalid Koser (ed.) *New African Diasporas*. London and New York: Routledge.

Richardson, Laurel. 1995. Narrative and Sociology. In John Van Mannen (ed.) *Representation in Ethnography*. London, California and New Delhi: Sage.

_____.1990. *Writing Strategies: Reaching Diverse Audiences*. California, London & New Delhi: Sage.

Rolston, Bill and Shannon, Michael. 2002. *Encounters: How Racism Came to Ireland*. Belfast: Beyond the Pale Publications.

Roof, Wade Clark (ed.) 1993. *Religion in the Nineties*. Newbury Park, Calif: Sage Periodicals.

Roof, W. and Hodge, D. (1980), Church Involvement in America. *Review of Religious Research*, 21 (Supplement), pp. 405-26.

Roth, P. 1989. *How Narratives Explain*. Paper presented to the University of Iowa Faculty Rhetoric Seminar (POROI), Iowa City.

Rotte, Ralph and Volger, Michael, 1997. *Determinants of International Migration: Empirical Evidence for Migration from Developing*

Countries to Germany. London: Discussion Paper Series, No. 1920. Centre for Economic Policy Research.

Sanneh, Lamin. 1993. *Encountering the West: Christianity and the Global Cultural Process. The African Dimension.* London. Marshall Pickering.

Sanctuary 2005. *A bi-monthly newsletter on asylum, refugee and migrant matters from a religious perspective published by Refugee & Migrant Project of Irish Bishops' Conference.* Maynooth, Ireland. January, No. 33.

_____.2006. January, No 36.

Sassen, Saskia. 1988. *The Mobility of Labour and Capital: A Study in International Investment and Labour Flow.* Cambridge: Cambridge University Press.

_____.1998b. *Globalisation and its Discontents.* New York: New Press.

Schelling, Thomas. 1971. Dynamic Models of Segregation. *Journal of Mathematical Sociology* 1:143-86.

Sennett, Richard. 1992. *The Origins of the Modern Ghetto.* Paper presented at Arden House Urban Forum on Place and Right. Harriman, NY. April.

Sherkat, Darren, E. 1997. Embedding Religious Choices: Integrating Preferences and Social Constraints into Rational Choice Theories of Religious Behaviour. In Lawrence A. Young (ed.) *Rational Choice Theory and Religion: Summary and Assessment.* New York: Routledge; pp. 65-86.

Silverman, David. 2003. Analyzing Talk and Text. In Norman K Denzin and Yvonna S. Lincoln (eds.) *Collecting and Interpreting Qualitative Materials.* London; New Delhi: Sage Publications.

Simmel, Georg. 1921. The Sociological Significance of the Stranger. In Robert E. Park and Ernest Burgess (eds.) *Introduction to the Science of Sociology.* Chicago: University of Chicago Press.

Simmons, Leo W. 1942. *Sun Chief. The Autobiography of a Hopi Indian.* New Haven: Yale University Press.

Smith, Suzanne and Mutwarasibo, Fidéle. 2000. *Africans in Ireland: Developing Communities.* Dublin: African Cultural Project.

Smith, T. L. 1978. Religion and Ethnicity in America. *America Historical Review,* 83: 1155 – 1185.

Spiller, Keith. 2002. *'Little Africa': Parnell Street, Food and Afro-Irish Identity.* (www.ucc.ie/ucc/depts/geography/stafhome/denis/spiller. htm - visited Dec).

Stark, Rodney and Bainbridge William Sims. 1996 [1978]. *A theory of Religion.* New Brunswick, New Jersey: Rutgers University Press.

Styan, David. 2003. La Nouvelle Vague? Recent Francophone African Settlement in London. In Khalid Koser (ed.) *New African Diasporas.* London and New York: Routledge.

Swatos William H Jr and Gustatson, Paul M.1992. Meaning, Continuity, and Change. In William Swatos (ed.) *Twentieth Century World Religious Movements in Neo-Weberian Perspective.* Lewiston, New York: Mellen.

Sweeney, Paul. 1998. *The Celtic Tiger: Ireland's Economic Miracle Explained.* Dublin: Oak Tree Press.

Ter Haar, Gerrie. 1994. Standing up for Jesus: A Survey of New Developments in Christianity in Ghana. *Exchange*, Vol. 23: 3, December.

_____.1998a. *Halfway to Paradise: African Christians in Europe.* Cardiff: Cardiff Academic Press.

_____.1998b. The African Diaspora in Europe: Some Important Themes and Issues. In Gerrie ter Haar (ed.) *Strangers and Sojourners: Religious Communities in the Diaspora.* Leuven: Peeters. pp. 37 – 58.

_____.1998c. African Christians in The Netherlands. In Gerrie ter Haar (ed.) *Strangers and Sojourners: Religious Communities in the Diaspora.* Leuven: Peeters; 153-171

_____.2003. Who Defines African Identity? A Concluding Analysis. In Gerrie ter Haar and James Cox (eds.) *Uniquely African? African Christian Identity from Cultural and Historical Perspectives.* Trenton, NJ: Africa World Press. pp. 215-40.

Thiong'o, Ngugi wa. 1993. *Moving the Centre: The Struggle for Cultural Freedoms.* London: John Currey Ltd.

Thomas, William and Florian Znaniecki. 1974 [1927]. *The Polish Peasant in Europe and America.* New York: Octagon Books.

Toulis, Nicole R. 1997. *Believing Identity: Pentecostalism and the Mediation of Jamaican Ethnicity and Gender in England.* Oxford: Berg.

Tróicare and the Irish Commission for Justice and Peace (ICJP). 2002. *Refugees and Asylum Seekers: A challenge to solidarity.* Dublin: Tróicare/ICJP.

Turner, Harold W. 1979. *Religious Innovations in Africa: Collected Essays on New Religious Movements.* Boston: G.K. Hall & Co.

Ugba, Abel. 2007a. Ireland. In Triandafyllidou and Gropas (eds.) *European Immigration: A Sourcebook.* Hampshire, UK, Burlington, US: Ashgate; pp. 169-183.

_____.2007b. African Pentecostals in Twenty-first century Ireland: Identity and Integration. In Fanning (ed.) *Immigration and Social Change in Ireland.* Manchester: Manchester University Press; 168-184.

_____.2006a. Between God and Ethnicity: Pentecostal African Immigrants in Twenty-first Century Ireland. *Irish Journal of Anthropology*, Vol. 9 (3), pp. 56 – 63.

_____.2006b. African Pentecostals in Twenty-first Century Ireland. *Studies*, Volume 95, No. 378, pp. 163-173.

_____.2005. Active Civic Participation of Immigrants in Ireland, a contribution to a project on *Immigrant Civic Participation in 25 EU Countries*: www.uni-oldenburg.de/politis-europe/download/Ireland.pdf (March 2005).

_____.2004. A Quantitative Profile Analysis of African Immigrants in Twenty-first Century Dublin. www.tcd.ie/Sociology/mphil/prelim-findings-2.pdf (Dec. 2004).

_____.2003a. From There to Here: An African view of Ireland and the Irish. *Asyland,* Magazine of the Irish Refugee Council: Spring 2003.

_____.2003b. African Churches in Ireland. *Asyland*, Magazine of the Irish Refugee Council: Autumn 2003; 10-11.

_____.2002. Mapping Minorities and their Media: The National Context – Ireland, a contribution to an EU project on *Diasporic Minorities and their Media in the EU* project: www.lse.ac.uk/Depts/Media/EMTEL/Minorities/reports.html.

UNHCR (United Nations High Commissioner for Refugees) 1997. *The State of the World's Refugees: In Search of Solutions.* Oxford: Oxford University Press.

United Nations. 1993. *The State of World Population, 1993.* New York: United Nations.

Van Mannen, John. 1995. An End to Innocence: The Ethnography of Ethnography. In John Van Mannen (ed.) *Representation in Ethnography*. London, California and New Delhi: Sage.

Vertovec, Steven. 2000. *Religion and Diaspora*, paper presented at the conference on 'New Landscapes of Religion in the West', School of Geography and the Environment, University of Oxford, 27-29 September 2000.

Wa Kabwe, Desire Kazadi and Segatti Aurelia. 2003. Paradoxical Expressions of a Return to the Homeland: Music and Literature among the Congolese (Zairian) Diaspora. In Khalid Koser (ed.) *New African Diasporas*. London and New York: Routledge.

Walcott, Harry F. 1995. Making a Study "More Ethnographic". In John Van Mannen (ed.) *Representation in Ethnography.* London, California and New Delhi: Sage.

Waldinger, Roger. 1993. The Ethnic Debate Revisited. *International Journal of Urban and Regional Research*. Vol. 17, No. 3: 444 – 452.

Wallis, Roy and Bruce, Steve. 1984. The Stark-Bainbridge Theory of Religion: A Critical Analysis and Counter Proposals. *Sociological Analysis* 45: 11-27.

_____.1986. *Sociological Theory, Religion and Collective Action.* Belfast: Queens University.

Warner, Stephen R. 1993. Work in Progress Towards a New Paradigm for the Sociological Study of Religion in the United States. *American Journal of Sociology* 98: 1044-93.

_____.1998. Immigration and Religious Communities in the United States. In R.S. Warner and J.G. Wittner (eds.) *Gatherings in Diaspora: Religious Communities and the New Immigration.* Philadelphia: Temple University Press; 1-34.

_____.2005. *A church of Our Own: Disestablishment and Diversity in American Religion.* New Brunswick, New Jersey and London: Rutgers University Press.

Warner, Stephen R and Wittner, Judith G. 1998 (eds.) *Gatherings in Diaspora: Religious Communities and the New Immigration.* Philadelphia: Temple University Press.

Washington, Joseph R. 1984. *Black Sects and Cults.* Lanham and London: University Press of America.

Weber, Max. 1978 [1922]. *Economy and Society.* Berkeley: University of California Press.

_____.1930. *The Protestant Ethic and the Spirit of Capitalism.* London: Allen and Unwin.

_____.1965. The *Sociology of Religion.* London: Methuen.

Weiner, Myron, 1995. *The Global Migration Crisis: Challenge to States and to Human Rights.* New York: HarperCollins.

Wellman, Barry. 1979. The Community Question: The Intimate Networks of East Yorkers. *American Journal of Sociology* 84: 1201-1231.

Westermann, Diedrich. 1937. *Africa and Christianity.* London: Oxford University Press.

White Elisa Joy. 2002. *On Dublin's African Diaspora Spaces,* a paper delivered at a seminar on 'Re-Mapping Dublin: Spatial Narratives of Racialised Ethnic Minorities and Diasporic Communities in a Changing City', organised by the MPhil in Ethnic and Racial Studies, Dept of Sociology, Trinity College, Dublin, Feb. 2002.

Williams, Raymond B. 1992. Sacred Threads of Several Textures. In R.B. Williams (ed.) *A Sacred Thread: Modern Transmission of Hindu Traditions in India and Abroad.* Chambersburg: Anima; pp. 228-57.

Williams, Raymond. B. 1988. *Religion and Immigrants from India and Pakistan.* Cambridge: Cambridge University Press.

Wilmore, Gayraud S. 1983. *Black Religion and Black Radicalism: An Interpretation of the Religious History of Afro-American People.* Maryknoll (NY): Orbis.

Wilson, Bryan R. 1966. *Religion and Secular Society.* London: Watts.

Winter, Alan. J. 1996. Symbolic Ethnicity or Religion among Jews in the United States: A Test of Gansian Hypotheses. *Review of Religious Research,* Vol. 37, No. 3, pp. 137-151.

Wirth, Louis. 1969. *The Ghetto*. Chicago and London: University of Chicago Press.

Wolf, Margery. 1992. *A Thrice Told Tale: Feminism, Postmodernism and Ethnographic Responsibility*. Stanford: Stanford University.

Woodward, Kath. 2002. *Understanding Identity*. London: Arnold.

_____.2004. (ed.) *Questioning Identity: Gender, Class, Ethnicity*. London and New York: Routledge and The Open University.

Wuthnow, R.1993. *Christianity in the Twenty First Century*, Oxford: Oxford University Press.

Zhou, Min. 1992. *Chinatown: The Socio-economic Potential of an Urban Enclave*. Philadelphia: Temple University Press.

Zhou, Min and John R. Logan. 1991. In and Out of Chinatown: Residential Mobility and Segregation of New York City's Chinese. *Social Forces* 70:387-407.

Zlotnik, Hania. 2001. Past Trends in International Migration and their Implications for Future Prospects. In Saddique M.A.B (ed.) *International Migration into the Twenty-first Century*. Chetenham: Edward Elgar Publishing Limited.

NEWSPAPERS

Beesley, Arthur. 2000a. Net Spread Across Globe in Trawl for Skills to Satisfy Starving Economy. *The Irish Times*, December 22.

_____.2000b. Finding Employees is an Increasingly Difficult Task. *The Irish Times*, November 24.

_____.2000c. FAS Consider Overseas Offices. *The Irish Times*, December 04.

_____.2000d. Jobless Rate Below 5% for the First Time. *The Irish Times*, June 08.

Brennan, Ciaran. 2001. Unemployment Rate Below 4% but Jobs Rise Slows. *The Irish Times*, February 22.

Brennock, Mark and Haughey, Nuala. 2003. Judges Apologise to Non-nationals for Remarks about Immigrants. *The Irish Times*: February 21.

Browne, Vincent. 2003. Judge Fairly that you be not Judged. *The Irish Times*, February 26.

Butler, Patrick. 2003. *FLAC* Criticises Direct Provision. *The Irish Times*, July 17.

Crosby, Judith. 2001. 108 Cases under Scrutiny for Breaches of Labour laws. *The Irish Times*, June 8.

Cullen, Paul. 1997. EU Refugee Treaty Takes Effect, but Ireland still has no Law on Asylum. Dublin: *The Irish Times*, August 29.

_____.2002. Vibrant Africans Overcome the Threat of Racism. *The Irish Times*, July 30.

Deegan, Gordon. 2004. Nigerian Doctor Seeks Seat on Town Council. *The Irish Times.* March 22.

De Rosa, Roisin. 2000. Nigerians march against Racism. *An Phoblacht/ Republican News.* April. 27.

Donnellan, Eithne. 2003. Driving our Nurses away. *The Irish Times,* July 12.

Dooley, Raymond. 2003. State is Obliged to Protect Irish-born Children. *The Irish Times,* November. 21.

Field, Elizabeth. 2000. Food from a Different World. *The Irish Times,* March 11.

Freyne, Patrick. 1998. Where to Buy your Fufu and your Pfumbwa. *The Irish Times,* January 29.

Goldstone, Katrina. 2003. Letter to the editor page. *The Irish Times.* January 17.

Guardian. 2003a (published in Lagos, Nigeria). *PFN Seeks Appointment of Members into Federal, State Cabinets.* May 30.

_____.2003b. *Adeboye, at Inauguration Service, says Nigeria will be Great.* May 26.

Haughey, Nuala.2000a. Ignorance and Poverty add to Racial Tensions in Dublin. *The Irish Times,* May 06.

_____.2000b. Refugee Group Chairman Urges Action after Assault. *The Irish Times,* December 04.

_____.2000c. State Contesting Right of non-EU Parents of Irish Children to Stay. *The Irish Times,* January 9.

_____.2001. Legal Service for Refugees Resumes Business after Staffing Problems. *The Irish Times,* April 05.

_____.2002a. Foreign Worker Scheme Suspended to Stem Abuse. *The Irish Times,* October 30.

_____.2002b. Nigerians are Flocking to their own Churches. *The Irish Times,* October. 28.

_____.2002c. Operation Strikes Fear in Illegal Immigrants. *The Irish Times,* July 17.

_____.2003a. Employers told number of Work Permits to be cut from Next Year. *The Irish Times,* September 13.

_____.2003b. FLAC Censures Asylum Seeker Housing Scheme. *The Irish Times,* July 11.

_____.2003c. State Housing for new Asylum Seekers. *The Irish Times,* June 12.

_____.2003d. Residents of Limbo. *The Irish Times,* June 7. Holland, Kitty. 2004a. Rule Change for Spouses of Non-EU Nurses Welcomed. *The Irish Times,* January 07.

_____.2004b. Bill on Citizenship Rights to be Enacted by Christmas. *The Irish Times,* September 30.

Kelly, Olivia. 2001. Mono: New Faces for Ireland. *The Irish Times*: April 04.

Lucey, Anne. 2001. Employers Angered at New Rules over Work Permits. *The Irish Times*, December 31.

McCann, Tom. 2000. Using Faith to Feel at Home. *The Irish Times*. October 14.

McGarry, Patsy. 2004. Immigrants Praised for 'Huge Impact' on Church. *The Irish Times*, February 25.

McGrath, Brendan, 2000. Foreigners Offered Cash to Relocate at FA'S Job Fairs. *The Irish Times*, October 9.

Media Guardian. 2006. *Dublin Heralds a New Era in Publishing for Immigrants.* March 12.

Metro Eireann, 2000. *New African Churches Arrive here with Vibrating Ovations.* June/July: p. 18.

O'Brien, Carl. 2003. PDs Act to Remove Rules Anomaly that Barred non-EU Members. *The Irish Times*: December 04.

_____.2005. Residency for Nearly 17,000 Under New Parent Law. *The Irish Times*, December 27.

Okamura, Kusi. 2003. Stepping into the Limelight. *The Irish Times*, October 22.

Olusola, Josephine. 2002. Stop Telling me to go Back Home - This is my Home. *The Irish Times*, July 30.

O'Toole, Fintan. 2002. The Desire to be Seen Doing Something. *The Irish Times*, July 20.

Pollak, Andy. 1999. Welcome to Dublin, unless you're Black. *The Irish Times*, April 24.

The Irish Times. 2002. *Irish-Born Deportees.* Editorial. April 10.

_____.2007. Ireland's First Black Mayor Set to be Elected in Portlaoise. Dublin: June 28.

WEBSITES

www.christianitytoday.com: Official website of Christianity Today (visited Jul. 2004).

www.orac.ie: official website of the Office of Refugee Application Commissioner, Ireland's official refugee and asylum seeker agency (visited Dec. 2005).

www.unhcr.org: Official website of the United Nations High Commission (visited in 2005). www.akidwa.ie: Official website of AkiDwA, the African Women's Network (visited 2006).

www.africacentre.ie: Official website of Africa Centre (visited 2006).

www.entemp.ie: Official website of the Department of Enterprise, Trade and Employment (visited 2004).

www.environ.ie: Official website of the Department of Environment, Heritage and Local Government. (visited in 2005).

www.justice.ie: Official website of the Department of Justice, Equality and Law Reform. (visited in 2005).

www.metroeireann.com: Website of *Metro Eireann*. (visited in 2004).

INDEX

Index